COCKNEY RHYMING SLANG
A POLITICALLY INCORRECT GUIDE

COMPILED BY IAN HALL

TABLE ~~OF~~ CONTENTS

INTRODUCTION...

Okay, if you can't take a joke, can't see the funny side of things, or get bent out of shape for the smallest reason, this book is probably NOT for you. This book is NOT going to be remotely 'Politically Correct'... in any way, shape or form.

The title alone warns you for goodness sake...

However, from its outset the very nature of Cockney Rhyming Slang was to obfuscate, to openly hide secrets, to pass on information within the hearing range of the uninitiated. In actual fact, Rhyming Slang was invented to make the sharing of the Politically Incorrect easier.

In more modern times, the role of Rhyming Slang has become more mainstream than its original purpose, but its core has stayed true; we still use Rhyming Slang in place of the taboo phrases that we really want to use. From the many dictionaries available the people 'in-the-know' point out people's big noses with glee, comment on their dress, ethnicity, sexual preference, and revel in others ignorance of them doing so.

But Rhyming Slang is more than just a slagging tool; it's a way to avoid openly mentioning the more uncomfortable aspects of your life. It's a method of talking openly about what ails you, your hemorrhoids, your lack of a sex life, your recent risqué adventures. It's a way to politely allude to Junior's recent brush with the law and his subsequent incarceration... and it's done with skill, guile and a fair amount of humor.

Now... there are some pure howlers in here; phrases that you wouldn't say in ANY kind of company... but I include them, because they're part of the greater picture.

To summarize... NO... this is NOT a politically correct book; by its subject matter it simply can't be.

You have been cautioned... and now more than once.

In case you haven't actually taken the hint, in the warnings below, (which I have called 'Disclaimers'), I expand the cautions in more detail. If, after reading them, you still wish to continue into the stinking comedic morass which we call Cockney Rhyming Slang, then by all means plough right in.
In the interests of transparency let's start with 'rude' words...

DISCLAIMER 1: RUDE WORDS...

I'm afraid there are rude words in this dictionary. If you read on from here, and are offended, it's your fault, you have been warned right from the start. I never set out to be rude, but I HAVE to include these words in both the actual slang and in some definitions. Let's face it, people use rude words, and some slang is used as an alternative for that rude or foul language. I accept that some slang is downright bawdy and some ridiculously offensive, but again, I make no apologies for its inclusion.

So, take this warning, I don't know what level of rudeness you, the reader, wants, so I stuck it all in.

Now, for everyone's benefit, I did throw an 'asterisk' into the middle of the two worst ones, the 'F' bomb, and the 'C' word, but since slang is often used as an alternative to swear words, or to refer to certain words, I've kept it to a single 'asterisk'.

I hope you understand.

DISCLAIMER 2: NOT SO RUDE WORDS...

Yup, in here you'll find ALL the stuff we don't like talking about... and believe it or not... THAT'S THE POINT!

We sometimes use Rhyming Slang to avoid embarrassing other people, and in a fair amount of situations, to avoid embarrassing ourselves.

We use slang to point out certain issues in our own world without mentioning anyone by name... IT'S THE LANGUAGE OF GOSSIP!

We use slang to talk man to man, woman to woman, generation to generation, without involving those 'not in the know'.

We use slang to impart secrets... it's a CODE! And like bow-ties, codes are fun.

And like secret agents, if we can cut across a conversation, make a point, without anyone knowing what we just said... THAT'S THE WHOLE POINT!

DISCLAIMER 3; ONE BIG SLAGGING MATCH...

Okay, this is another warning to stop reading right now.

Because if you don't like insults, you've opened the wrong book!

Now, we know all colours of skin have been insulted at one point in time, and even amongst one color, there are so many discriminatory divisions you'd hardly believe it.

(And, yes, I do realize that I spelled 'color' two different ways.... It was a deliberate mistake; see 'Disclaimer 7'.)

Inside these august covers are racial slurs, ethnic barbs, insults by gender or lack of it, and insults by country, region, continent and city.

We have 1001 different ways to poke fun at body shape, pose and size. Think you've heard every 'gay' insult; think again. You've not even scraped the scum off the surface.

And Rhyming Slang is a great vehicle to deliver a put-down. Think you're the height of fashion? Think you're the bees-knees in the 'correct' dress code? A true proponent of Cockney Rhyming Slang will bring you down to earth with a bump.

Using every rhyme possible, this book will give you a million ways to insult the person sitting right next to you, and unless they've also bought the book, they'll be oblivious to every joyous poetic barb.

So again... If you're soft-skinned about this kind of stuff... don't read any further. I don't want you to read the book, be offended, then take me to court over it. Because if I see you in court, I'll win. And why will I win?

All the stuff you've just read will be labelled 'Exhibit One'!

DISCLAIMER 4: KEEPING IT IN ALPHABETICAL ORDER...

Alphabetical Order; this book has been written in fits and starts since I began the idea, a couple of years back. I am making no claims for the absolute perfect Oxford Alphabetical-ness of the individual definitions. Believe me, I tried my very best.

However, I'm only human, so if I made some small critical a-z error, it's probably not a big one, so... GO BITE ME.

DISCLAIMER 5: *MALE ORIENTATION...*

I'll make no bones about it, Cockney Rhyming Slang is male oriented; there are more phrases to describe good looking women than men. This is probably a historical aspect, and stems from the predominantly male work force in markets, fairs and in the illegal professions.

This, however, does not mean that this language can't be used by women, quite the contrary, but both in media and historically, it's been a 'guy thing'.

Another aspect of the male use is perhaps deeper rooted. Women are the subtle sex, the calm, demure, secretive ones who impart nuances across the table with the wink, a smile or eye flicker. Males have always been the bull in the china shop, blustering their hormones across the room in a show of loud brash bravado.

I mean, you girls even go to the toilet together to discuss such stuff... when us guys go for a pee, we men just brag about our particular 'flow', see who can pee highest up the wall, and read the ribald graffiti... usually out loud.

Come on, we're simple creatures really.

DISCLAIMER 6: *DOES IT RHYME AT ALL?*

There are many of the rhymes that simply don't. Yup, they don't actually rhyme in 'proper' English, but when you use the word in a particular London accent, they're close, so get over it.

For instance, the word, 'toss', from the phrase, "I don't care the toss of a coin", is one slang term that fits in with the not 'particularly rhyming' category. For the word 'toss', the rhyme 'Kate Moss' works fine. But 'Iron Horse', seems to miss the point, until you slur all the words, cockney style.

I've tried to explain the accent later, but like so many, it doesn't work unless you hear it. Phone me. Or bite me, watch a Michael Caine movie, or phone him, whatever's easier.

DISCLAIMER 7: ENGLISH OR AMERICAN?

Yeah, here you got me. I raise my hands in surrender, and cop to the major crime of mixing my nationality. I'm Scottish, born in Edinburgh, and lived in the UK for 40 years. BUT... I did come to live in America, and in the last 20 years, my 'Scottishness' has mellowed. When I go back to the UK these days, I am now lambasted for my 'Americanness'.
(Yeah, we globe-trotting types can never win)
So, forgive my ass (arse) if I use 'color' instead of 'colour', or 'harbour' instead of 'harbor'. Bite me. I won't harbor a grudge, and my face won't turn a reddish colour.
This Author's got dual citizenship, the language is definitively British, but the biggest readership will probably be 'foreigners'.
"So is this guide going to be in American English, or English English?" I hear you ask.
It's a dictionary of English phrases... and it's gonna be read more by Americans than British... that's all I'm sayin'!
However, since the Cockney accent is now being referred to as 'Estuary English' to encompass both sides of the Thames River, I feel emboldened to be the first to call my particular mishmash... 'ATLANTIC ENGLISH'!

DISCLAIMER 8: MY EXAMPLES OF THE SLANG...

In every definition, I have given at least one example of the slang in plain everyday speech. I make no bones about it, these are by no means the only way to use the phrase, and I take little credit for the originality; some of these are common phrases, and I have heard them in everyday speech from an early age.
And the subject matter in the examples? If I have 328 different rhymes of 'needing to go to the toilet', then how many different ways can I say... "I need to go to the toilet"?

So... the examples are not Shakespeare in their make-up, they're just very basic examples of speech. And if I get too repetitive in my examples... go bite me... again. Or write a new one, and email it to me.

DISCLAIMER 9: YOUR FAVORITE IS MISSING...

If I've missed your favorite rhyme out, don't let your heart be troubled, don't get your knickers in a twist, don't run to your safe-space, and don't write a letter to your local politician... just drop me an email and I'll set your rhyme aside for future editions. I might even give you credit for it if I'm in a generous mood. Or I might not.

Heck, why not just pick one of the many thousand rhyming phrases, and tell all your friends that YOU sent it in to me, and I published it for you, anonymously.

Heck, tell them you wrote the book, and that 'Ian Hall' is your pen name... it'll be our secret.

I won't tell on you. I promise.

Yours
IAN HALL

RHYMING SLANG; THE HISTORY...

If there is one thing modern linguists can agree upon, it is that slang is universal. Each country has its own dictionary, and some countries have many different regional varieties. Some of these regional, territorial or community languages are intelligible outside the border or group; I'm Scottish, born and bred, yet there are places in Scotland I only understand one word in five!

And these slang languages are not divided by geographical borders either; individual trades have their own glossaries... thieves, merchants, military men, robbers, gypsies and many other groups and professions have had their 'secret' languages for centuries.

In France, the secret language of highwaymen, housebreakers, and pickpockets is called Argot, and is mentioned in Victor Hugo's Les Miserables, written in 1862. In Holland it is called Bargoensis, and in Low Germany it was known as Gypseria. Elsewhere in Germany, the slang is called Rothivalsch, or Eed Italian. In Italy, brigands who robbed trains used a language called Oergo. The slang of the thieves in South Africa who hounded the Hottentots is termed cuze-cat, and is probably where the term and lingual basis for African American 'scat' slang originated. According to Hotten (An author of slang in 1858), 'The brigands and more romantic rascals of Spain, term their private tongue Ger-mania, or 'Bobbers Language'.

In Britain, slang was referred to as 'Cant', and was considered a vile perversion of the proper English gentleman's tongue.

(It was said to be named after a Scottish preacher, Andrew Cant, who from his pulpit blasted the congregation in a dialect only understood by them.)

RHYMING SLANG...

The rhyming version, originating in Britain, however is purely based on the English language, and is unique among all other secret languages in that it relies completely on rhyme as its essential core.

It was once thought that the unique form of rhyming slang we now glibly call 'Cockney', was originally found in inner London, but there is some controversy if it was restricted to the area which is now commonly known as the East End, or indeed if it started there at all. The true Cockney's definition of their region has traditionally been... "Anyone born within the sound of the Bow Bells", the church bells belonging to the Church of St Mary Le Bow, on the London street called simply, Cheapside.

Basically, it is the north-east quarter of London, to the north of the River Thames.

But the origins of the slang language itself have been called into some question.

In 1858, John Camden Hotten (a London writer and publisher) wrote a book entitled...

A Dictionary of Modern Slang, Cant, and Vulgar Words: Used at the Present Day in the Streets of London, the Universities of Oxford and Cambridge, the Houses of Parliament, the Dens of St. Giles, and the Palaces of St. James : Preceded by a History of Cant and Vulgar Language : with Glossaries of Two Secret Languages, Spoken by the Wandering Tribes of London, the Costermongers, and the Patterers.

It was reprinted in 1859 and again posthumously, and set out mostly the difference between Cant (vulgar) language, and Slang (a fluid culturally centric) language. At the end of the book, he gave a glossary of 150 examples of 'rhyming slang', but despite him being a Londoner, and living and working in the area, amazingly did not credit the actual Cockney region as the source. In fact he makes the point that the language was NOT limited to London (or any particular part of it), but that perhaps 20,000 practitioners of 'rhyming Cant' were using the language across the length and breadth of Britain from around 1835. He also states quite clearly that the class of vagabonds using the language was mostly 'Patterers' (A user of verbal patter to sell); typically market or street sellers/vendors of the time. These 'merchants' used rhyming slang in their sing-song sales spiel to pass on messages between themselves and also to intrigue and attract prospective customers.

So... There seems to be a possibility that the term 'Cockney' was added/affiliated to the general Rhyming Slang at some later stage. It wouldn't be the first time that a region or country would call a generic item their own. (Witness my own Scotland's undying identification of tartan and the bagpipes)

Hotten also defines Cockney as simply thus; "COCKNEY; a native of London".

Now, John Camden Hotten, a Londoner and something of an expert on local and British slang as a whole, was surely in a fine place to know

However... although the residents and descendants of the Cockney region cling onto Cockney Rhyming Slang as their own, it is now broadly considered to belong to all residents of London... all nine million of them... and while this may rile the 'true' Cockney, perhaps it is just history re-adjusting itself.

Anyway...

There is no doubt that a rhyming slang language originated in the English working classes somewhere between 1820 and 1835, including (but definitely not restricted to) the Cockney region, where it took its modern name.

One thing is certain; the explosion of rhyming slang in London came at a time when the city was changing...

1829; Sir Robert Peel establishes the first Police Force.

1829; The Rocket (the first steam train) was designed by Robert Stephenson.

1830; The Industrial Revolution; although this was a fluid date rather than a fixed one. (Historian Eric Hobsbawm held that the Industrial Revolution began in Britain in the 1780's and was not fully felt in both populace and economy until the 1830's or 1840's.)

1830; The Liverpool and Manchester Railway opened.

This opened one of the expansion routes for rhyming slang... London workers flocked to the railway works, and were forced to work alongside Irish immigrants. Now known as navvies (Navigators) the jovial rhyming language prospered. It is no accident that many Irish rhymes are quoted by Hotten in 1858, and most of these rhymes are people's names, belying the immediacy of the contact.

The second expansion for the rhyming language came with the prison sentence of deportation. With transportation to the colonies being a popular punishment for the British working classes, the rhyming language spread to Australia, where it was added to, bastardized, and transformed.

The prisoners, once having served their sentence, often had little interest in returning to the land of their crimes, and many settled in the growing towns of Australia. An expert in the local times wrote that a rather large gathering of 'Cockneys' had taken root in Sydney.

These freed prisoners either stayed in Australia, or moved to the other growing bastion of the English language; America. These quasi-Australians both settled on the west coast, and spread eastwards, meeting their cousins driving west. The language they brought with them was fresh, vibrant, and humorous. It caught on immediately, and was called Australian Rhyming Slang by the Americans they encountered.

The California gold-rush in 1848, and the Yukon gold rush of 1896 ensured that the jocular rhyming language was in America to stay, and many books have been written giving glossaries of examples.

The first American volume of rhyming slang was compiled by criminal turned author, Chicago May, in 1928, but without doubt, the most important volume of American Rhyming Slang was published in 1944.

Professor of English at Louisville University, David W. Maurer, exchanged views with Sidney J. Baker, an expert on the Australian language, and together they published an article in **American Speech** magazine. The tome, entitled, **Australian Rhyming Argot in the American Underworld**, cemented all controversy regarding rhyming slang in America, giving hundreds of examples.

Cockney rhyming slang had indeed travelled around the world. But in America, the name of the slang had changed. It was now officially 'Australian Rhyming Slang'.

To cement this, it should be mentioned at this point that American actor Cary Grant used rhyming slang first in film, in

1943. In **Mr Lucky**, his character tries to teach rhyming slang to Laraine Day, and he labels it as 'Australian rhyming slang'.

THE ORIGINS...

It is a standard belief that rhyming slang originated in the seedier sides of London life, the criminal underground, but it has been proven not to be the case. Most of the old rhymes refer to normal everyday life, and everyday jobs. So while the criminals may have made use of rhyming slang to pass hidden messages, it is now not considered to have originated in their ranks.

From the early examples in Hotten's book, it seems that market traders, street sellers, manual workers, factory workers, millers, dockworkers and sailors were the first users, and probably the main instigators of rhyming slang.

However, with the establishment of the first police force in 1929, the thieves in London were the first to face Sir Robert Peel's men in blue, and the thieves' use of rhyming slang became so prevalent that it became necessary for the police to learn the basics of this language and examples of the rhymes were included in the newest law enforcement manuals.

According to Hotten, it became common among many of the working-class, becoming a badge of their status, and a matter of some pride. The 'Toffs' may have had their education and their airs and graces, but the working class had its new code, and as the phrases were bandied around, the Toffs looked on in bewilderment.

As the slang spread through British streets many aspects of 'Cockney' English became a more endemic part of the general London accent. In typical modern terms, it has now been termed 'Estuary English'.

The industrial revolution spread the populace across the country, and the growth of the British Empire in the Victorian Era took the British accent, and thus the slang the people used, to the four corners of the world.

In 1846, even the Oxford English Dictionary included 'joanna' as a meaning for 'piano', (with local phrasing it makes more sense; Jo-ann'er, and pee-ann'er)

In the same dictionary in 1857, it listed 'Barnet', as being a person's hair (Barnet Fair – hair). (Barnet Fair was an annual horse and entertainment fair in Barnet, London, from 1558 to 1881)

So, throughout Victorian London, as rhyming slang grew into acceptance, Charles Dickens in his novels dealt with the common man in London, and the rough accent grew through countless Penny Dreadful's available on the street corners of the day.

It was a time of social climbing, a time of enlightenment, and a time of the growth of language as children began to be educated on a general level.

BUT WHY USE IT AT ALL?

Slang has long been used to disguise taboo words in a spoken sentence that might cause embarrassment to either the user or those in earshot.

For instance, if two market traders were ogling the large breasts of a customer, they're hardly likely to blurt out, "Look at the tits on her!" in case the customer overheard. However, if they said, "Looks like Bristol City's playing good recently," it might pass unnoticed by the customer, allowing the fellow trader perhaps to reply, "Fancy an ice cream later? Raspberry Ripple's always been my favorite." Referring to her prominent nipples.

Sitting in mixed company, it can be used to pass messages from only one person to another; it's really difficult to attract your mate's attention to the girl playing darts, or to pass comment on someone's dress or big nose; Cockney Rhyming Slang allows this to happen unobtrusively.

It comes as no surprise that a lot of the definitions deal with body parts or medical conditions; there's nothing worse than folks talking about their hemorrhoids, bunions, warts or worse, but the slang diminishes the trauma, and even makes folks see the funny side of it all. There's a huge difference between talking about the diabolic consequences of AIDS, and talking about 'buckets an' spades', or shortened to just 'buckets'!

Toilet functions, another civil taboo, also take up a fair amount of the phrases in the book. No matter what actually happens in a

20

toilet, there's a rhyme to accurately tell everyone all the grisly details without mentioning the gruesome particulars. Whether you're bursting to go, or just done the deed, whether you just did a wee tinkle, or had a nuclear explosive incident, there are a thousand rhymes to tell everyone all about it in colorful rhyming detail.

Additionally, slang has also been used extensively to discuss a person's sexual antics (or lack thereof), and sexual proclivities, with equal anonymity. Comments on gayness, promiscuousness, sexual acts and such, litter the dictionary with comic abandon.

There are also a fair amount of the rhymes relating to derogatory personal descriptions that simply wouldn't be put up with in polite company, but using the slang, these slip below the average radar. From big feet to obvious wigs, from hooked noses to knobbly knees, you'll find a rhyme to point out everyone's Achilles heel.

Throw in a few racist rhymes, for almost every nationality and skin colour, and you've probably covered the whole gamut.

If you haven't realized it already, you'll soon find out there's nothing 'politically correct' in Cockney Rhyming Slang.

I make no bones, and don't apologize for it.

WELL KNOWN COCKNEY ACTORS...

Michael Caine was born in Rotherhithe, London, and brought up in Southwark, just a few miles away, both south of the Thames, with his father being a fish market porter. When he came to stardom, he kept his own accent in many of his films, like **Alfie, Get Carter**, and **The Italian Job**, ensuring the world would hear the cockney accent, and learn to love it.

Bob Hoskins was brought up in Finsbury Park, London, just a few miles west of the Bow Bells limits, but his accent has never died. Films like **The Long Good Friday, Mona Lisa**, and countless TV appearances have kept this Londoner in work.

Ray Winstone was born in Hackney, London, and his cockney accent is rough and natural. From his debut in the violent prison film, **Scum,** to **Quadrophenia, Sexy Beast**, and **Sweeney Todd**, this hard working actor never let go of his cockney roots.

Terrance Stamp was born in Stepney, London, and spent his childhood on Canal Road and in Plaistow, West Ham. From playing arch villain General Zod in **Superman**, then hard hitting parts in **The Hit**, and **The Limey** brought a harsh London Accent into the box office.

Tim Roth began life in Dulwich, London, south of the Thames, but still in central London. His accent is part of his psyche. From a skinhead in **Made in Britain** to Tarantino's **Reservoir Dogs** and **Pulp Fiction,** his familiar tones are never far away.

Lennie James might have been born in Nottingham, but he was raised in London, and for 8 years in care... he's the true hard-case Londoner, and has played the part from Guy Ritchie's **Snatch** to Matthew McConaughey's **Sahara**. On the small screen, he's mesmerized us with hard hitting performances from **Jericho, Line of Duty**, to the part of Morgan Jones in **The Walking Dead.**

Alan Ford is one of the lesser well-known London actors. But if you see his face, you'd recognize him immediately. He grew up in Walworth, in South London, and has a special place in the Cockney Rhyming Slang heritage.

Ford narrated and appeared in Guy Ritchie's **Lock, Stock and Two Smoking Barrels**, and, in 2000, had a star role as crime boss 'Brick Top' in Ritchie's follow-up, **Snatch**. Then, in the pinnacle of lampooning, he appeared in the 2012 film, **Cockneys vs Zombies**.

I need say no more.

Warren Mitchell was born in Stoke Newington, and apart from his many serious roles, he will always be remembered as Alf Garnett, the grumpy father in the sit-com, **'Til Death Us Do Part'**. He spewed his London accent with pride, and was never far from his well-worn sky-blue and claret West Ham scarf.

Barbara Windsor, born in Shoreditch, London, and initially known as the busty blond of the 'Carry On' films, found her place in BBC TV's soap, **Eastenders**, set in East End London.

David Jason's father worked as a porter at the London fish market, and although he has starred in many series since, Jason will be best remembered as Del-Boy (Derek) Trotter in **Only Fools and Horses**. Set in London, it lasted 80 episodes, and its episodes and specials spanned 22 years of British culture. I have cried myself laughing at many of their escapades.

Mike Reid, born in Hackney, his family moved to Tottenham during the blitz, and he played many the TV and movie stunt double in the 60's and 70's. Making his name as a comedian, he starred in children's television as the host of **Runaround**, before hitting Guy Ritchie's movie, **Snatch**, and a recurring role in BBC's **Eastenders** as pub owner Frank Butcher.

Rising star **Danny Dyer** was born in Custom House, London, and has already starred in a plethora of films showcasing his rough accent, and at the time of writing is in BBC's **Eastenders**.

Special Mention... Dennis Waterman. No single cockney has probably done more in television to promote the cockney accent than this man. Born in Clapham, London, he played Oliver on stage at age 13, but his first main role was as Detective Sergeant George Carter in the police series, **The Sweeney** (53 episodes and 2 spin-off feature films), set in London. He followed this with a starring role in **Minder,** (114 episodes) as bodyguard Terry McCann, to old-timer George Cole. With many other TV shows and appearances, he more recently revisited his 'cockney-ness' in 107 episodes of the BBC TV police procedural, **New Tricks** (2003 to 2015). Set in modern London, Waterman never missed a cockney slang insert, and does not always explain the references to his cast members (and therefore the watching audience).

Special Mention... Chas & Dave. In music, no-one has done more to promote the London vernacular. They have been credited with inventing a new musical style titled 'rockney'; a cross between 'rock' and 'cockney'. They have peppered the British charts with 8 Top 20 hits from 1975 to 2013. From their Cockney Rhyming Slang song **'Rabbit'** to **'Snooker Loopy',** they have delighted British audiences for years.

AND... Chas & Dave are the only actual mentioned Cockneys to have their own rhyme; Chas & Dave – SHAVE.

Who has not seen clips or watched some version of George Bernard Shaw's re-hash of Greek mythology's tale of the sculptor falling in love with his statue, which then comes alive.

Shaw's version of **Pygmalion**, first performed in Vienna in 1913, took the London/Cockney accent from London to New York in just a few months. Shaw's sad ending was changed to a happier one to boost attendances, and Shaw (grumbling all the way to the bank) protested the happy ending until 1938.

In 1956 **Pygmalion** was first performed on Broadway as a musical (now called **My Fair Lady)** starring Rex Harrison and Julie Andrews. The pair opened two years later in the West End of London, and the musical has been running around the world ever since.

The 1964 movie, also entitled **My Fair Lady**, brought the Cockney accent to the world, delivered by an exceptional Audrey Hepburn as Eliza Doolittle.

Now... Julie Andrews v's Audrey Hepburn...

It was a tough fight, but despite the fact of Julie Andrews having played the part on stage for six years, Hepburn was chosen to give the film a better box office name. Hepburn already had many exceptional films under her belt, and Andrews had no film experience whatsoever. Hepburn's vocals, however, were dubbed by Marni Nixon, as Hepburn did not possess the register for the songs.

Julie Andrews did extract her revenge... Although **My Fair Lady** won eight 1964 Oscars, (Including Rex Harrison for Best Actor) Julie Andrews won the 1964 Best Actress Oscar for her debut film, **Mary Poppins**... which leads us to another Cockney snippet...

Yeah, who could write a book about Cockney accents and not mention Dick Van Dyke's monstrosity in **Mary Poppins**? The film was Disney's biggest to date, taking in a staggering $102 million (In comparison to My fair Lady's $72 million).

There you go... mentioned.

Funnily enough it is the American actor Cary Grant who uses it first in the film, **Mr Lucky** in 1943. His character tries to teach rhyming slang to Laraine Day, but labels it as *'Australian rhyming slang'*.

Sidney Poitier, in the 1967 movie, **To Sir With Love,** teaches rhyming slang to Lulu and other members of his scoffing class. The movie is set in North East London, and is still considered a classic.

Michael Caine must be considered the biggest London accent movie draw. He began acting in 1956, but it was the 1960's that broke him worldwide... and he did them all with his London accent mostly intact. In 1964, he clipped his accent alongside Stanley baker in the wonderful story of Rorke's Drift, **ZULU**. The next year, he was the quintessential British spy as Harry Palmer in **The Ipcress File**. In 1966 he starred in the title role of **Alfie**, the London wide boy, narrating his way through the world's problems. He played Harry Palmer again in **Funeral In Berlin** also in 1966, and the following year in the **Billion Dollar Brain**.

In 1969, he hit a double with **The Italian Job**, putting the British car, the mini, on the map, and cementing his own accent.

For rhyming slang lovers, Quincey Jones' closing song of the movie, is called *"Getta Bloomin' Move On"* a.k.a. *"The Self Preservation Society"* and uses a host of rhyming slang terms... (German Bands, Boat Race, Barnet Fair, Dickie Dirt, Peckham Rye, Gregory Peck, Jam Jar, Tickety Boo, Almond Rocks, Daisy Roots, Hampstead Heath, Whistle and Flute, Lah-di-dahs, and Plates of Meat). I would have loved to have been a fly on the wall as American Quincy Jones wrote the lyrics of that one.

Then came what came to be called The Great Rhyming Slang Hiatus...

(Okay, I just coined the phrase myself, but, hey, it may catch on.)

In 1998, just when you thought rhyming slang had died... along came prospective film maker, Guy Ritchie.

The film, **Lock, Stock, and Two Smoking Barrels** took the London crime film genre onto a new level, and introduced Jason Statham and hard-man footballer Vinnie Jones to an unsuspecting world market. The movie has so many Cockney Rhyming Slang phrases; it almost needs subtitles for the British audience, never mind those abroad. The film has the honour of having more rhyming phrases than any other world-distributed movie release.

After the immediate success of his debut film, Ritchie went on to produce a short-lived Channel 4 television series based on the film, called **Lock Stock...** it had seven episodes and heavily featured Cockney Rhyming Slang, making it difficult at times to understand. It had a mediocre cast, but introduced another ex-footballer, Londoner Bradley Walsh, to the acting genre. If the London accent had been forgotten since Bob Hoskins' **The Long Good Friday**, it was now back with a vengeance.

Ritchie followed **Lock Stock** with another crime heist films, **Snatch** (2000). Capitalizing on Lock Stock's success, it starred a plethora of London talent... Jason Statham, Alan Ford, Lennie James, Vinnie Jones, comedian Mike Reid, and Puerto Rican star Benicio del Toro, not to mention a stellar garbled Irish-ish diatribe from Brad Pitt.

The best Rhyming slang line came from Alan Ford... "You stop me again when I'm walking, an' I'll cut your f*cking Jacobs off!" (Jacobs'Crackers = knackers= testicles.)

Revolver (2005), and **RocknRolla** (2008), followed... 'Estuary English' was officially back in style.

After the runaway success of **Lock Stock**..., director Steven Soderbergh brought the London accent to America with **The Limey** the following year (1999). It starred Terrance Stamp in the title role, coming to America to look into the death of his daughter.

Sexy Beast followed starring Ray Winstone, Ben Kingsley and Ian McShane. Full of tension between the two leading stars, it's a masterpiece of the genre.

With London accents in **Ocean's Eleven** (2001), and **Austin Powers in Goldmember** (2002), there was a lull before **It's All Gone Pete Tong** (2004), came to the screen. Using a Cockney

Rhyming Slang term for the actual title (It's All Gone Wrong) gave viewers a taste of what was inside.

If some of the films gave homage to rhyming slang, **Cockneys vs Zombies** (2012) lampooned it, the most memorable of which is when one character calls the zombies, 'Trafalgars'. Giving the explanation he cites; "Trafalgar Square... Fox and Hare... Hairy Cheek... Five Day Week... Weak and Feeble... Pins and Needles... Needle and Stitch... Abercrombie and Fitch... Abercrombie... Zombie".

A 10th degree of separation Cockney Rhyming Slang...

Shut up.

It works for me.

COCKNEY RHYMING SLANG ON THE SMALL SCREEN...

In Britain, after the release of **The Italian Job** movie, rhyming slang hit the small screen. London based programs used the formula regularly. **Steptoe and Son** (1970–74) with Harry H. Corbett and Wilfrid Brambell were a spellbinding partnership, but **Not On Your Nellie** (1974–75), starring Hylda Baker, started the trend of using rhyming slang phrases as TV titles. **The Sweeney** (1975–78) comes from the phrase 'Sweeney Todd' (Flying Squad).

Rhyming slang is mentioned in **The Fall and Rise of Reginald Perrin** (1976–79), **The Good Life** (1975–78), **The Jeffersons** (1976), **Mind Your Language** (1977–79), **Citizen Smith** (1977–80), **Minder** (1979–94), **Only Fools and Horses** (1981–91), and **EastEnders** (1985-).

WE ALL USE RHYMING SLANG...

WE JUST DON'T KNOW WE'RE DOING IT!

In most English speaking countries, to some degree the rhyming slang has permeated the common vernacular to the stage where people don't realize they are using it.

For example...

1. The noise you make with your lips, imitating a fart, is commonly called a 'raspberry', or 'blowing a raspberry'. But few realize they are using Cockney Rhyming Slang, because 'raspberry tart' is actually Cockney Rhyming Slang for 'fart'. "Ow, that smells awful. Someone's just dropped a raspberry tart!"

2. Hippies all over the world in the 60's and 70's referred to money, cash, as 'bread'. "Hey man, got any bread on you, we need smokes!" But little did those long haired surfer-types realize they were using Cockney Rhyming Slang. Yup, the slang term, 'Bread & Honey', means money.

3. The word 'scarper', meaning to run away, usually from a nefarious situation, wasn't in the English dictionary in the 1800's. The phrase's original link was Scapa Flow, a natural harbour in the Shetland Islands used in WW1 as the base for the British Northern Fleet, and where the Germans scuttled their WW1 fleet. The name only became known outside the Shetland Islands during the war, 1914-1918. In Cockney Rhyming Slang, 'Scarpa Flow' means 'go' (run away), and so the phrase 'to scarper' has become a perfectly acceptable English term.

4. When someone asks to see something, to examine it for themselves, the phrase "Give me a butchers, then." is often used. Cockney Rhyming Slang for 'look', is 'butcher's hook'.

5. In my own childhood, I was a bit of a tall boy, easily outstripping both mum and dad. When my show size overtook his, dad often referred to my large feet as 'plates of meat', probably never knowing he was using rhyming slang.

And that brings us to a very important aspect of the language...

THE TECHNICAL SIDE...

Cockney Rhyming Slang at its most simplest uses a common or contrived phrase, whose last word is used as a rhyme to infer another everyday word or phrase. This usage is Cockney Rhyming Slang at its very simplest, and for the sake of the book it is what I have termed 1st degree of separation, or simply '1st degree'.

1ST DEGREE COCKNEY RHYMING SLANG... (1D)

This is by far the most commonly heard and used (when the full phrase and rhyme is included in the speech).
Example; "He went up the Apples and Pears."
Meaning... He went up the stairs.
(- 'stairs', is 'Apples and Pears')
This is by far the most popular usage by the novice, where the whole phrase and rhyme remains in the sentence, and in a lot of cases, even though you might not know the actual phrase, you may perhaps still ascertain the meaning of the sentence.

2ND DEGREE COCKNEY RHYMING SLANG...(2D)

Still commonly heard and spoken (when the rhyming part has been dropped)...
When users of the language truncate the phrase, just the rhyming word is used.
"Lend me a Godiva, then." In Cockney Rhyming Slang, a fiver (British five pound note) is a 'Lady Godiva', but in this case only the rhyming part of the original phrase has been spoken.
However, even at this stage, it's hardly a secret language for those with imagination.
But when the rhyming part is dropped, it starts to get interesting.

"Lend me a Lady, then." is a far more obscure phrase than the one above.

Shortening slang phrases is not specific to Cockney Rhyming Slang. Even general slang phrases like "He went ape-shit!", meaning he 'lost his cool', can be abbreviated to "He went ape!" The meaning is still understood by those in the know.

Example; "He kicked me in the Alberts!"

Meaning... He kicked me in the testicles (balls).

(- testicles (balls) is 'Albert Halls', but in this case the rhyming part ('Halls') is dropped, leaving the user with a brand new slang term)

However, there are still times when the meaning of the 'non-rhyme' can be gleaned just by the words around it.

WHERE TO USE 2ND DEGREE...

There are no hard and fast rules as to when to use either the First Degree or Second... in fact some folks use a mix of the two, but what I find, is most people will use what sounds the best under the circumstances. Some phrasings sound good with the whole rhyme, some sound pithy and succinct with the non-rhyme part only.

There are some phrases in Cockney Rhyming Slang that are NEVER shortened, especially when there are a lot of phrases that involve the same root word; the listener would never know exactly which meaning was being offered. There are some that naturally are shortened, just because it sounds good. Unfortunately in this morass of rules we find there are no rules, and in this volume there are only my rudimentary guidelines.

However... it's when a slang sentence incorporates two or more elements of rhyming slang the meaning begins to become obscure for the uninitiated.

Try this one...

"Some fridge fancied a bit of posh with me trouble last night. I punched him right in the mincer and gave him an ocean liner for his soapies."

Translated...

"Some fridge (fridge freezer – geezer) fancied a bit of posh (posh & becks – sex) with me trouble (trouble & strife - wife) last night. I punched him right in the mincer (mince pie – eye) and gave him an ocean liner (shiner) for his soapies (soapy bubbles – troubles)."

In the above example lies the original purpose of using the slang. Even in friendly social circles, the user can state quite anonymous phrases using this form of coded speech.

3RD DEGREE COCKNEY RHYMING SLANG...(3D)

This is very rare. This is when the original rhyme has been dropped, and the other part of the original phrase has also been dropped, to be replaced by another word associated with the original phrase.

Example; "Calm down, mate, keep your Elvis."

Meaning... keep your hair on.

('hair-on' is Aaron. But the original Aaron has been dropped being replaced by Elvis, an obvious associated word, although 'Elvis' was never in the original rhyming slang.)

4TH DEGREE COCKNEY RHYMING SLANG????... (4D)

Believe it or not... I actually found a few examples... And I'm being told it's quite common in places.

'Macca'; Cockney Rhyming Slang for... CRAP (shit).

This is technically a very convoluted third degree, but if there ever 'was' an example of fourth degree Cockney Rhyming Slang, this is it.

Here's the explanation.

1D; Pony & Trap is rhyme for 'crap'.

2D; Pony is the abbreviated form of Pony & Trap.

3D; Macaroni rhymes with pony.

4D? Macca is short for macaroni.

Example... "Get the next round in, I'm off for a quick macca."

USE WITH CARE...

With so many similar rhymes meaning the same thing, and with many of the rhymes having more than one meaning, sometimes the user has to be careful on which to use, or which to abbreviate. For example, the rhyme, 'Jack the Ripper', can be used to mean Kipper (a smoked haddock), slipper, or stripper. Now even if we did not abbreviate, this could be easily misinterpreted.

Imagine coming home and saying to your wife, "Oh, I love me jack the ripper with a knob of butter on top."

SO IS IT JUST RHYME?

Absolutely not. It's not all bollocks and bluster... there's subtlety in the language too, and even from the earliest examples, the subtlety is not lost. And it's not just myself that's noticed it...

Ghil'ad Zuckermann, an Israeli linguist and professor at the University of Adelaide, Australia, has studied Cockney Rhyming Slang and found that it falls into two distinct categories.

The most basic and common form of Cockney Rhyming Slang is formed from rhyme only, where the actual rhyme has no connection with its meaning or definition. This form is by far the most prevalent, and perhaps covers 80-90% of the slang language.

However, Zuckermann proposed that there is another, a far more subtle style, which he called a 'phono-semantic' rhyming slang. This higher level incorporates some form of link between the Cockney Rhyming Slang phrase and the subsequent meaning. Clever rhymers form a string connection (jocular, subtle or truthful) with their subject matter and their rhyming phrases.

Take the already used example of, 'Apples and Pears'. The meaning of this particular Cockney Rhyming Slang is 'stairs', and refers to any kind of staircase. However, the word, stairs, also describes the idea of gradation from the front of a shop display to the back. In the barrows of the market stalls, samples of fruit and vegetables (such as apples and pears) are presented in steps and stairs to show the fruit off to its full potential. Hence, we can assume the phrase was originated by the traders in the market stalls; part of their secret language.

The phrase, Sorrowful Tale, is rhyme for 'Three Months in Jail', and the link is subtle and almost melancholic.

Another early example is 'Satin and Silk', the Cockney Rhyming Slang for milk. The rhyme is suggestive of its smoothness.

This higher level of 'phono-semantic' rhyming slang has also carried on the some of the more modern phrases.

Take the rhyming slang term, 'Euan Blair' (British Prime Minister's son), and the meaning, 'Leicester Square' (a square in London). The connection looks innocuous at first, but when we find out that underage (16) Euan Blair was found drunk by police in Leicester Square in 2000, we realize that a master rhyming slang-er has been quickly at work.

AND IT'S NOT A DEAD LANGUAGE...

No, it's not. Although most of its phrasing comes from Victorian London and the turn of the twentieth century, Cockney Rhyming Slang is very alive and well. New examples of modern rhymes are appearing every week, meaning the language is being used and adapted by the younger adults and children.

'Barrack Obama's', is Cockney Rhyming Slang for 'pajamas'.

'Bacardi Breezer', is a 'geezer', or bloke.

There are mentions of the web, the internet, cell phones and space travel.

With new social groups striving to achieve their own identity, Cockney Rhyming Slang has never been more popular. Some of the old personality's names die, but new ones emerge to take their place. For example, the famous British 'curry', so long described as a 'Ruby Murray' (Irish singer of the 1940's) has now been deposed (at least north of Hadrian's Wall) by Scotland's tennis champion, 'Andy Murray', but the meaning is the same.

"Fancy a Ruby/Andy Murray?" "Sure, remember the fried rice!"

Rhyming slang, although almost 200 years old, is alive and kicking today, and hopefully our little book will bring its intricacies and humor to a new audience.

COCKNEY RHYMING SLANG OVERSEAS...

In the US, the first TV show to regularly feature some form of rhyming slang was the Saturday morning children's show The Bugaloos (1970–72), with the character of Harmony (Wayne Laryea) often incorporating it in his dialogue.

Most English speaking countries now employ their own form of rhyming slang. Outside the UK, it is strongest amongst ex-patriots in Australia, New Zealand, and to a lesser degree, Canada.

Many examples in Australian rhyming slang were noted in the novels written at the turn of the 1900's.

However, the modern phrases are frowned upon by the Cockney stalwarts, and insist that the more modern rhyming slang doesn't originate from the Cockney's themselves. So now Cockney Rhyming Slang is used loosely to collectively gather all English rhyming slang phrases.

SCOTTISH RHYMING FOOTBALL SLANG...

As a Scot, I'd be remiss in not giving my own country a small mention, and indeed my favorite sport... football.

In Scottish football, a number of clubs have nicknames taken directly from rhyming slang.

Partick Thistle, nicknamed 'The Jags', are known as the "Harry Rags".

Glasgow Rangers, (sorry, I almost gagged just writing their name) nicknamed 'The Gers', are known as the "Teddy Bears", rhyming somewhat with 'Gers'.

Edinburgh's second best team, Heart of Midlothian, commonly called just 'Hearts', have the rhyming slang nickname, the "Jam Tarts". They also play in an awful color of burgundy red, like old moldy strawberry jam, which they insist on being termed 'maroon'.

And last, but by no means least, my own Edinburgh team, the fantastic and super Hibernian, their name truncated to just 'Hibs', are nicknamed "The Cabbage" which comes from Cabbage and Ribs being the rhyming slang for Hibs (and the fact they play in Green).

(I hope I got through the last segment without showing bias in any way)

HOW TO ACTUALLY SAY IT ALL...

THE LONDONER'S VOWELS...

THE FUNNY 'A'... AW and AY.
Using the 'A' to 'AW' change, words like raspberry, father, bastard, half, become 'r-aw-spberry', f-aw-ther', 'b-aw-stard', and 'h-aw-f'.
The 'AY' affects different words like handbag, and in this case, twice... 'h-ay-ndb-ay-g'. (A little like a southern USA person would say 'Kay'nsas')

THE QUEER 'E'...
This is a funny one, with no real rules. The 'E' in certain words, like trousers, is changed into a definite 'I' sound (now pronounced trous-i-s). However, the 'ER' in father becomes an 'A', morphing the word into 'fath-a'

THE FUNNY 'I'...
The letter 'I' can be used two ways... in most London accents words like lips, chips, Britain, or litter, the sound is unchanged. But in words like China, minder, climb, decider, the 'I' in the middle of a word can be pronounced 'OI', (OY). The word, 'decided' sounds normal enough, but Londoners would pronounce it as dec-oi-ded. Using the 'AY' change, the country (and the rhyming slang for 'mate) China, would be pronounced Ch-oi-na, Play-te, someone climbing up a cliff would be described as a cl-oi-mer, (cl-oi-ma) and tight becomes 't-oi-ght'. (Using the 'R' contraction to follow, the money note, 'a fiver', becomes 'a foi-v-a'.)

THE FUNNY 'O'...
Basically some 'O' can be pronounced as 'OW', and there doesn't seem to be a rule. Rope becomes rowp, no becomes now.
Other words containing 'O's are also battered around a bit.
London can be pronounced, Lunnin.
"I'm a Londoner", becomes the almost unreadable, "Oi'm a Lunnin-a."

THE WEIRD 'OU'...

A simple word like 'trousers' becomes a morass. The 'OU' changes to a long 'A' sound as in the word, 'lamb'. And the 'E' part is pronounced 'I', as in the word 'tit'. The final version of trousers sounds like 'tr-a-z-i-s'.

LONDON'S POSSESSIVE PRONOUNS...

It's somewhat difficult to give a realistic example of an accent when you are limited to the written word, although I've tried in all of the definitions to be as close as possible.

After completing the volume, I found there's a couple of words to mention in particular.

MY... In London, this has been bastardized over the years to sound like 'ME'. (In Scotland, and in various parts of northern England, this is slightly altered to sound like 'MA'. For example the English phrase, "I can't take my eyes off her, she's gorgeous." becomes cockney, "I can't take me bleedin' eyes owf 'er. She's love-erly". (Again, in Scotland this would be... "I canna tak' ma eyes aff 'er.")

When 'me' becomes expanded, it makes 'myself', become me'self'... and if that gets contracted, it becomes, 'me'sel''. (In Scotland it would be 'ma'sel'')

YOUR and ... Similarly, 'your' becomes 'yer'.

HER and HIM... Just dropping the first letter makes a huge difference it the way we pronounce these... becoming "er', and "im', in the process.

HERS and HIS... The plurals, contract to 'ers and 'is.

GOING TO, and WANT TO... Contract these and you get 'gonna', and 'wanna'.

I AM... This is a more complex one. It contracts to sound like this... 'OY-IM'. The phrase... 'I'm going to smash your face in', has no accent at all written into it (apart from what your imagination gives it). But, put on a deep London accent and it becomes crystal clear... "Oi'm gonna smash yer faice in!"

CAN'T, DON'T, and WON'T... These are quite simple, becoming canna, dinna, and winna. (Once again in Scots, canny, dinny, and winny)

I hope you get the difference. Just imagine Michael Caine saying everything in parenthesis (sorry, inverted commas) that might help. For the Scottish stuff, pretend you're Craig Ferguson.

OTHER LONDON PRONUNCIATIONS...

The letter 'H'... is often dropped in London street speech... Harry, Honey, and Handbag are pronounced 'arry, 'unny, and 'andbag, respectively.

ER... gets cropped to a guttural stop which sounds very much like a mix of the 'A' sound in the word 'land', and the 'U' sound in the word, 'up'. It is usually written as an 'a'. In this way geezer becomes, geeza, freezer becomes freeza, and runner becomes runna. Combining the 'A' rule from above, the word, newspaper, would be pronounced as 'news-pay-pa'.

R... Oh boy, where do we begin. The word 'horse', sounds innocuous enough, but the letter 'r' gets lost somehow, making the sound like 'hoe-se'. (Incidentally, the word 'lost', also gets changed to 'loe-st', almost 'lowest'. 'Lost and Found would approximately sound like 'lowest an' fanned'.)

TH... Whether it's at the beginning or end of a word, the 'TH' sound gets slanged/lazified to 'F'. (For example, thunder is pronounced 'funder', and if we use the 'ER' contraction above, we get 'funda'). 'With' becomes 'wif'. Similarly words like Ruth, tooth, truth, etc, can be pronounced 'Roof', 'toof', and 'troof'.

TH... in the middle of a word is basterdized differently, almost into a 'V' sound. Father becomes faw-ver, and bothered becomes bovvered.

THE OLD BRITISH MONETARY SYSTEM...

Despite my urgent need to get on to the definitions, I feel it only right to waffle just a little about the old British monetary system before it went decimal in 1971. Hopefully this will shed some light on the coins and terms of the dictionary definitions which deal with 'old-money'; Pounds, Shillings and pennies.

Farthing Coin - Quarter of a penny, used until 1960.
Halfpenny Coin – Half a penny, used until 1971.
Penny Coin – A penny, large copper coin, twelve pennies made a shilling. 240 pennies made a pound.
Threepence Coin – Threepence coin, usually called a 'thruppeny bit', it was thick and twelve sided. Four thruppences made a shilling.
Sixpence Coin – Six penny coin, small thin, silver colored. Two sixpences made a shilling.
Shilling Coin – Usually called a 'bob', or 'one bob bit'. Twenty shillings made a pound.
Two Shilling Coin – Yup, this was called a 'two bob bit', or a florin.
Half Crown Coin – This is where it gets slightly confusing. This is a two and a half shilling coin. It helps in this case to think American; the half-crown is actually a quarter of a pound.
Crown Coin – rarely used in service, mostly for commemorative issues.
(I hope the above made sense.)

THINGS TO REMEMBER ABOUT THE UNITED KINGDOM...

THE UNITED KINGDOM...
This collective term ('united') means everything... England, Scotland, Wales, Northern Ireland, and all the islands around them, Including the Hebrides, Shetlands, Orkneys, Isle of Man, Isle of Wight and Channel Islands.

GREAT BRITAIN means England, Scotland, Wales and all the islands around them. (BUT NOT Northern Ireland)
ENGLAND just means England.
WALES is a country, and is NOT part of ENGLAND. (Well, it kinda is, but it's NOT, RIGHT!)

THE WAR...

(Now, this is *mucho importante*...)
England didn't fight Hitler on its own... the rest of us, 'Brits', get pissed off when folks say *England* when they mean the whole of the UNITED KINGDOM. (Sorry, was I shouting?)

DRIVING...

YES, we Brits drive on the LEFT side of the road, but so do OTHER countries; Australia, Japan, India, Indonesia, many African countries, the Caribbean, Guyana, Suriname, and French Guyana.

BEER...

Let's face it, no guy ANYWHERE goes into a bar and orders a 'beer'. That's just for movies that don't want to mention one particular brand, offending all the others.
In most bars, even a slightly discerning guy would take a quick look to see what was on offer, and order by name, or by pointing to it. (Guys in new places have often covered up their ignorance by just pointing... probably works for most things... newspapers, beer, whores, etc etc...)
In Britain it's the same, but obviously different. In the UK, even bog-standard mainstream beer is divided into lager, light, mild, amber, dark, bitter, pale ale, and stout. There may be 'real ales' for sale, and the definition for those would take a whole book to peruse, but again, these would be ordered by name. Very few men, even when in company, would just say 'lager', and NO BRIT would just say 'beer', unless the person being addressed already knew what brand of 'beer' he was referring to. British barmen are well used to men approaching the bar and asking... "What have you got?" It could be a more specific question... "Give me a lager, what have you got?" Oh, and unless you're a poser (and I

have been from time to time) Brits rarely drink American beer...
cos it's mostly shite.

And that brings me to the absolute best joke about American
beer... It goes as thus...

"Why is drinking American beer like having sex in a canoe?
"I dunno."
"Because it's f*cking close to water!"
Oh, come on, that was funny!

To continue...
CIDER is alcoholic, wonderful, and if bought from farms is called
SCRUMPY. There is NO non-alcoholic cider in the UK. That's
called Apple Juice.
BRITS eat Chinese and Indian foods (Curries) by the bucket-
load, and fish and chips by the ton. We grew up on it, and we
miss it whenever we go anywhere else.
BRITS drink tea like it was cannabis juice. AND tea is the cure-all
for ANYTHING. "Oh, you just lost your husband in a terrible
driving accident... Don't fret, love, I'll put the kettle on."

No More Waffle
Okay, the introduction's over, let's get on with the actual
dictionary. Over 300 pages of definitions.
We love you all, and hope you have a great time.

PART ONE:
COCKNEY TO ENGLISH

Abergavenny – PENNY. (Origins; Welsh town)
1D. "I'm stone cold broke, not an abergavenny to me name."

Able and Willing – SHILLING.
1D. "An able an' willing for a mars bar? On your bike!"

Abraham Lincoln – STINKIN'. (Origins; American President)
2D. "Wow, I was abraham drunk last night, got a real head this morning."

Abraham's Willing – SHILLING.
2D. "Can you spare me an Abraham? I'm stony."
(OLD; Included in Hotten's 1858 Rhyming Slang Glossary)

Ace of Spades – AIDS (immune deficiency disease).
1D. "Watch out for him, he's got the ace of spades."
3D. "I'm off to jimmy's funeral. Motorhead got him in the end."
(Rock band, Motorhead, had the hit, 'Ace of Spades.)

Ache and Pain – RAIN.
1D. "Look outside, not ache and pain again!"

Acid Trip – RIP.
2D. "Crikey, I just got an acid in me trousers with that nail."

Acker Bilk – MILK. (Origins; 60's band leader and clarinetist, and had the #1 hit, 'Stranger on the Shore')
1D. "Hey mum? Got any Acker Bilk in the house?"

Adam and Eve – BELIEVE. (Origins; Biblical characters)
1D "Would you Adam and Eve it? Tom got married."

Adam and the Ants – PANTS (trousers). (Origins; British pop band)
2D. "Hey, have you seen my good Adams? I can't find 'em."

Adam Faith – SAFE (pronounced Adam Faiff). (Origins; 60's British singer/actor)
1D. "Let's put our valuables in the hotel's Adam Faith!"

Adrian Chiles – PILES Hemmorroids). (Origins; British TV/Radio presenter)
1D. "One sniff of rain, and me adrian chiles are out in force."

Adrian Mole – DOLE (Social Security). (Origins; teenage book/TV character)
2D. "I'm not working anymore; I'm on the adrian yet again."

Adrian Quist – PISSED. (Origins; Australian Tennis player)
1D. "Man, I was adrian quist last night."

Air Miles – PILES (Hemorrhoids).
1D. "My air miles are giving me gip today."

Airs and Graces – BRACES (suspenders in USA).
1D. "'Ave you seen my airs an' graces, love? I'll lose me adams without 'em."

Aesop's Fable – BUS TIMETABLE.
2D. "Have you seen my aesops anywhere?"

After Eight Mint – SKINT. (Origins; British thin mint confectionary)
2D. "I'm fully after eight tonight, buy us a beer."

Ain't It a Treat – STREET.
2D. "What's the news on the ain't it? What's the buzz?"

Air Gunner – STUNNER.
1D. "have you seen Frank's bird, she's an air gunner."

Ajax – TAX. (Origins; sink cleaner)
1D. "Always pay yer ajax's; it's the law, dude."

AJ Hackett – JACKET. (Origins; New Zealand guy who introduced bungie jumping.)
1D. "Got myself a new aj hacket last week, good cut too."

Alacompain – RAIN. (Origins; probably French... *a la campaigne*)
1D. "Oh no, not alacompain again... I'm sick of this."
(OLD; Included in Hotten's 1858 Rhyming Slang Glossary)

A La Mode – CODE.
2D. "Hey, Larry, we've got to talk a la mode, behind the rub-a-dub".

Al Capone – TELEPHONE. (Origins; American 1930's gangster)
1D. "I'll speak to you tomorrow, call you on the al capone."

Al Caponed – STONED (drunk or high). (Origins; American 1930's gangster)
1D. "Look at him, he's al caponed, falling all over the place."

Al Pachino – CAPPUCHINO. (Origins; American actor)
1D. "I'm off for a coffee. Either a laté or an al pachino."

Al Roker – TOKER. (Origins; American TV presenter)
2D. "Watch out, that guy is a real al roker."

Alan Border – OUT OF ORDER. (Origins; Australian cricketer)
2D. "Look at him bumping her Thruppeny bits, he's bang Allan."

Alan Knott – HOT. (Origins; English cricketer)
1D. "Don't touch the sausage rolls, they're really alan knott."

Alan Ladd – BAD. (Origins; American actor)
2D. "Don't trust Steve; as far as wooden pews is concerned, he's all alan."

Alan Minter – PRINTER. (Origins; English Boxer)
1D "Got me a new alan minter yesterday… an Epson."

Alan Minter – SPLINTER. (Origins; English Boxer)
2D. "Picked up this two by four and got a terrible Alan in me finger."

Alan Pardew – FLU (influenza). (Origins; English football manager)
1D. "Even after my jab, I still caught the alan pardew."

Alan Whicker – NICKER (British pound). (Origins; famous English TV personality)
1D. "Hey mate, lend me an alan wicker 'til Friday."

Alan Whicker(s) – KNICKERS (underpants, panties). (Origins; famous English TV personality)
2D "The elastics snapped in me alans!"

Albert Hall(s) – BALLS (testicles). (Origins; concert venue in London)
2D "Oh, unfair, he kicked me in the Alberts!"

Alderman's Nail – TAIL.
2D. "He's always wagging his alderman's. Can't keep it in his callards."

Alexander the Great – PLATE. (Origins; Ancient king of Macedonia)
2D. "Pass me yer alexander, I'll dish out the chicken."

Alexei Sayle – EMAIL. (Origins; Irreverent British comedian)
1D. "Drop me an alexei sayle, and I'll get back to you with the details."

Alex Nash – SLASH (urinate).
1D. "I'm off down the alley for a quick alex nash."

Alf Garnet – BARNET (hair). (Origins; British actor and West Ham supporter)
2D. "Whad'ya think of the new alf?, got it going, huh?"

Alfie Moon – COON (a person of black colour).
2D. "Look at her, she's always hanging out with the alfies."

Alfred the Great – WEIGHT. (Origins; Ancient English king)
2D. "Come on, guess the alfred of the baby. Win a score!"

Alger Hiss – PISS. (Origins; American accused of spying)
1D. "I'm off into the ditch for an alger hiss."

Ali McGraw – SCORE. (both game score, and 'what's up?', 'what's happening?')
1D. "Spurs, West ham, what was the ali mcgraw?"
2D. "I've not seen you for a while, what's the Ali, mate?"

Alibi Ike – BIKE. (Origins; film starring Joe E. Brown and Olivia de Havilland)
2D. "On yer alibi, mate, get yourself gone!"

Alice Bands – HANDS. (Origins; a stiff hair band)
1D. "She's not my problem now; she's out of my alice bands."

All Afloat – COAT.
1D. "Someone's nick me all afloat; it was on me chair."
(OLD; Included in Hotten's 1858 Rhyming Slang Glossary)

All Behind – BLIND.
1D. "He got hit in the war, poor bugger, he's all behind now."

Alligator – LATER.
1D. "What are you doing alligator? Going out?"

All Night Rave – SHAVE.

47

2D. "Got me a new razor, gives me a real close all night."

All Time Looser – BOOZER (bar, pub).
2D. "Nothing new this weekend, going to the all-time as usual."

Almond Rocks – SOCKS.
1D. "Got me some new insulated almond rocks yesterday, real cosy."

Alphonse – PONCE (pimp; one who lives off a prostitute's wages).
1D. "Oh, he's got his girl on the game, a right alphonse."

Alphonse – PONCE (sissy, an effeminate man).
2D. "Don't go too hard on him, he's an alphonse."

Amsterdam – TRAFFIC JAM. (Origins; city in the Netherlands)
1D. "There was a serious amsterdam down town this morning; bomb scare."

Anchor Spreadable – INCREDIBLE. (Origins; a British brand of butter).
2D. "Gor blimey, look at her pins, they're anchor spreadable."

Ancient Greek – FREAK.
1D. "What an ancient greek, he's into glam rock!"

Ancient Greek – REEK.
2D. "This ancient's of conspiracy, I've got a bad feeling about this."

Andy Caine – RAIN.
1D. "Look at the andy caine, it's coming down like cats and dogs."

Andy Farley – CHARLIE (cocaine).
2D. "I'm off to davy's, going to hampden me an ounce of Charlie."

Andy McNab – CAB. (Origins; ex-SAS, author of Bravo Two Zero)

48

1D. "I'm off down the boozer, call be an Andy McNab."

Andy McNab(s) – CRABS. (Origins; ex-SAS writer, author of Bravo Two Zero)
2D. "Don't touch her, she's got a case of Andy's."

Andy McNab(s) – KEBAB. (Origins; ex-SAS writer, author of Bravo Two Zero)
3D. "I'm off down the kebab shop, going to get me a bravo two-zero."

Andy Murray – CURRY. (Origins; Scottish tennis player)
1D. "I'm having an andy murray tonight; what do you want?"

Andy Pandy – BRANDY. (Origins; 60's British children's TV character)
1D. "What cha' having then? Make mine an andy pandy."

Andy Pandy – DANDY. (Origins; 60's British children's TV character)
2D. "Oh, that's fine and andy."

Andy Pandy – SHANDY. (Origins; 60's British children's TV character)
1D. "Oh, get me an andy pandy, it's too hot for proper beer."

Anekka Rice – PRICE. (Origins; British TV personality)
2D. "What was the anneka of your tin flutes, then?"

Angela Merkel – CIRCLE. (Origins; German Prime Minister)
1D. "I'm totally lost, mate, going round in angela merkels."

Angus Deayton – CHEATIN'. (Origins; British TV presenter/comedian)
1D. "I caught Dennis angus deaton'ing on his missus last night."

Angus MacGyver – SKIVER (shirks work).
1D. "He's useless, a real angus macgyver."

Ann Boleyn – GIN. (Origins; Henry VIII's second wife)
2D. "You have a beer, I'll have an Ann."

Ann Frank – WANK. (Origins; German diarist)
1D. "I don't like Darren, he's a bit of an ann frank."

Annie May Wong – PONG/STRONG.
2D. "That cheese is a bit Annie May!"

Ant and Dec(s) – CHEQUE. (Origins; British TV personalities)
1D. "I gotta go round the ham, cash a couple of and & decs".

Ant and Dec(s) – ORAL SEX. (Origins; British TV personalities)
2D. "I scored last night; a little ant in the alley behind the rub-a-dub dub".

Anthea Turner – EARNER. (Origins; TV presenter)
1D. "I'm doing bar work twice a week, it a good anthea turner."

Anthony Blunt – C*NT.
2D. "He can be a right Anthony when he wants to be."

Anti-Septic – YANK, (American). This is a 'kind' of 2nd degree rhyme. Septic Tank means 'Yank' so the 2nd degree would become 'septic', "I like him, he's a septic." Anti-yank would simply be the opposite; 'anti septic'.
2D. "Can't stand summer in London; too many rich septics for my liking."

Any Racket – PENNY FAGGOT.
1D. "Oh look at the sign, they're doing any rackets!"
(OLD; Included in Hotten's 1858 Rhyming Slang Glossary)

Appeny Dip – SHIP. (Origins; halfpenny)
1D. "I have to fly; I can't stand the appeny dip. I get seasick."

Apple Bobbing – 'robbing'.
1D. "I can't stand him, he's an apple bobbing git."

Apple Cider - SPIDER.
2D. "Hit that Apple before it gets under the bed!"

Apple Core – SCORE (team score, or, the latest news).
2D. "Hello mate, not seen you for a while. What's the apple?"

Apple Fritter – BITTER (beer).
2D. "I've tried the new apple but I prefer my old salmon."

Apple Fritter – SHITTER (your bum, or where you go to 'poo').
1D. "Oh, had a curry last night, my apple fritter's a bit nippy this morning!"

Apple Pie – SKY.
2D. "Apple's a bit on the dark side, looks like rain."

Apples and Pears – STAIRS.
1D. "I'm going up the apples and pears to bed."
(OLD; Included in Hotten's 1858 Rhyming Slang Glossary)

April Fools – POOLS (football betting).
1D. "That's it for another weekend, filled out the april fools."

April Fools – STOOLS.
2D. "I looked round the bar, not a single empty april in sight."

April in Paris – ARSE (ARIS) (short for Aristotle). (This one's a convoluted 3rd degree… a combination of bottle and glass – arse, and Aristotle - bottle)
3D. "I'm 'aving terrible trouble with me Aris."

April Showers – FLOWERS.
2D. "I plum forgot it was our anniversary, so I picked some aprils on the way home."

Arabian Nights – SHITES (diarrhea). (Origins; old tales)
1D. "Ouch, bad curry last night, got me a bad case of the arabian nights."

Arethusa – BOOZER (pub, bar). (Origins; mythological character)
1D. "What you doin' later, paper? Going down the arethusa?"

Aristotle – BOTTLE (guts, courage).
2D. "He was askin' for it, so I gave him a good kick up the Aris."

Armitage Shank – BANK. [Origins; Armitage Shank makes toilet bowls, sinks)
2D "I'm off to the Armitage to see if the wanker will give me a dog and bone."

Armitage Shank – WANK. [Origins; Armitage Shank makes toilet bowls, sinks)
1D. "Me bird's off on holiday, so I'll have to make do with an armitage shank."

Army and Navy – GRAVY.
2D. "Mum? Can I have some army for my mashed taters?"

Arnold Palmer – FARMER. (Origins; American golfer) One of the clever, more convoluted ones; the rhyme, although also meaning 'farmer', also refers to a bad golfer who spends a lot of time 'cutting' the long grass around a course.
2D. "He's a 62 handicap, always out in the country; a right Arnold."

Artful Dodger – LODGER. (Origins; Dickens character)
2D. "Things are tight back home, we've taken in an artful to help pay the clark kent."
(OLD; Included in Hotten's 1858 Rhyming Slang Glossary)

Arthur Ashe – CASH. (Origins; American tennis player)
1D. "That flash bloke's not short of arthur ashe."

Arthur Ashe – SLASH (urination). (Origins; American tennis player)

2D. "Oh, got caught short; I'm nipping round the alley for an arthur."

Arthur Bliss – PISS. (Origins; English composer).
2D. "I'm just popping to the cadbury's for an arthur."

Arthur Conan Doyle – BOIL. (Origins; Scottish author)
2D. "Get that kettle on the arthur, I'm parched!"

Arthur Daley – OLD BAILEY, (high court). (Origins; character in TV/film 'Minder')
1D. "Kevin's up at the arthur daley next week; this is his last chance."

Arthur Fowler – GROWLER (vagina). (Origins; character in BBC TV soap 'Eastenders')
1D. "I hear she's got the prettiest arthur fowler; not that I've seen it!"

Arthur Scargill(ed) – GARGLED (drunk). (Origins; British miners leader)
2D. "He's had more than one too many; he's right authured."

Artichoke Ripe – SMOKE A PIPE.
2D. "I never could understand them's that artichoke ripe, seems stupid."
(OLD; Included in Hotten's 1858 Rhyming Slang Glossary)

Ascot Races – BRACES (Suspenders in USA). (Origins; horse racing venue)
1D. "If I forget me ascot races, my trousers will be down at me ankles."

Aston Villa – PILLOW (Pronounced 'pilla'). (Origins; English football team)
1D. "Oy, you, stop fighting with me aston villa!"

Atilla the Hun – TWO-ONE, (a football score).
2D. "What's the Arsenal score, bobby?" "Attilla, mate."

Atomic Kitten – SMITTEN. (Origins; Liverpool girl band)
2D. "Have you seen Sean lately? He's atomic over his new chick."

Aunt Mabel – TABLE.
1D. "You're always welcome here, mate. Get your plates under the aunt mabel."

Aunt Nell – BELL.
1D. "Hurry, we'll be late for school, I can almost hear the aunt nell."

Aunt Nell – SMELL.
1D. "Ooh, hold yur nose, there's a right aunt nell in here."

Auntie Annie – FANNY (backside, ass).
1D. "She's a lazy sod, at home on her auntie annie watching the goggle box."

Auntie Dot – HOT.
1D. "Man, I'm sweating like a pig; forgot how auntie dot it is here in Ibeza."

Auntie Ella – UMBRELLA.
1D. "Wonderful - it's just starting to rain and I left me auntie ella in the car."

Auntie Lilly – SILLY.
1D. "I feel right auntie lilly in this uniform, mate."

Auntie Nellie – BELLY.
1D. "This is the life, lying on me auntie nellie on the beach."

Auntie Nellie – TELLY (television).
1D. "Turn on the auntie nelly, let's see the news."

Austin Power – SHOWER. (Origins; US Mike Myers movie)
2D. "I need an austin before I got out tonight."

Axel Rose – NOSE. (Origins; American rock singer)

2D. "Yikes! Look at her axel! It's like Concorde!"

Ayers Rock – COCK (penis). (Origins; sandstone outcropping in the middle of Australia)
1D. "Ooh, I'm randy tonight, me ayers rock's quaking in me trousers."

Aylesbury Duck – F*CK. (Origins; a breed of white duck)
2D. "Sorry mate, not interested; I don't give an aylesbury!"

Ayrton Senna – TENNER. (Origins; Formula 1 racing driver)
2D. "Here, lend us an ayrton 'til Friday me old china."

B

Baa Lamb – TRAM.
1D. "I'll meet you downtown; I'll take the baa lamb."

Babbling Brook – COOK.
2D. "My missus couldn't babble to save her life."

Babbling Brook – CROOK.
2D. "He's always on the babble, nothing on the level."

Babe Ruth – TRUTH. (Origins; American baseball player)
1D. "She told me a load of mince pies, but I wanted to know the babe ruth."

Baby Paps - CAPS.
1D. "When the carriage came past, the men all took their baby paps off, real touching."
(OLD; Included in Hotten's 1858 Rhyming Slang Glossary)

Bacardi Breezer – FREEZER. (Origins; alcopop drink)
1D. "I took the turkey legs home; put them in the bacardi breezer."

Bacardi Breezer – GEEZER. (Origins; alcopop drink)
2D. "He's always been an awkward sod, a real funny bacardi."

Back and Front – C*NT.
1D. "He hit it too hard, made a real back and front of it."

Back to Front – C*NT.
2D. "He hit his missus, he's a total Back."

Bacon and Eggs – LEGS.
2D. "Man, she's got a lovely pair of bacons."

Bacon Bits – TITS.
1D. "Look over there, in the pink top. What a nice pair of bacon bits."

Bacon Bonce – NONCE.
1D. "Steer clear of that one, he's a well-known bacon bonce."
(Supposedly, NONCE is a code used by prison staff to save pedophiles from being beaten up; "Not On Normal Communal Exercise").

Bacon Butty – NUTTY. (Origins; bacon sandwich)
1D. "Steer clear mate, the whole family's bacon butty."

Bacon Rind – BLIND.
1D. "You must be bacon rind not to see she's a fruit cake."

Bacon Rind – MIND.
2D. "Are you out of your bacon?"- 'mind', also 'blind'. Are you completely bacon?

Bacon Sarnie – PAKISTANI.
1D. "We got new neighbors, a bunch of bacon sarnies."

Baden Powell – TOWEL. (Origins;; founder of scout movement)
1D. "Here, cover up your bits, wrap a baden powell around you."

Bag For Life – WIFE. (One of those 'clever' rhymes)
1D. "Ah well, ten o'clock, time to get home to the bag for life."

Bag of Fruit – SUIT.
1D. "Whad ya think. I got me a new bag o' fruit!"

Bag of Sand – A GRAND (1000 pounds).
1D. "He owes me a bag of sand, and he hasn't paid back a jack benny."

Bag of Yeast – BEAST.
1D. "Don't trust him, darlin', he's a real bag o' yeast."

Bag of Yeast – PRIEST.
2D. "I'm off to the chipped apple to have a word with the local bag."

Baked Bean – QUEEN.
1D. "He's as queer as a three quid note, a real baked bean."

Baked Beans – JEANS.
1D. "I'm off down Carnaby Street to get me a new pair of baked beans."

Baked Potat'er – LATER.
2D. "I'll see ya baked, mate."

Baker's Dozen – COUSIN.
1D. "I'm off to the wedding then, catch up with all the news from me baker's dozens."

Bale of Hay – GAY.
1D. "Watch out, it's a woofters bar, full of bales of hay."

Bale of Straw – RAW.
1D. "That steak's way underdone, mate, bale of straw."

Ball and Bat – TWAT, (vagina and idiot).
1D. "I never did trust Frank, he always behaved like a complete ball and bat."

Ballet Dancer – CHANCER.
1D. "Look at Albert; always the dodger, always the ballet dancer."

Ball of Chalk – WALK.
1D. "I'm off for a ball of chalk, need the exercise."

Balloon Car – SALOON BAR.
2D. "I'm off down the boozer, I'll be in the balloon."

Ballroom Blitz – TITS. (Origins; a song by the glam group, Sweet.)
2D. "Oh my, she's grown up well, got marvelous ballrooms."

Bambi and Thumper – TRUMPER, (an arsehole). (Origins; cartoon characters)
2D. "I can't stand the man, he's always been a bit of a bambi."
(This is probably a convoluted slur on Donald Trump, as the rhyme for TRUMP is a dump (shit))

Bamboo Shoots – BOOTS.
2D. "I can't find me bamboos after the last game."

Bananarama – DRAMA. (Origins; English pop group)
1D. "Oh hark at her, she's a real bananarama queen!"

Band in the Box – THE POX.
1D. "Kevin got a little hospital stay, band in the box I'm afraid."

Band of Hope – SOAP.
1D. "I'm trying out a new liquid band of hope."

Bangers and Mash – CASH.
2D. "I knew his cheques were dodgy, so I got him to pay me in bangers."

Bangers and Mash – SPLASH, (urinate).
1D. "Keep a look out, I'm jumping over the wall to have a bangers and mash."

Bangers and Mash – TRASH.
2D. "Clean out the car mum, I'm sick of all the bangers lying around."

Barack Obama's – PYJAMAS. (Origins; American President)
2D. "I'm off to bed, where's me barracks?"

Barb Wired – TIRED.
1D. "I'm exhausted, barb wired out of me mind."

Barclay's Bank – WANK, (masturbate).
2D. "We all barclays from time to time, admit it!"

Bargain Hunt – C*NT. (origins; TV antiques program)
1D. "Oh boy, he missed the penalty! He made a right bargain hunt of it!"

Barnaby Rudge – JUDGE.
2D. "Wish me luck; I'm up in front of the barnaby tomorrow morning."

Barnacle Bills – TESTICLES.
2D. "He kicked him in the barnacles, perfect shot!"

Barnet Fair – HAIR. (Origins; this was an annual horse and entertainment fair in Barnet, London, from 1558 to 1881)
2D. "She must be going out on the town; she's got her barnet done."
(OLD; Included in Hotten's 1858 Rhyming Slang Glossary)

Barn(ey) Owl – ROW (ruckus).
2D. "I had a bit of a barney with the geezer behind the counter."

Barney Marlin – DARLIN'.
1D. "Come on, buy some onions, be a barney marlin."

Barney Rubble – DOUBLE. (Origins; cartoon character, Flintstones)
1D. "Come on quick, down the pub! At the barney rubble."

Barney Rubble – TROUBLE. (Origins; Flintstones cartoon character)
2D. "Stay away from Stan. He's a whole heap of barney."

Bar of Soap – DOPE.)(Origins; American Rhyming Slang)

Bar of Soap – POPE.
1D. "I'm off to Wembley, going to see the bar of soap."

Barry Brown – FROWN. (Origins; American actor)
1D. "Look at his boat race, what a barry brown."

Barry Cluff – ROUGH.
1D. "I don't like the look of little Sandy; she's a bit barry clough for me."

Barry Crocker – SHOCKER. (Origins; Australian entertainer, sang the theme for soap, Neighbours)
1D. "West Ham played shit last night, four nil; what a barry crocker."

Barry Cryer – LIAR. (Origins; English comedian/actor)
1D. "Shut your cakehole, yer tellin' barry cryers."

Barry McGuigan – BIGGUN. (Origins; Irish boxer)
1D. "Best not mess with the bouncer on the door, he's a real barry mcguigan."

Barry Nash – SLASH, (urinate). (Origins; Irish hurling player)
1D. "Get a round in, I'm off for a barry nash."

Barry White – SHITE. (Origins; American soul singer)
1D. "That movie was terrible, total barry white."

Basement Jaxx – TRASH.
2D. "Hey, I love Kristine, don't basement talk her."

Basil Brush – THRUSH, (genital rash). (Origins; UK kids puppet fox)
2D. "The wife got her itch diagnosed this morning; a nasty case of basil."

Basil Fawlty – BALTI, (type of Indian curry). (Origins; John Cleese sitcom character)
1D. "We're off down the Bombay Spice for a basil fawlty."

Basin of Gravy – BABY.

2D. "Hey Vikki, hand the basin over, I'll feed her."

Bat and Ball – TALL.
1D. "She's six foot, a real bat and ball girl."

Bat and Wicket – TICKET.
2D. "I've got a bat for tonight's train."

Bath Tub – PUB.
1D. "I'm parched, off down the bath tub."

Bathroom Tap – JAP.
1D. "The new restaurant's authentic, chock full of bathroom taps."

Bathroom Tiles – PILES, (hemorrhoids).
2D. "Man, me bathrooms are giving me crap today."

Battle Cruiser – BOOZER, (pub).
2d. "I'm going to have a couple of drinks round the battle before I go to the party."

Battle Of The Nile – TILE, (hat). (Origins; famous British naval victory)
1D. "I had to nick me a new battle of the nile, someone filched mine."
(OLD; Included in Hotten's 1858 Rhyming Slang Glossary)

Battle of Saratoga – YOGA.
1D. "I'm getting dragged to me wife's new 'thing', bloody battle of saratoga."

Battle of Waterloo – STEW.
1D. "I'm off early, the wife's making my favorite battle of waterloo tonight."

Baydon Powell – TROWEL. (Origins; he invented the Scout movement)
2D. "I got a new job today, brickie, I even get a new baydon."

Bayne & Duckett – F*CK IT. (Origins; Scottish footwear store)
1D. "Bayne and duckett, will you take a look at the raspberry's on the blonde!"

Bazaar – BAR.
1D. "Saturday night, going out? Yup, down the usual bazaar."

Beam Me Up Scotty – TOTTY, (nice looking women). (Origins; Original Star Trek phrase)
2D. "Oh man, this place is crawling with birds, beam me ups everywhere."

Beans on Toast – EVENING POST, (newspaper).
1D. "Go out and buy the beans on toast will you son?"

Bear's Paw – SAW.
1D. "Pass me the bear's paw, will you?"

Beating Heart – TART.
1D. "Look, a couple of beating hearts just walked in."

Becks & Posh – NOSH (Food). (Origins; David Beckham & Posh Spice)
1D. "Fancy a bit of becks an' posh? This bar does a great ruby."

Bee Hive – DRIVE.
1D. "I reckon I'm going out in the country this weekend, have a little bee hive around."

Beecham's Powder – LOUDER. (Origins; UK indigestion remedy)
2D. "What, I can't shout any beechams, can I?"

Bees and Honey – MONEY.
2D. "That's a swanky bar, you can't go in there without any bees."

Bees Knees – BUSINESSES.

1D. "Look around, all these bees knees just waiting on me calling in."

Bees Wax – TAX.
2D. "I got the red letter yesterday, from the bees people."

Beetles and Ants – PANTS.
2D. "I haven't got a clean pair of beetles, dang it."

Beggar My Neighbour – LABOUR, (Exchange).
2D. "Got an appointment with the beggar my's this afternoon. Wish me some friar."

Behind With The Rent – BENT, (gay).
1D. "I was always wondering; you're not behind with the rent, are you?"

Belinda Carlisle's – PILES, (Hemorrhoids). (Origins; American singer)
1D. "Bloody rain again. It always brings out me belinda carlisles."

Bell Ringers – FINGERS.
1D. "My bell ringers are sore after the gardening yesterday."

Belt Buckle – CHUCKLE.
1D. "Oh we had a real belt buckle at the pub last night. Great craic."

Ben Cartwright – SHITE. (Origins; character in TV western Bonanza)
1D. "Where's the council gritter, I've got a ben cartwright to unload!"

Bended Knees – CHEESE.
1D, "Bended knees an' Branston Pickle; the best sarnie ever."

Ben Dover – HANGOVER.
1D. "I'got a real bad ben dover this morning, spewed twice."

Ben Flake – STEAK.
1D. "I love a thick ben flake at the weekends; nice change."
(OLD; Included in Hotten's 1858 Rhyming Slang Glossary)

Bendy Flex – SEX.
1D. "Had the best bendy flex of me life last night, in me dream!"

Bengal Lancer – CHANCER, (fraud).
2D. "I need three good workers for a quick job, an' no bengals."

Benny Hills – PILLS. (Origins; British comedian/actor)
2D. "I'm going to get Benny'd up before going out tonight."

Ben Sherman – GERMAN. (Origins; british clothing brand)
1D. "Lot of ben shermans in London this weekend for the big game."

Berkshire Hunt – C*NT.
2D. "Don't ever trust 'Enry, 'e's a right berk sometimes."

Berlin Walls – BALLS.
2D. "Me callards are too slack, and making me berlins wobble."

Bernard Langer – BANGER, (Sausage). (Origins; German golfer)
1D. "Oh bernard langers and mash, me favorite dinner."

Bernard Matthew – QUEUE. (Origins; English chicken producer)
1D. "Look at the length of the bernard matthew, lets hit the boozer for an hour."

Bernard Miles – PILES, (hemorrhoids). (Origins; British actor)
2D. "Typical; I get a party to go to, and me bernards play up."

Bernie Flint – SKINT, (broke). (Origins; English pop singer)
1D. "No extras for a while, I'm totally bernie flint."

Bernie Winter – PRINTER. (Origins; English comedian)
1D. "Get to office supplies, get me a new Bernie winter."

Bertie Auld – BALD. (Origins; Scottish footballer)
2D. "Look at poor Percy now, as bertie as a snooker ball."

Beryl Reid – WEED. (Origins; English comedienne)

Burt & Ernie – JOURNEY. (Origins; Muppet characters)
1D. "We've got a right little bert an' ernie planned, five countries in ten days."

Bethnal Greens – JEANS, (denim). (Origins; area in London)
2D. "New bethnals, new razor, not bernie, what can go wrong?

Better Off Dead – RED, (Communist).
1D. "He's been a better off dead since he was at school."

Betty Boo – POO. (Origins; cartoon character)
2D. "I'm bursting for a Betty, where's the khazi?"

Betty Grable – TABLE. (Origins; American actress)
1D. "Typical West Ham, bottom of the flipping betty grable."

Bexleyheath – TEETH. (Origins; area of SE London)
2D. "Take a look at my bexleys; just polished this morning."

Bib & Brace – FACE. (Origins; workman's overalls)
1D. "Look at the bib an' brace on that, looks like a flipping volcano."

Biffo the Bear – HAIR. (Origins; kids comic (Beano) character)
2D. "Me biffo's not looking its best today, bloody wind."

Big Ben – TEN. (Origins; tall clock tower in London)
1D. "What time's the russel harty? Big ben? Gotcha."

Big Bloke – COKE, (cocaine). (Origins; American Rhyming Slang)

Big Dippers – SLIPPERS. (Origins; carnival ride)
1D. "I love to get me feet into me big dippers after a hard day."

Bill & Ben – PEN. (Origins; UK TV kids show characters)
1D. "Have you seen my bill an' ben; the present from dad."

Bill & Ben – TEN. (Origins; UK TV kids show characters)
1D. "Shots of tequila, about bill and ben of 'em."

Bill & Benner – TENNER. (Origins; UK TV kids show characters)
2D. "I'm taking it easy tonight, I only got a bill with me."

Bill Murray – CURRY. (Origins; USA actor/comedian)
1D. "Fancy a bill murray when the pub closes?"

Bill Oddie – VODDY, (Vodka). (Origins; English comedian/TV presenter)
1D. "Barman? Two bill oddies 'n' coke, two mothers ruin."

Bill Roffie – COFFEE. (Origins; English footballer/manager)
1D. "I'm sticking to bill roffie, thanks very much. Last night was tragic."

Bill Wyman – HYMEN. (Origins; member of the Rolling Stones)
1D. "Think they're virgins? No way; not a bill wyman in the room."

Billie Hoke – COKE. (Origins; American Rhyming Slang)

Billie Piper – HYPER. (Origins; English actress)
1D. "I like Valerie, but she's a bit too billie piper for my taste."

Billie Piper – SNIPER. (Origins; English actress)
1D. "Look at Danny at the bar, checking out the new talent like a billie piper."

Billie Piper – WINDSCREEN WIPER. (Origins; English actress)

2D. "I can't see a bloody thin in this rain, I need new billies."

Billy Bunter – PUNTER, (customer, or person who gambles).
(Origins; UK comic character)
1D. "Hey, come through an' help, we got a queue of billy bunters."

Billy Button – MUTTON.
1D. "Oh, look at her, billy button dressed as lamb, an' no mistake."
(OLD; Included in Hotten's 1858 Rhyming Slang Glossary)

Billy Goat – THROAT.
1D. "I've got a real sore billy goat this morning."

Billy Hunt – SILLY C*NT. (Origins; too many Bill Hunts to be certain)
1D. "No, treble twenty, double tops, billy hunt."

Billy Jean – CLEAN.
1D. "Betty's got andy mcnabs? Nah, I'm pretty sure she's billy jean."

Billy Ocean – SUN TAN LOTION. (Origins; American singer)
1D. "Pass the billy ocean, love, sun's coming out."

Billy Ray Cyrus – VIRUS. (Origins; American singer)
2D. "Had to take the old car an' scooter to the shop, I think it's got a billy ray."

Billy Straw – 10-pound draw (a 2-gram bag of cannabis).
Based on the name of the British Home Secretary's son, William Straw

Bin Laden - GARDEN. (Origins; Saudi terrorist)
1D. "Maisie? Oh, she's working in the bin laden."

Bin Lid – KID.
1D. "Russel harty on Friday? Can I bring the bin lids?"

68

Bin Lid – QUID, (british pound).
2D. "Toss me a bin coin for the supermarket trolley."

Birch Broom – ROOM.
2D. "I had to get me another birch to lay me brown in."
(OLD; Included in Hotten's 1858 Rhyming Slang Glossary)

Bird Bath – LAUGH.
1D. "Tottenham for the cup? You're having a bird bath."

Bird Lime – TIME, (usually prison time).
2D. "Harry's doing 5 months bird in Pentonville."
(OLD; Included in Hotten's 1858 Rhyming Slang Glossary)

Bird's Nest – CHEST.
1D. "He wasn't breathin'! I had to punch him right on the bird's nest."

Biscuit & Cookie – BOOKIE.
1D. "I'm off down the biscuit an' nookie, got a cert on the two o'clock."

Biscuit & Cookie – NOOKIE, (sex).
2D. "I'm feeling good today, got me biscuit last night."

Biscuit & Cookie – ROOKIE.
2D. "Try the lost wallet trick on the new biscuit barman."

Biscuits and Cheese – KNEES.
2D. "I 'ate laying floor tile; on me biscuits all flippin' day."

Biscuit Tin – CHIN.
1D. "Look at the biscuit tin on Larry's bird! It's a ski slope!"

Bish Bash Bosh – WASH.
2D. "I'm going to have a quick bish-bash before I hit the town tonight."

Black & Decker – PECKER, (penis). (Origins; American tool manufacturer)
1D. "From the gossip, Fred's black an' decker don't work no more."

Blackpool Rock – COCK. (Origins; seaside resort confectionary)
1D. "She looks timid, but when she gets her hand on me blackpool rock..."

Blackpool Tower - SHOWER. (Origins; seaside resort copy of Eiffel Tower)
1D. "I'll nip up for a quick blackpool tower, you watch the game build up."

Bladder of Lard – CARD.
2D. "Gor blimey, it's 'er birthday, and I forgot a bladder, didn't I."

Blade of Grass – ARSE.
2D. "I'm done walking, I'm parking my blade in the first pub I come across."

Blind Date – LATE. (Origins; Cilla Black TV show)
3D. "It's past seven, Colin, you're a bit cilla tonight, ain't ya?"

Blind Mice – ICE.
2D. "It's your round, I'll have a gay and blind."

Blood Red – HEAD, (blow job).
1D. "See Carol, I hear she likes to give blood reds on a regular basis."

Bloody Mary – HAIRY.
1D. "The new landlord's a bit bloody mary, he's nearly a frigging monkey."

Blue Peter – HEATER. (Origins; Naval signal flag)
1D. "Oh, turn up the blue peter, it's parky outside."

Blushing Bride – GIRL GUIDE.

2D. "They don't half grow up quick, she's a blushing already."

Boat Race – FACE. (Origins; a rowing race along the Thames River in London, held every year between the two 'prestige' universities of Oxford and Cambridge)
2D. (A song by the Monks) "Nice legs, shame about the boat."
3D. "She's a nice girl, but shame about the Oxford and Cambridge." (The two universities who compete in the 'boat race')

Boba Fett – WET.
2D. "No raincoat, no auntie ella, I'm real boba, an'd no mistake."

Bobbins and Cotton - ROTTEN.
2D. "Oi, don't be bobbin, Roger, give the kid a chance."

Bobby & Dick – SICK.
1D. "I'm not going to school today mum, I'm real bobby an' dick."

Bobby Brown – TOWN. (Origins; WAY too many to chose from)
2D. "I'm going up bobby this afternoon, do some shoppin'."

Bobby Moore – SCORE. (Origins; English footballer)
1D. "I feel lucky tonight, Jim. I'm sure I'm going to bobby moore."

Bobby Moore – SURE. (Origins; English footballer)
2D. "No, Mount Etna's in Sicily, I'm absolutely bobby."

Bob Cryer – LIAR. (Origins; English politician)
1D. "Shut your cakehole, yer tellin' bob cryers."

Bob Dylan – VILLAIN. (Origins; American singer)
1D. "Oh yeah, if I tell him 'no', I'm the bob dylan."

Bo Diddley – KIDNEY. (Origins; American singer/musician)
1D. "Too much drink can affect your bo diddleys, they say."

Bob Hope – DOPE, (drugs). (Origins; American comedian)
1D. "I think you've been smoking some bob hope, kiddo."

Bob, My Pal – GAL, (girl).
1D. "Going out on the town tonight, jus' me an' bob, my pal."
(OLD; Included in Hotten's 1858 Rhyming Slang Glossary)

Bob McNab – CAB. (Origins; English footballer)
1D. "We're late, no time for tubing it, we'll have to call a bob mcnab."

Bob Marley – CHARLIE, (cocaine). (Origins; Jamaican singer/musician)
1D. "Hey Tommy, got any bob marley? I'm asking for a friend."

Bob Squash – WASH.
1D. "I need a bob squash, been gardening all day."

Bodie and Doyle – OIL. (Origins; UK TV show characters)
1D. "I changed the bodie an' doyle in the car today."

Boiled Beef & Carrot – CLARET, (blood).
2D. "Oh you should have seen 'is face, covered in boiled beef."

Boiler House – SPOUSE.
1D. "You should see the way he treats his poor boiler house, terrible."

Bombay Duck – F*CK. (Origins; Chinese chicken dish)
1D. "I don't give a bombay duck, I want another drink!"

Bonnets So Blue – IRISH STEW.
2D. "Oh, I love a bit of bonnets, and mashed taters."
(OLD; Included in Hotten's 1858 Rhyming Slang Glossary)

Bonney Fair – HAIR.
2D. "Say what you like about Shiela, she's got beautiful bonney."

Bonnie & Clyde – SNIDE. (Origins; American gangsters)
1D. "Oh don't pay attention to what I say, I'm just being bonnie an' clyde."

Boom & Mizzen – PRISON. (Origins; sailing ship's masts)
1D. "Old Charlie got nicked at last; he's in the boom an' mizzen for years now."

Bootlace – CHASE, (heroin).

Bo Peep – SLEEP. (Origins; nursery rhyme character)
1D. "I just can't seem to get any bo peep right now, it's way too warm."

Boracic Lint – SKINT, (broke). (Origins; old wound bressing)
2D. "Just paid the mechanics bill for the jam; I'm boracic now."

Boris Becker – PECKER, (penis). (Origins; German tennis player)
2D. "I don't trust Jim around anyone's wife, 'e can't keep his boris in 'is trousers."

Boris the Bold – COLD.
1D. "Typical me, summer comes and I catch a boris the bold."

Boris Karloff – COUGH. (Origins; English actor)
2D. "That's a real nasty boris you've got there me old son."

Born & Bred – DEAD.
1D. "I can't believe it, one day he's here, the next, born an' bred."

Borrow & Beg – EGG.
2D. "Give us a sarnie, two borrows, sunny side up."

Boss Hogg – BOG, (toilet). (Origins; American TV character)
1D. "Where's the boss hogg? I gotta take a barry white."

Botany Bay – RUN AWAY. (Origins; old prison destination in Australia)
1D. "I couldn't stand up to three of 'em. I had to botany bay."

Bottle & Glass – ARSE.

1D. "Slipped on the vincent price, and landed right on me bottle an' glass."

Bottle & Glass – CLASS.
2D. "He don't have the bottle to pull a tux off properly."

Bottles & Stoppers – COPPER, (policeman).
2D. "I'll have to watch out, I think the bottle's on to me!"

Bottle of Beer – EAR.
2D. "I smacked 'im right round the bottle for 'is cheek."

Bottle of Beer – QUEER, (gay).
1D. "I always knew he was bottle of beer; I got good gaydar."

Bottle of Cola – BOWLER.
1D. "He can bat, but he's a terrible bottle of cola."

Bottle of Glue – NUMBER '2', (poop).
1D. "Wait for me, I' got to do a quick bottle of glue."

Bottle of Pop – SHOP.
1D. "Me jam's in the flippin' bottle of pop... again!"

Bottle of Porter – DAUGHTER.
1D. "Me bottle of porter's in the family way, again."

Bottle of Rum – BUM.
2D. "Sit on your bottle, Will, I'll get the next round in."

Bottle of Sauce – HORSE.
1D. "Oliver's new bird has a boat race like a ugly bottle of sauce."

Bottle of Scotch – WRISTWATCH.
1D. "I was on eBay the other week, got me a new bottle of scotch."

Bottle of Spruce – TWOPENCE.
1D. "Work all day, and for what a measly bottle o' spruce."

Bottle of Water – QUARTER, (drugs).
2D. "Can yer sell me a bottle? I got the cash."

Bottomless Pit – SHIT.
2D. "I'm off for a bottomless, felt it coming for a while."

Boutros Boutros Gali – CHARLIE, (cocaine). (Origins; Egyptian politician)
2D. "You wouldn't know where I can get some boutros, would ya?"

Bow & Arrow – BARROW.
1D. "Look after me bow an' arrow for a bit, gotta take a leak."

Bow & Arrow – SPARROW.
2D. "I hate spring, new fricking bows everywhere."

Bowl of Chalk – WALK.
1D. "I'm off for a bowl of chalk… shake the cobwebs out."

Bowl of Fruit – SUIT.
1D. "Hey, you like me new bowl of fruit? Only cost me ten knicker!"

Bowler Hat – CHAT.
2D. "Long time no see; let's get together for a bowler sometime."

Bowler Hat – TWAT.
1D. "Look at the bowler hat on the corner, what a pillock."

Bowl the Hoop – SOUP.
1D. "I'm not sure what's in this bowl the hoop, but it hits the spot."
(OLD; Included in Hotten's 1858 Rhyming Slang Glossary)

Bows & Arrows – FARRAH'S, (brand of trousers).

1D. "My God, Harry's looking smart for a change, that's a nice pair of bow and arrows."

Box of Toys – NOISE.
2D. "Oh dear, listen to the box Sammy's car's making."

Brace & Bit – SHIT. (Origins; old type of drill)
1D. "I can feel a brace an' bit coming on, stop at the next exit."

Brace & Bit – OUTFIT, (drugs paraphanalia) (Origins; New Zealand Rhyming Slang)

Brace & Bit – TIT, (breast). (Origins; old type of drill)
2D. "Honest, I've never seen a bigger raspberry on a brace in my life!"

Brad Pitt – FIT. (Origins; American actor)
2D. "I've been going down the fatboy, gotta get brad to keep up with Elsie."

Brad Pitt – SHIT. (Origins; American actor)
1D. "Larry plays me hot and cold, he can be a real brad pitt sometimes."

Brad Pitt – TIT. (Origins; American actor)
2D. "Oh, corner table, now that's what I call a nice pair of brads."

Brady Bunch – LUNCH. (Origins; American TV show)
1D. "Have we decided on the brady bunch yet?"

Brahms & Liszt – PISSED, (drunk). (Origins; classical composers)
2D. "Hi honey, I'm home... but I may be a little brahms."

Bram Stoker – CHOKER, (to freeze up). (Origins; Irish author of Dracula)
1D. "Man, he never even looker confident, a real bram stoker."

Bram Stoker – JOKER. (Origins; Irish author of Dracula)

1D. "Let's get out of here, do you think I'm bram stoking?"

Brass Bands – HANDS.
1D. "Take your brass bands off my trouble!"

Brass Door – WHORE.
1D. "It's been so long, even a brass door's tempting."

Brass Flute – PROSTITUTE.
2D. "Look at the brasses on the corner, making the place untidy."

Brass Tacks – FACTS.
1D. "Okay, let's get down to the brass tacks here… from the beginning."

Bread & Butter – GUTTER.
1D. "Harry was shitfaced, I found him lying in the bread and butter."

Bread & Butter – NUTTER, (crazy).
2D. "Watch out for that scrot at the end of the bar, he's a real bread."

Bread & Cheese - SNEEZE.
1D. "Oh watch out, I think I'm going to bread an' cheese."

Bread & Honey – MONEY.
2D. "Bob'll buy us a drink, 'e's got bread."

Bread Knife – WIFE.
1D. "Im off to the cabin cruiser wif me bread knife tonight."

Brendan Grace – FACE. (Origins; Irish comedian)
1D. "Nice body, shame about the Brendan grace."

Brenda Lee – KEY. (Origins; American singer)
2D. "Where's me brenda's, love? I can't find 'em."

Brian Clough – PUFF, (gay). (Origins; English footballer/manager)
2D. "Tin roof warning! There's a brian in the room."

Brian Clough – TOUGH. (Origins; English footballer/manager)
1D. "I'm buying Sammy a drink, he's had it brian clough recently."

Brian O'linn – GIN.
1D. "Give me a snifter of brian o'linn, an' I'll be on me way."
(OLD; Included in Hotten's 1858 Rhyming Slang Glossary)

Bricks 'n' Mortar – DAUGHTER.
1D. Got a big day tomorrow, I'm taking me bricks and mortar car shopping."

Bride & Groom – LIVING ROOM.
1D. "Take them cups of rosie into the bride an' groom, there's a dear."

Brigham Young – TONGUE. (Origins; American religious leader)
2D. "I slipped the new bird some brigham last night, she loved it."

Bright & Breezy – EASY.
1D. "Five nil, I've never known a game so bright an' breezy."

Brighton Pier – QUEER, (gay). (Origins, south English seaside town)
"Oh, look at the tourists that just walked in, one's a bit of a Brighton."

Brighton Sands – HANDS. (Origins, south English seaside town)
1D. "Look at the state of me brighton sands! I 'ate gardening!"

Briney Marlin – DARLIN'. (Origins; saltwater fish)
2D. "You look absolutely lovely tonight, me old briney."

Bristol Cities – TITS, (breasts). (Origins; This is worth a read; sailing ships used to trade between Bristol (England) and Bristol (Virginia). The trip was colloquially called going 'between the Bristols', and also probably described what the sailors would do to their wives or prostitutes when they got to port.)
2D. "Look at the barmaid, now she's got a lovely set of bristols."

Bristol City – TITTY. (Origins; English soccer club)
2D. "Let's go inside, they've got strippers. Didn't know this was a Bristol bar."

Bristol & West – CHEST. (Origins; British Building Society (credit union))
1D. "Watch out, nine o'clock, Bristol and west warning."

Britney Spears – BEERS. (Origins; American singer)
2D. "Come on Charlie, get the britney's in, your round!"

Britney Spears – EARS. (Origins; American singer)
1D. "Oh, look at the britney spears on that poor bloke, his head's got handles!"

Britney Spears – TEARS. (Origins; American singer)
1D. "Don't watch it to the end, there were Britney spears everywhere."

British Rail – MAIL. (Origins; UK National train company)
1D. "Did we get any british rail this morning, love?"

Brixton Riot – DIET. (Origins; area of London)
2D. "I'm going on a brixton, me tousers are way too tight."

Bromley By Bows – TOES, (run away). (Origins; area of east London)
2D. "I'm not fighting, I'm having it away on me bromleys."

Brown Bess – YES, (the affirmative). (Origins; British standard musket for years)
1D. "If he asks me to marry him, I'm saying brown bess."

(OLD; Included in Hotten's 1858 Rhyming Slang Glossary)

Brown Bread – DEAD.
1D. "I'm telling you, mate, that parrot is brown bread."
3D. "I saw the body on the road mate, no doubt, he was hovis for sure."
(Hovis is a brand of UK bread)

Brown Joe – NO, (the negative).
2D. "If he wants to put the rent up again, I'm saying 'brown joe'."
(OLD; Included in Hotten's 1858 Rhyming Slang Glossary)

Bruce Lee – KEY. (Origins; American Kung Fu star/actor)
2D. "Have you seen me brucies anywhere, love?"

Bruce Lee – PEE. (Origins; American Kung Fu star/actor)
1D. "I gotta go do a quick bruce lee, back in a tick."

Bruce Lee – TEA. (Origins; American Kung Fu star/actor)
2D. "Just what I needed on a cold day, love, a nice cuppa bruce."

Brussel Sprout – NOWT, (nothing).
1D. "I'm doing absolutely brussel sprout this weekend."

Brussel Sprout – SHOUT.
2D. "If you're going down the boozer on Saturday, give's a brussel."

Brussel Sprout – SCOUT.
1D. "New boozer, I'm going in to brussel sprout it for us."

Brussel Sprout – TOUT (sell).
2D. "I got no ticket, so keep your minces peeled for a brussel."

Bubble and Squeak – BEAK, (nose). (Origins; British dish, mashed potatoes and cabbage)
1D. "Slammed the door in my face! Nearly took me bubble an' squeak off!"

Bubble and Squeak – GREEK. (Origins; British dish, mashed potatoes and cabbage)
2D. "Old Zorba's not a bad bloke, considering he's a bubble."

Bubble and Squeak – WEEK. (Origins; British dish, mashed potatoes and cabbage)
2D. "This one was a hard bubble, I'll need a pint come Saturday."

Bubble Bath – LAUGH.
2D. "Fat Larry play football? You're 'avin a bubble aren't ya?

Bucket & Pail – JAIL.
2D. "One more time for drunk an' disorderly, an' I get seven days in the bucket."

Bucket of Water – DAUGHTER.
1D. "I'm taking me bucket o' water up town on Saturday to see 'er favorite band."

Bucket & Spades – AIDS.
1D. "Too bad about young Nicky, that bucket an' spades is a terrible thing."

Buddy Holly – VOLLEY. (Origins; American singer)
1D. "He called me a sherman, so I gave him a buddy holly right back."

Bugs Bunny – MONEY. (Origins; cartoon character)
2D. "I've got some bugs in me davey and I'm off down the rub-a-dub-dub."

Bull & Cow – ROW, (argument).
2D. "Oh, me and Allie 'ad a right bull last night in the cabin.".
(OLD; Included in Hotten's 1858 Rhyming Slang Glossary)

Bullock Bladder – LADDER.
2D. "Looks like Stan the window cleaner's in at Maisies, he's left 'is bullock outside."

Bullock's Horn – PAWN.
1D. "I'm boracic, I had to take me best Fender to the bullock's horn last week.

Bumble Bee – ECSTACY, ('E').
2D. "I scored some bumble for the weekend, going to be a corker!"

Bunny Ears – TEARS.
1D. "Man, she cried like a baby, real bunny ears too!"

Bunsen Burner – EARNER, (a job that pays good money). (Origins; lab equipment)
2D. "The jobs kinda dirty, but it's a nice little bunsen."

Burnt Cinder – WINDOW.
1D. "I got so mad, I threw 'is insects an' ants out the burnt cinder."

Burton on Trent – RENT. (Origins; town in Staffordshire, England)
2D. That landlord's a right bitch, he's only gone an' raised me burton again."

Bushel & Peck – CHEQUE.
1D. "I gave him a bushel an' peck. I hope it doesn't bounce."

Bushel & Peck – NECK.
2D. "Sandra's got a bushel like a swan."

Bushey Park – LARK, (prank). (Origins; town in Hertfordshire, near London)
1D. "Oh, it was a bushey park alright, we laughed our heads off."
(OLD; Included in Hotten's 1858 Rhyming Slang Glossary)

Buster Keaton – MEETING, (meetin'). (Origins; American actor)
1D. "Remember, big day Saturday, see you at the buster keaton."

Bus Timetable – FABLE, (pack of lies).
1D. "He gave me a great excuse, but the whole thing was a bus timetable."

Butchers Hook – LOOK.
2D. "You've cut yourself? Give us a butchers, then."

Butter Flap – CAP.
1D. "So I doffed me old butter flap and walked in to 'is office."
(OLD; Included in Hotten's 1858 Rhyming Slang Glossary)

C

Cab Rank – BANK.
1D. "I'm off down the cab rank, see the sherman tanker for a loan."

Cabin Cruiser – BOOZER, (bar, pub).
2D. "Where's Danny? Off down the cabin early?"

Cadbury's Log – BOG. (Origins; British dessert)
1D. "We can't do gardening today, the grass is like a cadbury's log."

Cadbury's Flake – MISTAKE. (Origins; British chocolate bar)
1D. "God, he's missed a council gritter! What a cadbury's flake!"

Cadbury's Fudge – JUDGE. (Origins; British chocolate bar)
1D. "He's up in court today, I hope the cadbury's fudge goes light on 'im."

Cadbury's Snack – BACK.
2D. "Lor' love a duck, me cadbury's playing me up something rotten."

Cadbury's Swirl – GIRL. (Origins; British chocolate bar)
2D. "Come sit on me lap, me old Cadbury."

Cain & Abel – TABLE. (Origins; Bible characters)
2D. "Sit yourself down at the cain and I'll bring your tommy."
(OLD; Included in Hotten's 1858 Rhyming Slang Glossary)

Callard & Bowsers – TROUSERS. (Origins; UK Toffee maker)
2D. "Hold on, I'm just pulling up me callards".
3D. "'e was caught with 'is lards down!"

Calvin Klein – FINE. (Origins; Fashion Mogul)
2D. "I'm feeling calvin today."

Calvin Klein – WINE. (Origins; Fashion Mogul)
2D. "Pass me the wine list, I fancy a glass of calvin with my meal."

Camden Town – A BROWN, (halfpenny).
2D. "I found a Camden in the street today, mu luck's in!"
(OLD; Included in Hotten's 1858 Rhyming Slang Glossary)

Camel's Hump – DUMP, (defecation).
2D. "hang on guys, I'm just going for a quick camels."

Canal Boat – TOTE, (carry).
2D. Man, I'm loaded today, hands full, I can't canal another thing."

Canary – FAIRY, (gay man).
1D. "Look at that canary, he's even got a pink handbag!"

Canary Wharf – DWARF. (Origins; Area of London)
2D. "I can't believe Jimmy's just five foot one, what a canary!"

Candlesticks – ZITS.
1D. "He's got bad acne; candlesticks all over."

Candle Wax – TAX.
1D. "I'm off down to town hall, pay me candle wax bill."

Candle Wick – DICK, (penis).
2D. "Great night last night, me candle's all tingly."

Canoes – SHOES.
1D. "Look at the canoes on him! Must be size 14's, what a pair of boats."

Can of Oil – BOIL, (blemish).
2D. "She'd be nice looking, but only once her canov's clears up."

Canterbury Tales – WALES. (Origins; book by Geoffrey Chaucer)
1D. "Going off to canterbury tales for me 'olidays, Cardiff."

Can't Keep Still – TREADMILL.
1D. "I bought me'self a can't keep still the other month; an expensive coat rack."

Cape of Good Hope – SOAP. (Origins; Southern tip of Africa)
1D. "Went to the bog to wash me hands; no cape of good hope!"

Captain Cook – BOOK. (Origins; British naval explorer)
1D. "He's going to be a clever 'un; always got his hovis in a captain cook."

Captain Cook – LOOK. (Origins; British naval explorer)
2D. "I just went over there to take a captain."

Captain Hook – BOOK. (Origins; character from Peter Pan)
1D. "Tommy went to court; the damn cadbury's threw the captain hook at him."

Captain Hook – LOOK. (Origins; character from Peter Pan)
2D. "Blimey, take a cadbury's at this, it's terrible."

Captain Kirk – TURK. (Origins; Original Star Trek captain)
1D. "He looks a bit tanned, maybe got a bit captain kirk in him somewhere."

Captain Kirk – WORK. (Origins; Original Star Trek captain)
2D. "Ah well, Monday morning... off to captain again."

Car & Scooter – COMPUTER.
1D. "Gor blimey, this internet's getting popular; I ain't even got a car and scooter!"

Cardboard Box – POX.

1D. "Steer clear of Mary for a few months, not unless you want the cardboard box."

Carpet Pile – SMILE.
1D. "Luv a duck, look at the carpet smile on her; she must have got some last night!"

Carpet & Rugs – JUGS, (breasts).
2D. "Yup, that Veronica's sure went and grown up; lovely pair of carpets on her now."

Carving Knife – WIFE.
2D. "I left the carver on her own tonight, she's a bit moby."

Casa Blanca – WANKER.
1D. "Tommy's a right casa blanca, he's gone and got nicked again."

Cash & Carried – MARRIED.
2D. "You gotta feel sorry for Dave; poor bloke got cashed at the weekend."

Castle Rag – FLAG, (fourpence).
1D. "Dirty sod gave me a castle rag after all that work."
(OLD; Included in Hotten's 1858 Rhyming Slang Glossary)
(From Hotten's book, he mentions that the populace hated the fourpence piece, as it encouraged the reduction of a tip from sixpence)

Cat & Cages – WAGES.
1D. "I'm off down the cabin cruiser, got me cats and cages today."

Cat & Dog – BOG, (toilet).
1D. "Get a round in, mate. I'm gonna splash in the cat and dog."

Cat & Mouse – HOUSE.
2D. "I went 'round to his cat to wake him up."
(OLD; Included in Hotten's 1858 Rhyming Slang Glossary)

Catherine Zeta Jones – MOANS.
2D. "We were in the middle of it, nice and quiet, then she goes all catherine zeta on me!"

Cattle Truck – F*CK.
1D. "I don't give a cattle truck anymore, she can piss off."

Cellar Flap – TAP, (borrow).
1D. "I'm calling into Tommy's, see if I can cellar flap a godiva 'til Friday."

Central Heating – MEETING.
1D. "I gotta go in early today, there's a central heating at eight."

Centre Half – SCARF. (Origins; football position)
1D. "You seem your centre half? It's the first game of the season."

C'est La Vie – PEE, (urinate). (Origins; French for 'That's life')
2D. "I'm nipping into the café for a quick c'est la; I'm bursting."

Chairman Mao – COW, (throw a fit). (Origins; Chinese leader)
2D. "It's only a trip to Manchester, don't have a chairman."

Chalfonts St Giles – PILES, (Hemorrhoids). (Origins; town just outside London)
2D. "Me chalfonts are worse, I'll be going to the docs soon."

Chalk Farm – ARM. (Origins; area of London)
1D. "I bashed me flippin' chalk farm in the doorway, real sore."
(OLD; Included in Hotten's 1858 Rhyming Slang Glossary)

Chandelier – QUEER.
1D. "Oops, must be queens night out, look at the chandeliers that have just walked in."

Charing Cross – HORSE. (Origins; London station junction)
1D. "It was a riot right enough, police on charing crosses and everything."

Charing Crosser – TOSSER, (wanker). (Origins; person from Charing Cross, London)
1D. "Bunch of Arsenal supporters, charing crossers, the lot of 'em."

Charlie Brown – CLOWN. (Origins; cartoon character)
2D. "Christ, there's a streaker on the park, what a proper charlie."

Charlie Bucket – F*CK IT. (Origins; Roald Dahl character)
1D. "If they score again, I'm off home, charlie bucket."

Charlie Chan – TAN. (Origins; fictional character by Earl Derr Biggers)
1D. "The Jones's are just back from Tenerife, look at their charlie chan."

Charlie Chester – CHILD MOLESTER. (Origins; English comedian)
1D. "Have you seen 'is young bird? He's a right Charlie Chester."

Charlie Dicken – Chicken. (Origins; short for Charles Dickens)
1D. "Missus 'as got charlie dicken in the oven, I'm off home early."

Charlie Drake – STEAK. (Origins; British comedian)
1D. "I think I'll have the charlie drake, please, well done."

Charlie Hunt – C*NT. (Origins; none found)
1D. "I tried to fix the door hinges, but I made a total charlie hunt of it."

Charley Lancaster – HANDKERCHER, (handkerchief).
2D. "I was glad I had a charley with me, all that crying and stuff."
(OLD; Included in Hotten's 1858 Rhyming Slang Glossary)

Charlie Nash – SLASH, (urinate). (Origins; Northern Irish Boxer)
1D. "Sorry, two pints, and I gotta take a charlie nash."

Charlie Prescott – WAISTCOAT. (Origins; none found)
1D. "Like me new whistle, it's got a charlie prescott too."
(OLD; Included in Hotten's 1858 Rhyming Slang Glossary)

Charlie Pride – RIDE. (Origins; American country singer)
1D. "We're going to take a charlie pride on the cross channel ferry this weekend."

Charlie Ronce – PONCE, (effeminate or gay man).
1D. "I know Howard's a charlie ronce, but he's harmless."

Charles Fox – BOX. (Origins; too many to choose from)
1D. "So what's on the olde charles fox tonight then?"

Charm & Flattery – BATTERY.
2D. "Me kareem died last night, mechanic said it needed a new charm."

Chas & Dave – SHAVE. (Origins; Cockney singers)
1D. "You need a flipping chas an' dave, an' no mistake."

Cheddar Cheese – KEYS.
2D. "Got me hackneys, got me cheddars, got me dosh, I'm sorted."

Cheerful Giver – LIVER, (meat).
2D. "We're havin' cheerful an' onions for dinner tonight. I can't wait."

Cheese & Ham – SCRAM, (run away).
1D. "You broke the window, we better cheese an' ham."

Cheese & Kisses – MISSUS, (wife).
"I'm off up town, meeting the cheese an' kisses for lunch."

Cheese & Rice – JESUS CHRIST.
1D. "They missed again, cheese an' rice! Come on Hammers!"

Cheese Bap – JAP.
1D. "Those cheese baps were pure shits during the war."

Cheese Rind – FOUR OF A KIND.
1D. "I won this hand for sure, cheese rind, kings."

Cheesy Quaver – FAVOUR. (Origins; British crisp snack)
2D. "Do me a cheesy, Bob. Get the TV onto the footy."

Cheesy Quaver – RAVER. (Origins; British crisp snack)
1D. "Gladys may look calm, but she a bit of a cheesy quaver when she gets drunk."

Cheggers Plays Pop – SHOP. (Origins; British TV programme)
2D. "Oi, Charlie, mind the cheggers for a mo, I gotta take an ogden."

Chelsea Blue – JEW. (Origins; London football team)
1D. "Must be a conference in town, lots of chelsea blues around."

Chelsea Pier – QUEER. (Origins; pier on the Thames in London)
1D. "I've never seen anything more Chelsea pier than that wot just walked in."

Cheltenham Bold – COLD. (Origins; town with racecourse west of London)
1D. "Gloves and scarf weather; cheltenham bold outside."

Cherie Blair – PENALTY FARE. (Origins; British Prime Minister's wife)
1D. "Got slapped with a cherie blair yesterday; should have bought a ticket before I went."
('Penalty Fare' is an on-the-spot fine for travelling in a train, and not having previously bought a ticket.)

Cherry Hogg – DOG.

2D. "I'm mad, my cherry got off its lead again."

Cherry Pie – LIE.
1D. "Told a couple of cherry pies to the wife last night, think I got away with it."

Cherry Ripe – PIPE. (Origins; this is an Australian chocolate bar; could be Aussie slang)
"I love me cherry ripe, I could smoke all day."
(OLD; Included in Hotten's 1858 Rhyming Slang Glossary)

Cheryl Crow – SNOW. (Origins; American singer)
1D. "I hate winter, it's forecast cheryl flippin' crow tomorrow."

Chevy Chase – FACE. (Origins; the origin is widely thought to be the American actor/comedian, but the rhyme is probably referring to a 16th century ballad, and this is probably where the comedian took his name)
2D. "Not only a nice body, but a cute chevy too."
(OLD; Included in Hotten's 1858 Rhyming Slang Glossary)

Chewy Toffee – COFFEE.
2D. "Me an' me cheese are going out for a cuppa chewy."

Chew The Fat – CHAT.
1D. "I love the pub… the beer, the laughs, chewin' the fat."

Chicken & Rice – NICE.
1D. "That new jam jar of yours is chicken an' rice, mate."

Chicken Curry – WORRY.
1D. "Come on love, don't chicken curry over it, that never changed anything!"

Chicken Dinner – WINNER.
2D. "I did good today at the old gee-gees; two chickens and a couple of each ways."

Chicken Dipper – SLIPPER.

1D. "This is a night to draw the curtains, put me chicken dippers on, an' watch the auntie Nellie."

Chicken Dipper – STRIPPER.
2D. "That chicken should have jacked it years ago; mutton undressed as lamb."

Chicken Jalfrezi – CRAZY. (Origins; Indian Curry dish)
1D. "No bull, Holly just went all chicken jalfrezi on her man, for nothing!"

Chicken Oriental – MENTAL. (Origins; Indian Curry dish)
1D. "It was totally chicken oriental in the nuclear sub on Saturday night."

Chicken Plucker – F*CKER.
1D. "I hate Reed; he's a dirty chicken plucker all the way through."

China Plate – MATE, (friend).
2D. "How are you doing, my old china? Not seen ya for a while."

Chinese Blind – MIND.
2D. "Lend you a paul mckenna? You're out of your chinese mate."

Chinese Chippy – NIPPY, (cold weather). (Origins; some Chinese take-aways in the UK double as fish and chip shops)
2D. "You know winter's comin', there's a bit of Chinese in the air."

Chip Butty – NUTTY. (Origins; a French Fry sandwich)
1D. "The whole idea of shifting the stadium is chip butty, mate."

Chipmunks – TRUNKS.
1D. "Don't forget to pack me chipmunks for the beach, love."

Chipped Apple – CHAPEL.

1D. "I'll have to go to the chipped apple now, that's where Dot's getting cashed."

Chips & Peas – KNEES. (Origins; in English fish & chip shops, they sell mushy peas)
1D. "Love, I'm on me chips an' peas, don't take me to your mums."

Chitty Chitty Bang Bang – COCKNEY RHYMING SLANG. (Origins; movie)
2D. "We're all about chitty chitty in this book, ain't we?"

Choc Ice – DICE. (Origins; British ice cream bar)
1D. "I lost a few lady godivas on the choc ice tables last night."

Chocolate Frog – WOG, (person of color, not black).
2D. "There's a reggae festival in Hyde park, lots of chocolates around."

Chocolate Fudge – JUDGE.
1D. "I'm up on Monday, let's see what the chocolate fudge decides."

Christian Slater – LATER. (Origins; American actor)
1D. "I'm off home, I'll see you christian slater."

Christian Ziege – EAGER. (Origins; German footballer/manager)
1D. "Check out Linda, beavering away, I like her, she's a bit christian ziege."

Christmas Card – RAILWAY GUARD.
1D. "We've no tickets, look out for the christmas cards."

Christmas Crackered – KNACKERED, (exhausted). (Origins; Christmas decoration)
1D. "I'm completely christmas crackered, I need my scratcher, pronto."

Christmas Eve – BELIEVE. (Origins; day before Christmas)
1D. "I don't christmas eve it, Harriet drinking beer!"

Chump (Or Chunk) Of Wood – NO GOOD.
1D. "Keep a watch on Opie, he's up to a chump of wood."
(OLD; Included in Hotten's 1858 Rhyming Slang Glossary)

Church Pews – SHOES. (Origins; long benches in churches)
1D. "I'm off to get me church pews re-soled, they're pretty bare."

Church Boys – CUSTOMS AND EXCISE.
1D. "I got me American parcel stopped by the church boys, bastards."

Cilla Black – BACK. (Origins; British TV star/singer)
2D. "Oh, look, Albert an' Steph are cilla from their hols."

Cinderella – STELLA, (Artois, beer). (Origins; children's story character)
1D. "Get a round in, Norrie! Three cinderellas!"

Circus and Clown – BROWN.
2D. "Abe's almost gone feckin' circus on us, weather in Spain must have been good."

Clair Rayners – TRAINERS. (Origins; author/TV personality)
1D. "Whad ya think of me new Claire Rayners?"

Clark Gable – TABLE. (Origins; American actor)
1D. "Okay, cards on the clark gable, I don't want to go to your darky's."

Clark Kent – BENT. (Origins; Superman character)
1D. "Never seen a more obvious one, clark kent as a nine bob note."

Clark Kent – RENT. (Origins; Superman character)
2D. "Sorry Dave, I'm having a tough time coming up with this month's clark."

Clement Freuds – HEMORROIDS. (Origins; TV chef/personality)
2D. "Me clements ain't half giving me problems!"

Clever Mike – BIKE.
1D. "I'm on me clever mike, away from here."

Clickety Click – 66.
1D. "Ah well, I hit the big clickety click next month."

Clonakilty – GUILTY. (Origins: town in Ireland)
1D. "He was banged up for a year, jury found him clonakilty."

Clothes Peg – EGG.
1D. "I love me boiled clothes peg in the morning."

Clothes Pegs – LEGS.
1D. "Look at the clothes pegs on 'er. The skirt's the width of a belt."

Clucking Bell – F*CKING HELL.
1D. "Clucking bell, that was a close one, 5-4 after 95 ninutes."

Coals & Coke – BROKE.
2D. "I heard the juice machine at the café is coals for the summer."

Coat & Badge – CADGE (borrow).
1D. "Hey Billy, can I coat an' badge a jacket from you, I lost mine."

Coat Hanger – CLANGER, (spoken mistake).
1D. "He only went an said his secret girlfriend's name out loud, a real coat hanger."

Cobbler's Awls – BALLS, (testicles).
2D. "I don't believe a word he says, he talks cobblers most of the time."

Cock & Hen – TEN.
2D. "Big round, after a tip, I didn't get any change from a cock."

Cock Linnet – MINUTE, (time). (Origins; bird)
1D. "Hold on a cock linnet, tell me that again?"

Cock Sparrow – ARROW. (Origins; bird)
1D. "Looks like Davey's been hit by cupids little cock sparrow."

Cock Sparrow – BARROW. (Origins; bird)
2D. "Bill? He's wheeling his cock 'round the market somewheres."

Cockle & Mussels – BRUSSELS, (sprouts).
1D. "Fried Cockles an' mussels with brown gravy… smashing!"

Cockney Rhyme – TIME.
1D. "I ain't got the cockney rhyme for this, get on wi' it!"

Cockroach – COACH.
1D. "Brighton Pier by ten in the morning, lovely cockroach ride."

Cocoa – SAY SO. (Said facetiously; related to the definition below)
1D. "Berlins in France? Okay kiddo if you cocoa."

Cocoa Drink – THINK. (Said facetiously; related to the definition above)
1D. "You're not drunk. Yes. I cocoa drink the same mate."

Cod & Plaice – FACE.
2D. "Sammy's new bird has a cod like a bag of windjammers."

Coffee Stalls – BALLS.
2D. "From what I heard, he got his coffees slapped real hard after that last time."

Cold Chill – OLD BILL, (police).

1D. "Watch out, the cold chill have got undercovers walking round."

Collar and Cuff – PUFF, (gay, effeminate man).
2D. "There's a couple of collars in the corner, all close and cuddly."

Crowded Space – SUITCASE.
2D. "We got our crowdeds all packed, Lanzarotte tomorrow!"

Colney Hatch – MATCH. (Origins; small area in north London)
1D. "You going to the big colney hatch? Should be a cracker."

Colonel Gadaffi – CAFÉ. (Origins; Libyan dictator)
1D. "Panic over; I found him down at a Carnaby Street colonel gadaffi."

Comedy Dave – RAVE. (Origins; BBC Radio 1 DJ)
2D. "Are you coming to the comedy on Friday night?"

Conan Doyle – BOIL. (Origins; Author of Sherlock Holmes)
2D. "He's got a conan on his firemans the size of me eye!"

Condoleezza Rice – PRICE. (Origins; American politician)
2D. "I'll buy Bill's jam jar, as long as the condoleeza's right."

Connaught Ranger – STRANGER. (Origins; Irish regiment in the British Army)
1D. "See ya later Henry, don't be a connaught ranger again, okay?"

Constantino Rocca – SHOCKER, (disaster). (Origins; Italian golfer)
2D. "I played golf at Troon yesterday; it was a complete constantino."

Coochie Coo – ZOO.
2D. "We're off to the coochie; they've got new performing seals."

Cooking Fat – CAT.
1D. "Has the cooking fat done a runner? Not seen her for ages."

Copacabana – SPANNER, (wrench). (Origins; Resort in Brazil)
2D. "Pass me the copa, the nine sixteenths."

Cop a flower pot – COP IT HOT, (get into big trouble).
1D. "Jimmy copped a flower pot on Saturday, fighting, got nicked, and hit a bottle."

Corned Beef – TEETH, (pronounced, 'teef').
1D. "Bloody spoon hit me corned beef; bloody sore too."
3D. "I got so mad, I smacked 'im in the fray bentos."
(Fray Bentos makes corned beef in the UK.)

Corn on the Cob – JOB.
2D. "How can Valerie afford booze, she ain't got a corn."

Corned Beef – DEAF, (pronounced 'deef').
1D. "You didn't hear the siren? Are you corned beef?"

Cornish Pastie – NASTY. (Origin; meat pastry made in Cornwall)
2D. "Don't order the ruby curry here, it's totally cornish!"

Cough & Drag – FAG, (cigarette).
1D. "Boss, is it alright if I nip out for a quick cough and drag?"

Council Gritter – SHITTER.
1D. "He kicked me so hard, right in the council gritter too."

Council Gritter – SITTER, (easy chance to score).
2D. "Five yards out, an' he misses; what a council!"

Council Houses – TROUSERS.
1D. "Come an' see this, Kev's only wearing pink council houses!"

Country Cousin – DOZEN.
1D. "Get me eggs when you're at the store, a country cousin!"

Cousin Kyle – PEDOPHILE. (Origins; cartoon character in South Parks)
1D. "You better watch yourself, mate. You'll turn into a cousin kyle."

Covent Garden – A FARDEN, (Cockney pronunciation of farthing (quarter penny)). (Origins; district of London)
1D. "Get out, don't come back until you have a covent garden in your dirty hand."
(OLD; Included in Hotten's 1858 Rhyming Slang Glossary)

Cow & Calf – HALF.
1D. "It's hot. I could use a cow and calf of cold gary right now."

Cow & Calf – LAUGH.
1D. "Hammers win the title? You're having a cows calf, ain't you?"
(OLD; Included in Hotten's 1858 Rhyming Slang Glossary)

Cows and Kisses – MISSUS, (wife).
2D. "Oops, best behavior lads, the cows just walked in."
(OLD; Included in Hotten's 1858 Rhyming Slang Glossary)

Cow's Lick – CATHOLIC.
1D. "Nah, it'll never work, he's a proddy, she's a cow's lick."

Crash & Blunder – THUNDER.
1D. "What a storm last night; did you hear all the crash and blunder?"

Cream Cookie – BOOKIE, (betting shop).
1D. "I'm off down the cream cookie to place my bets."

Cream Crackered – KNACKERED, (exhausted).
1D. "I can't do another thing, I'm cream crackered, mate."

Cream Crackers – KNACKERS, (testicles).
1D. "And I swear she kicked him right in the cream crackers."

Creamed Rice – NICE.
1D. "She went out with him? That was creamed rice of her."

Cribbage Pegs – LEGS.
1D. "Ooh, look at the pegs on that beauty."

Crispy Duck – F*CK. (Origins; Chinese dish)
1D. "I don't give a crispy duck! I want him gone by tomorrow!"

Crosby Stills & Nash – CASH. (Origins; harmony group)
2D. "Look at the watch that bloke; he's not short of some Crosby."

Crosby Stills Nash & Young – TONGUE. (Origins; harmony group)
2D. "After I slipped her the crosby stills, she went wild on me."

Crown Jewels – TOOLS.
2D. "I'm ready, got me tiling crowns in the truck, lets go."

Crust of Bread – HEAD.
2D. "Come on ref! Use your crust mate, no penalty!"

Cucumbers – NUMBERS.
1D. "I don't rank him, he's only there to make up the cucumbers."

Cuddle & Kiss – HISS.
1D. "Then the tyre went cuddle an' kiss on me, an' I was stranded."

Cuddle & Kiss – MISS.
2D. "Five yards! How the crispy could he cuddle that council!?"

Cuff Link – DRINK.
1D. "Just one cuff link for me tonight, I'm driving."

C*nt Flap – SLAP.

1D. "I just gave her a c*nt flap around the north an' south. An' she's left me."

Cupid's Dart – FART.
2D. "I let loose the biggest cupid's in me life; interview over."

Currant Bun – FUN.
1D. "Hey Harry, let's have some currant bun with the new waitress."

Currant Bun – NUN.
2D. "Some of me meanest teachers were the currents at the convent."

Currant Bun – SON.
1D. "Hold on a minute, me old currant bun, you ain't eighteen yet."

Currant Bun – SUN, (British daily newspaper).
2D. "You got the currant, George? I'll swap for the Mirror."

Currant Cakey – SHAKY.
1D. "His job's bloody currant cakey, no wins in ten games."

Currants And Plums – THRUMS, (slang for threepence).
1D. "I love the old currants and thrums coins, good looking money."
(OLD; Included in Hotten's 1858 Rhyming Slang Glossary)

Custard & Jelly – TELLY, (television).
2D. Bloody Nora. As usual, there's nothing special on the custard tonight."

Cut & Carried – MARRIED. (Origins; 'cut' financially from her family, and 'carried' by her husband)
1D. "Tom's only got 'imself cut & carried, Las Vegas job, last week."

Cuts & Scratches – MATCHES.

2D. "Got any cuts on yer? I wanna light up."

Cutty Sark – LOAN SHARK. (Origins; fast tea-trade sailing ship)
2D. "I'm stoney, had to go down to Nobby, the cutty last night."

Cynthia Payne – RAIN. (Origins; modern UK brothel madam)
2D. "Black clouds coming our way; looks like some cynthia's on the books."

D

Dad's Army – BARMY. (Origins; UK TV Comedy Show)
1D. "Oh my god, look at Gordon, he's gone all dad's army on the barman."

Daffadown Dilly – SILLY. (Origins; a common name for narcissus, the daffodil family)
2D. "Don't be so daffadown, Tottenham will never win the league."

Daffy Duck – F*CK. (Origins, US Cartoon)
2D. "I don't give a daffy for your opinion; I'm right."

Daft & Barmy – ARMY.
1D. "The silly buggers gone and joined the daft and barmy, didn't he."

Daily Mail – TALE. (Origins;, UK Newspaper)
1D. "Don't listen to his daily mail, he's a deep fat fryer."

Dairylea – WEE, (urine). (Origins; UK Processed Cheese)
1D. "David, get your backside down here, you've dribbled dairylea on the toilet seat again!"

Daisy Roots – BOOTS. (Origins; mentioned in the lyrics of, "My Old Man's a Dustman", recorded by Lonnie Donegan in the 1950s)
2D. "Come on Lawrence, you can't go out in the rain without your daisies."

Dame Edna Everage – BEVERAGE. (Origins; Australian comedian)
2D. "I don't like coffee, I'm off to get a proper dame edna."

Dame Judy Dench – STENCH. (Origins; UK Actress)
2D. "Gor blimey, Pat, what's the judy in here? Somebody died?"

Damien Duff – ROUGH. (Origins; Irish football coach)
2D. "Oh, this boozer's honkin'; way too Damien for me."

Damien Hirst – DEGREE, (a university degree; first). (Origins; English artist)
1D. "Our Sarah did well at Leeds; got herself a damien hirst."

Damon Hill – PILL.

Dancing Bears – STAIRS.
1D. "Watch out for kids toys on the dancing bears, they're deathtraps."
3D. "Go on, get yourself up the daisy dancers to bed."

Dancing Fleas – KEYS.
1D. "Anyone see my dancing fleas? I can't leave without them."

Dangermouse – SPOUSE. (Origins; British cartoon in the 80's)
1D. "I'm off home, the dangermouse is waiting."
3D. "Where's the penfold tonight?" (Penfold was Dangermouse's companion.)

Daniel Boone – SPOON.
2D. "Oh, custard smells great, where's me Daniel?"

Daniel Fergus McGrain – TRAIN. (Origins; Scottish footballer)
1D. "I'm off on the danny mcgrain this weekend; going down to Blackpool."

Danny Glover – LOVER. (Origins; American actor)
1D. "I've got a new danny glover, real nice lass from Yorkshire."

Danny La Rue – CLUE. (Origins; UK television and cabaret Star)
2D. Don't worry about Shayne, she ain't got a danny."

Danny Marr – CAR.

1D. "I've got to find a smaller danny marr, the price of petrol's way too high."

Darby and Joan – MOAN. (Origins; slang for old folks club)
2D. "Man, that Linda's a bit of a darby-joaner, she won't shut up."

Darius Rucker – F*CKER. (Origins; American singer/songwriter)
2D. "Wow, that new fridge, he's a nasty darius, to be sure."

Darling Daughter – WATER.
2D. "Here, barkeep, pass me a glass of darling, an' a bit of blind!"

Darky Cox – BOX.
2D. "What's on the darky tonight then?"

Darky's Bum – MUM.
2D. "I don't like Charlie's darky; she's a bitch."

Darren Day – GAY. (Origins; English singer)
1D. "You don't have to worry about Cedric, mum, he's totally darren day."

Darren Gough – COUGH. (Origins; English cricketer)
2D. I've had a cold for a week, and this darren is killing me."

Davey Crocket – POCKET. (Origins; American frontiersman)
2D. "Always watch yer daveys when Ali's around; he's a real piece of work."

David Batty – TATTY, (old, worn). (Origins; English footballer)
1D. "Man, that t-shirt's as old as the hills; really david batty."

David Blaine – INSANE. (Origins; American illusionist)
1D. "Larry lost it last night, waving his arms, hitting walls, really david blaine."

David Boon – SPOON. (Origins; Australian cricketer)

1D. "Where's your david boon's mum, gotta set the table for the desert."

David Bowie – BLOWY, (windy). (Origins; British rock singer)
1D. "Crikey, the weather's a bit david bowie today."

David Gower – SHOWER. (Origins; English cricketer)
1D. "I'm having a david gower before going out tonight."

David Hockney – COCKNEY. (Origins; English painter)
1D. "Born in the west end, total david hockney, me."

David Jason – MASON. (Origins; British actor)
2D. "He's always been a weird 'un, a david, and creepy."

David Mellor – STELLA, (Atrois beer). (Origins; UK politician)
1D. "I'm drinking david mellor tonight, I like the Belgian stuff."

David Starkey – PARKY, (cold). (Origins; English TV historian)
1D. "Get yer coat on, it's david starkey outside tonight."

Davina McCalls – BALLS, (testicles). (Origins; British TV presenter)
2D. "I just grabbed him by the davinas and watched him grimace."

Dawn French – STENCH. (Origins; UK comedienne/actress)
1D. "Davie, the dawn french in your bedroom is making me downright moby."

Dawson's Creek – STREAK. (Origins; American TV program)
1D. "Oh, great day at the footie, a dawsons creeker just before halftime."

Day and Night – LIGHT (Ale).
1D. "Three pints of day and night, barman, and one fer yersel'."

Day Trippers – SLIPPERS.
1D. "Can't wait to get home, get me feet into me day trippers."

Day's Dawning – MORNING.
2D. "Ooh, days, worst part of the day."

Dead Horse – SAUCE.
1D. "Pass the dead horse, mum, yeah, the red stuff."

Dead Loss – BOSS.
1D. "Our dead boss at work is a real toe-rag."

Dear Ringer – MINGER, (smelly).
1D. "Toby wasn't half a dead ringer today at work; he needs an introduction to cape o' good."

Deaf & Dumb – BUM.
1D. "Slipped on the ice, fell right on me deaf an' dum."

Deep Fat Fryer – LIAR.
1D. "You spoke to the queen? You deep fat fryer, you."

Deep Sea Diver – FIVER, (5 pounds).
1D. "I found a deep sea diver in me pocket this morning."

Deep Sea Glider – CIDER.
2D. "Come on, a quick pint of deep sea will do your head the world of good."

De La Soul – DOLE, (welfare). (Origins; American pop band)
1D. "Damn, I've been on the de la soul for three months now."

Dennis & Gnasher – BADGER. (Origins; cartoon characters)
1D. "Man, talk about weird; I hit a dennis an' gnasher with the car last night."

Dennis Law – DRAW, (tie). (Origins; Scottish footballer)
2D. "That game was almost a waste of time, a goal-less dennis."

Dental Flosser – TOSSER, (wanker).
1D. "Mickey's a total dental flosser, a waste of space."

Derby Kelly – BELLY. (Origins; lyrics from old cockney song 'Boiled Beef and Carrots')
2D. "Go on Jim, get that beer in your derby, you'll feel better."

Derek Randall – LOVE HANDLE. (Origins; English cricketer)
1D. "Gor, look at the derek randalls on that blonde."

Derry and Toms – BOMBS. (Origins; London department store)
1D. "During the blitz, there were derry an' toms dropping like rain."

Desmond Hacket – JACKET. (Origins; Daily Express sports reporter]
2D. "Look at 'Arry. 'E's got 'imself a new desmond."

Desmond Tutu – 2ND CLASS HONORS, (university). (Origins; South African cleric/activist)
2D. "Lorraine got word of her degree, a desmond."

Desperate Dans – CANS, (headphones). (Origins; comic character)
2D. "Let's get ye set up, get in the studio, an' put your desperates on."

Diamond Rocks – SOCKS.
1D. "New rhythm an' blues means new diamond rocks too."

Dibs & Dabs – CRABS.
1D. "Going to the beach? Watch out for the dibs an' dabs!"

Dick Emery – MEMORY. (Origins; British actor/comedian)
1D. "You bought a tiddley wink once? I must be losing me dick emery."

Dick Van Dyke – BIKE. (Origins; American singer/actor)
1D. "On yer dick van dyke, mate, go on, get lost."

Dicky Bird – WORD. (Origins; could be the cricket umpire, doubtful)
1D. "He left the bar without so much as a dicky bird to anyone."

Dickie Bird – 3RD CLASS HONORS, (university). (Origins; could be the cricket umpire, doubtful)
1D. "MY son Brian got a dickie bird at Oxford."

Dickory Dock – CLOCK.
2D. "What's the time on the olde dickory, barman?"

Dickory Dock – TAXI METER.
2D. "That's us at Padding Station, mate. Dickory Dock says it's a godiva."

Dicky Dirt – SHIRT.
1D. "Gawd, just spilled kansas & missouri down me dicky dirt."

Didgeridoo – SCREW, (prison officer). (Origins; Australian musical instrument)
1D. "Watch out, Charlie, the digeridoos are on the warpath."

Didn't Outa – DAUGHTER.
1D. "He brought his didn't oughta to the rub a dub last night."

Dig a Grave – SHAVE.
1D. "Think I'll go to the barbers, get a proper dig a grave for a change."

Ding Dong – BONG.
1D. "I'll never understand the new ding dong craze."

Ding Dong – SONG.
1D. "Come on Henry, get up and give us a ding dong."

Ding Dong Bell – HELL. (Origins; nursery rhyme lyric)
2D. "Oh this rap music is pure ding dong. Let's go."

Dinky Do – 22-TWENTY TWO.

2D. "I won dinky squid at the horses on Saturday."

Dinky Doos – SHOES.
1D. "Oh, check out the new dinky doos that Sandra's sporting."

Dinner Plate – MATE.
2D. "Ah, I'll lend you a bruce, no problem, me old dinner."

Dirty Beast – PRIEST.
1D. "Did you hear about the dirty beast at St Francis? Terrible news."

Dirty Den – TEN, (pounds). (Origins; Eastenders character)
1D. "I got a dirty den to last me all night, I'll start with water."

Dixie Deans – JEANS. (Origins; Scottish footballer)
2D. "I gone an' ripped me dixies! What a disaster."

Do As You Likey – PIKEY, (gypsy, traveler).
1D. "A bunch of do as you likey's moved in on the open ground behind Safeway."
(Another one of those clever rhymes. Traveling people in the UK are considered dirty and as thieves because they camp for a while, (doing what they like),then move on leaving a mess behind them.)

Do No Harm – ALARM.
2D. "Leg it, lads. The do-no will have the space hoppers here in minutes."

Doctor Crippen – BREAD AND DRIPPING, (dessert). (Origins; American murderer)
1D. "I love a bit of doctor Crippen for me lunch."

Doctor Dre – GAY. (Origins; American rap artist)
1D. "I think Greta's a bit of a closet doctor dre."

Dodge & Swerve – PERVE, (pervert).

2D. "I marked him as a dodge the first time I laid me minces on 'im."

Dog & Bone – PHONE.
1D. "I talked to the bird on the dog an' bone last night, she sounded fine."

Dog & Boned – STONED.
1D. "Look at Pete; he's dog an' boned off his arse."

Dog & Lead – WEED.
1D. "I'm off down the market to meet Garry, get meself some dog an' lead."

Dog's Eye – MEAT PIE.
2D. "Lunch? Get me one of those kate dogs from Gregs."

Dog's Knob – JOB.
1D. "Got meself a new dog's knob, didn't I. Good little earner too."

Dog's Meat – FEET.
2D. "Oh Nancy, me dogs are ready for me kippers, I can tell you."

Dolly Mixtures – PICTURES, (cinema). (Origins; British candy)
1D. "I'm off to the dolly mixtures to see the latest flick."

Dolly Pegs – LEGS. (Origins; type of clothes peg)
1D. "Eyes left, mate, look at the dolly pegs on that one over the street."

Do Me Goods – WOODS.
1D. "I hate walkin' in the do me goods, way too creepy for me."
(Another clever one... the rhyme also means the cigarette brand Woodbines which were given to the British troops in the First World War, way before their harmful effects were known.)

Donald Duck – LUCK. (Origins; cartoon character)

1D. "I'm taking my rabbits foot with me, see if I can change me donald duck."

Donald Duck – F*CK. (Origins; cartoon character)
2D. "Sorry James, I don't give a flying Donald where you sleep; just not here."

Donald Ducking – CLUCKING, (craving more heroin). (Origins; cartoon character)
1D. "Look at the state of Kathleen; she's been donald ducking for days now."

Donald Peers – EARS. (Origins; Welsh singer)
1D. "Cock a butchers at that guy's donald peers. Man he should have a pilots licince."

Donald Trump – DUMP, (shit). (Origins; American tycoon/President)
2D. "I'm sorry, I've got to go for a donald."

Donald Trump – HUMP, (huff). (Origins; American tycoon/President)
1D. "Oh don't pay attention to Dennis, he's got the donald trump about something."

Doner Kebab – STAB. (Origins; Greek fast food)
2D. "Jackie only went and donered him. She's in the big house."

Donkey Kong – LONG. (Origins; video game)
1D. "So have you been waiting donkey kong?"

Donkeys Ears – YEARS.
2D. "I think I've been waiting for the right woman for donkey's."

Donnie Darko – SPARKO, (asleep). (Origins; movie by Richard Kelly)
2D. "Is he hovis or just Donnie?"

Don Revie – BEVVY, (drink). (Origins; footballer/manager)

1D. "Fancy a don revie tonight? Or just a beer or two?"

Doogie Howsers – TROUSERS. (Origins; American TV show)
2D. "I'm not taking doogies on my hols, just shorts."

Doris Day – GAY. (Origins; American actress)
2D. "I'm quite convinced that Cyn is well doris."

Dorothy Squires – TYRES. (Origins; Welsh singer)
1D. "I had to get new Dorothy squires for me jam, they were well bertie."

Dot & Dash – CASH. (Origins; the basis of Morse Code)
1D. "Have you got any dot an' dash on yer?"

Dot Cotton – ROTTEN. (Origins; character from BBC soap, Eastenders)
2D. "Got a sore weasel, and I feel a bit dot, to tell the truth."

Double Dutch – CRUTCH. (Origins; a hard-to-understand language)
2D. "Harry's broke 'is clothes peg. He'll be using a double for months."

Double Yolker – JOKER. (Origins; egg with two yolks)
1D. "Who's the double yoker on the door then?"

Doug McClure – WHORE, (pronounced whoor). (Origins; American actor)
1D. "I wouldn't be seen dead with Bea, she's a doug mclure for sure."

Douglas Hurd – 3rd CLASS HONOURS, (university). (Origins; British politician)
1D. "Jimmy did well, got his douglas hurd at Cambridge last year."

Douglas Hurd – TURD, (shit). (Origins; British politician)
2D. "Come on, get a move on, I need to dump a Douglas soon."

Dover Harbour – BARBER. (Origins; channel port)
2D. "I'm off to the dover to get me barnet sorted out, it's a mess."

Down The Drains – BRAINS.
1D. "Look at Liv; she's not got the down the drains she was born with."

Doyly Carte – FART. (Origins; opera company)
2D. "Colin, you dozy crispy? Have you just dropped a d'oyly?"

Drip Dry – CRY.
1D. "She went 'ome an' had a good old drip dry about him."

Drum & Bass – FACE.
1D. "You're Bill from Mrs Hall's class; I never forget a drum an' bass."

Drum & Bass – PLACE.
2D. "Homeless, don't worry, you can doss at my drum for a couple of days."

Drum & Fife – KNIFE. (Origins; type of marching band)
1D. "Gor, they ban guns, not they's taking me drum an' fife's away too."

Drum Roll – HOLE, (house).
2D. "Come on lads, let's pop 'round to my drum an' have a beer or six."

Duane Eddies – READIES, (cash). (Origins; American guitarist)
2D. "Hey Stan, you still got that haddock for sale? I got the duane's."

Duchess of Fife – WIFE.
2D. "I left the duchess at home, she's busy knitting for the nipper."

Duck and Dive – JIVE.

1D. "Man can that lady duck an' dive, she's a natural."

Duck and Dive – SKIVE.
1D. "Lenny ain't got any kind of gumption; he's a duck an' diver thru an' thru."
(Another clever one, linking ducking and diving, to skiving, the very act of doing so)

Ducks Arse – GRASS.
2D. "I'm looking to score some ducks this weekend, any ideas?"

Dudley Moore – SCORE, (£20). (Origins; British actor)
2D. "You couldn't spare a Dudley until Friday, could ya?"

Dudley Moore's – SORES. (Origins; British actor)
1D. "Me shingles are gone, but the dudley moore's still itch."

Duke & Daisy – CHICKEN JAHLFREZI. (Origins; a type of Indian Curry)
1D. "I'll bring home some duke an' daisy for dinner tonight."

Duke of Argyles – PILES, (hemorrhoids). (Origins; Scottish landowner)
2D. "Oh, me dukes are feckin' painful right now."

Duke of Kent – BENT. (Origins; English landowner)
1D. "That guy's as duke of kent as a nine bob note."

Duke of Kent – RENT. (Origins; English landowner)
2D. "Sorry Charlie, I can't afford to pay the Duke this week."

Duke of Montrose – NOSE. (Origins; Scottish landowner)
1D. "His duke o' montrose is so big, he looks like a donkey!"

Duke of Spain – RAIN.
1D. "Oh no, not more duke o' spain forecasted. I'm soaked thru."

Duke of York – CHALK. (Origins; English landowner)
2D. "Teacher threw a lump of duke at me today!"

116

Duke of York – CORK. (Origins; English landowner)
1D. "I've only told this to three people, so keep a duke of york on it."

Duke of York – FORK. (Origins; English landowner)
2D. "Keep your fingers out of your food, use a drum an' duke."

Dunkirk – WORK. (Origins; town in France)
1D. "Big panics at me Dunkirk, someone's on the take."

Dunlop Tyre – LIAR. (Origins; British tyre manufacturer)
2D. "Watch out for Trevor, 'e's a bit of a Dunlop."

Dustbin Lids – KIDS.
2D. "When the dustbin's outnumber you, it's time to stop."

Dusty Bin – CHIN. (Origins; TV game show character)
1D. "He's got drool dripping down his dusty bin, what a plonker."

Dwight Yorke – PORK. (Origins; English footballer)
1D. "Got some nice stew at home, dwight york an bangers."

E

Early Doors – DRAWERS, (knickers).
2D. "No earlies today, I'm going knickerless, commando!"

Early Hour(s) – FLOWERS.
"Been drinking all day, I've got to get me trouble some earlies."

Ear 'Ole – DOLE, (unemployment).
1D. If I get the tin tack I'm going straight on the ear'ole an' no mistake."

Earwig – TWIG, (understand).
1D. "He's always hanging around the door, earwigging conversations."

Easter Bunny – FUNNY.
2D. "Oh yeah, very easter, Benny. Stop larking around."

East and West – VEST.
"Where's me east and west, mum? I can't see 'em."

East Wests – BREASTS.
2D. "Ooh, luv a duck, take a butchers at her easts."

Easy Rider – CIDER.
1D. "Hey, landlord, three pints of easy rider please."

Eau de Cologne – PHONE.
"If you want to go to the footie on Saturday, give me a blow on the eau."

Eddie Grundies – UNDIES, (underwear). (Origins; character in the radio soap, The Archers)
1D. "Cathy? Have you seen my eddie grundies? I can't find 'em."

Eddy Grant – PLANT. (Origins; Guyanese musician)
2D. "I don't trust jack at all, I think he's a police eddie."

Edgar Allen Poes –TOES. (Origins; American writer)
2D. "He took off on his edgar allen's, fast as a rocket."

Edinburgh Fringe – MINGE, (vagina). (Origins; City festival)
1D. "She's a real cracker. Can you imagine the edinburgh fringe on 'er?"

Edna Everage – BEVERAGE. (Origins; Australian comedian's character)
2D. "I think I'll partake in some adult ednas tonight, maybe many."

Edward Heath – TEETH. (Origins; British Prime Minister)
2D. "Did you see that punch? He got smacked in right the edwards."

Efan Ekuku – POO POO. (Origins; English/Nigerian footballer)
2D. "I'm going to sky-dive; don't efan ekuku the idea, my mind's made up."

Egg & Spoon – COON, (black person).
1D. "There's a bunch of egg an' spoons sitting in our favorite corner."

Eggs & Kippers – SLIPPERS.
1D. "That's a good wife, dinner on the table, eggs an' kippers by the fire."

Egg Yoke – JOKE.
2D. "He doesn't know it yet, but the egg's on him!"

Egyptian Hall – BALL, (dance).
1D. "Did you get an invite to the Duke's Egyptian hall?"
(OLD; Included in Hotten's 1858 Rhyming Slang Glossary)

Eiffel Tower – SHOWER. (Origins; big tower in Paris)
1D. "I have to take a quick eiffel tower before I go out."

Eighteen Pence – SENSE.
1D. "She ain't got the eighteen pence she was born with."

Elastic Bands – HANDS.
2D. "Great goalkeeper; 'e's got great elastics."

Elephant & Castle – ARSEHOLE. (Origins; London suburb)
2D. "George always has been a bit of an elephant."

Elephant And Castle – PARCEL. (Origins; London suburb)
1D. "I gotta take this elephant an' castle down to the post office."

Elephants Trunk – DRUNK.
2D. "He shouldn't be driving home, he's well elephant's."
(OLD; Included in Hotten's 1858 Rhyming Slang Glossary)

Elizabeth Regina – VAGINA. (Origins; British Queen's full name)
2D. "Gor, her jeans are so tight, you can butcher her elizabeth!"

Elliot Ness – MESS. (origins; American prohibition agent)
2D. "My mum says me bedroom's a right Elliot these days."

Elmer Fudd – SPUD, (potato). (Origins; cartoon character)
2D. "She's cooking me favorite dinner, bernards an' elmers."

Elsie Tanner – SPANNER, (wrench). (Origins; UK soap character)
2D. "Pass me the big elsie, would ya? The one inch."

Emma Freuds – HEMORRHOIDS. (Origins; BBC DJ on Radio 1)
2D. "Yeah, it's raining, an' me Emma's are playing me up again."

Empire State – MATE. (Origins; building in New York, USA)
2D. "Come on, me old empire, lets hurry up, boozer's open."

Engineers & Stokers – BROKERS.
1D. "I'm off down me engineers an' stokers this afternoon, heady stuff."

English Lit – SHIT.
1D. "I really don't give an english lit for rap music."

Epsom Races – PAIR OF BRACES, (suspenders).
1D. "That's some snazzy epsom races, Billy. Did yer knick 'em?"
(OLD; Included in Hotten's 1858 Rhyming Slang Glossary)

Ernie Marsh – GRASS.
1D. "Have you got any ernie marsh on yer? I'm needin' some."

Errol Flynn – CHIN. (Origins; American actor)
1D. "Oh look, Scotty grew a beard to hide his Errol Flynn."

Ertha Kitt – SHIT. (Origins; American singer/actress)
1D. "Oh, get to the boozer pronto, I'm bursting on an ertha kitt."

Ertha Kitts – TITS. (Origins; American singer/actress)
"Oh, look at Bonnie; she's had a boob job; nice erthas."

Ethan Hunt – C*NT. (Origins; character in Mission Impossible)
2D. "I don't like Barney; he can be a right ethan when he puts his mind to it."

Euan Blair – LEICESTER SQUARE. (Origins; British Prime Minister's son)
1D. "I'll meet you all at euan blair at noon."
(A great example of a modern cutting satirical rhyme; Prime Minister Tony Blair's underage son (he was 16) was found drunk in Leicester Square by police.)

Evening Breeze – CHEESE.
1D. "Look, they've laid on nibbles; evening breeze an' crackers."

Everton Toffee – COFFEE.
2D. "I'll have an everton, no, I changed me mind. An al pachino."

(OLD; Included in Hotten's 1858 Rhyming Slang Glossary)

Ewan McGregor – BEGGAR.
2D. "There's more ewans every year on these streets."

Eyes of Blue – TRUE.
1D. "Connie's a looker? Never spoke a more eyes of blue word, mate."

Eye Lash – SLASH, (urinate).
1D. "Gotta wiz for a quick eye lash, mates. Back in a tick."

Eyes Front – C*NT.
1D. "I'll be keeping me eyes peeled for some eyes front tonight, it's been a while."

F

Fainting Fits – TITS.
2D. "I wouldn't mind getting me hands on her faintings."

Faith & Hope – SOAP.
2D. "I finally found a brand of faith that me trouble likes."

Fakey Ned – BED.
2D. "I'm off up to me fakey, I'm done in."

False Start – FART.
1D. "Thought I needed the crapper, but it was just a false start."

Falun Gong – WRONG. (Origins; Chinese spiritual practice)
1D. "I thought it'd be a home win, but I was falun gong."

Family Tree – LAVATORY.
1D. "I need to find a family tree, I'm touching cloth."

Fanny Blair – HAIR.
2D. "Gawd, Ginnie's got a great head of fanny."
(OLD; Included in Hotten's 1858 Rhyming Slang Glossary)

Fanny Craddock – HADDOCK. (Origins; British TV chef)
2D. "Oi, Toni! Fanny and chips for two!"

Far East – PRIEST.
1D. "I need to do me confession, you know, squalk to the far east."

Farmers Daughter – QUARTER.
2D. "My mum wants me to get her three farmers of boiled ham."

Farmer Giles – PILES, (hemmoroids). (Origins; Tolkien character)
1D. "Celebration time, I got rid of me farmer giles."

Farmers Pig – WIG.
1D. "Oh Jimminy. Look at the farmers pig on the guy that just walked in."

Farmers Truck – F*CK.
2D. "I don't give one flying farmers what he says, he's guilty."

Fat and Skinny – MINI, (car or skirt).
2D. "Oh, watcha, look at the fatboy on the gal that just crossed the street."

Fat Boy Slim - GYM. (Origins; American rap artist)
2D. "I'm going down to the fatboy, loose some pork."

Father Ted – DEAD. (Origins; irreverent TV comedy character)
1D. "It was sudden. I think he was father ted before he hit the floor."

Fawlty Tower – SHOWER. (Origins; TV comedy)
1D. "I'm going to grab a fawlty tower before hitting the sack."

Feather & Flip – KIP (sleep).
1D. "I'm going to have a feather an' flip before going out tonight."

Fergal Sharkey – CAR KEY. (Origins; Irish singer)
2D. "I can't find the feargal, we can't leave!"

Fergal Sharkey – DARKEY. (Origins; Irish singer)
1D. "Lennie's new girl is a bit of a feargal sharkie."

Ferret & Stoat – THROAT.
1D. "Her hands went right for me ferret an' stoat, quick as you like."

Fibre of Your Fabric – LOOT.

124

4D. "C'mon, let me feel the fibre of your fabric."
(This is another 4th degree rarity and is listed here on that strength. 1D. Whistle & Flute = suit. 2D. Suit's made of fabric. 3D. Fibre of Your Fabric = the feel of your suit. 4D. (the meaning changes) Fibre of Your Fabric = loot (money).)

Fiddle and Flute – SUIT.
2D. "Hey, check out my new fiddle, Saville Row, well, nearly."

Fiddle De Dee – PEE, (wee).
1D. "Hold on, there's a doorway, I need a fiddle de dee, don't I."

Field of Wheat – STREET.
1D. "What's the word on the fields of wheat, then?"

Fife & Drum – BUM.
1D. "Cop a feel of that fife an' drum, and you'll get your coupon slapped."

Filter Tips – LIPS.
1D. "She's got luscious filter tips, ain't she?"

Fine & Dandy – BRANDY.
2D. "A snifter? A drop of fine would suit me dandy."

Finger & Thumb – MUM.
1D. "How's your finger an' thumb keepin these days, Rodney?"

Finger & Thumb – RUM.
2D. "It's a bit Baltic outside, I think I'll start with a thimble of finger."
(OLD; Included in Hotten's 1858 Rhyming Slang Glossary)

Finlay Quaye – GAY. (Origins; Scottish musician)
2D. "I'm thinking that Carrie's man could be a wee bit on the finlay side."

Finsbury Park – ARC, (theater light). (Origins; district in London)

2D. "I like it when it goes dark, then one finsbury lights the hero."

Finsbury Park – MARK. (Origins; district in London)
1D. "Oh, that whisky sure hit the Finsbury park."

Fireman's Hose – NOSE.
2D. "Oh, crap. Look at the size of the fireman on 'is boat!"

First Aid Kits – TITS.
1D. "Fine pair of first aid kits, eyes right!"

First of May – GAY.
2D. "Lionel's a raving first, no bones about it."

Fish & Chips – HIPS.
1D. "Swing yer fish 'n' chips, come on do the bump!"

Fish & Chips – TIPS.
2D. "Come on Chuck, you're in wi' the trainer. Any good fish?"

Fish Hook – BOOK.
1D. "I hope you're having fun reading this fish hook."

Fish 'n' Taters – LATERS.
1D. "Yup, I'm off home too, see ya fish 'n' taters!"

Fisherman's Daughter – WATER.
2D. "Hand me some of that fisherman's, I'm parched."

Fishing Rod – PC PLOD, (policeman).
1D. "Hold on, here comes the old fishing rod, just turned the jack."

Five to Four – SURE.
"We'll beat them to nil, that's five to four."
(An unsuspecting clever one. If we take the five to four as betting odds, it's almost an even money shot.)

Five to Two – JEW.
1D. "Trust them five to twos to have a different Sabbath from everybody else."

Fizzy Drink – CHINK.
2D. "Where we going when the pub closes? Indian or fizzy?"

Flag Unfurled – A MAN OF THE WORLD.
1D. "Look at the Admiral... now that's a flag unfurled."
(OLD; Included in Hotten's 1858 Rhyming Slang Glossary)

Fleas & Itches – PICTURES, (cinema).
3D. "So what's the latest down at the fleapit then?"
(Another clever rhyme; in the early days, the cinema was often the cause of head lice in children, and I still remember my mum calling our local cinema, 'The Fleapit'.)

Flea and Louise – BAD HOUSE.
1D. "Oh, don't go to the poor house here, that's a fea an' louise."
(OLD; Included in Hotten's 1858 Rhyming Slang Glossary)

Fleetwood Mac – BACK. (Origins; multi-national pop band)
2D. "Oh, scratch me fleetwood for a bit, I got an itch."
3D. "Oh, me mick's playing me up rotten today." (Mick Fleetwood is the band's drummer)

Flight Lieutenant Biggles – GIGGLES. (Origins; Capt W.E. Johns book character)
2D. "Oh, don't mind Sadie, she's got the flight lieutenants."

Flounder & Dab – CAB, (taxi). (Origins; two kinds of flat fish)
2D. "Nip outside an' see if you can flag down a flounder for me."
(OLD; Included in Hotten's 1858 Rhyming Slang Glossary)

Flowers & Frolics - BOLLOCKS.
1D. "Oh that newspaper's a load of old flowers an' frolics."

Flowery Dell – CELL.

2D. "January, yup, Davie's still got three more years in the flower."

Fluffy Bunny – MONEY.
2D. "Any fluffy stuff on yer tonight? I'm boracic."

Fly My Kite – LIGHT.
2D. "Have yer got a fly by for me pipe? Mine's gone out."
(OLD; Included in Hotten's 1858 Rhyming Slang Glossary)

Fly a Kite – SHITE.
1D. "I'm going to fly a kite, back in a mo."

Fly By Nights – TIGHTS.
2D. "We were at it before we knew it, she dropped 'er alans an fly by's in seconds."

Foot Pump – DUMP.
1D. "I gotta take a foot pump, back in ten."

Fore & Aft – DAFT. (Origins; nautical terms for front and back)
1D. "Come on Stan, don't act all fore an' aft. Get yourself together."

Forest Gump – DUMP, (shit). (Origins; movie character)
2D. "You're going, hold on, I just got to have a forrest first".

Forsythe Saga – LAGER. (Origins; BBC television drama)
2D. "Your round? Mine's a forsythe an' lime."

Forty Four – WHORE.
1D. "We were doing fine, then after two drinks, she goes all forty-fourish on me."

Four by Four – WHORE.
2D. "I ve not had some posh for so long, I'm considering a four by."
3D. "Nice bunch of fence posts sitting in the corner."

Four by Two – JEW.
1D. "They had to get hitched in a synagogue, he's a four by two, see."
Trivia; four inches by two inches was the piece of rag given to the troops in WW1 to clean the bore of their Lee Enfield rifle.

Four by Two – POO.
2D. "Where's the khazi in this place, I feel a four by coming on strong."

Four Minute Miles – PILES, (hemorrhoids).
1D. "Ooh, me four minute miles are packing a punch today."
3D. "Me sir rogers are feckin' killin' me."
(Roger Bannister was the first person to beat the four minute mile)

Four Seasons – REASONS.
1D. "I forkin' love Ian Drury. Four seasons to be cheerful!"

Four Wheeler – SHEILA.
1D. "You should see the four wheelers go barmy on Saturday nights."
(Little piece of Aussie Rhyming Slang, Shielas being the Aussie term for 'women'.)

Francis Drakes – BRAKES.
1D. "I tried to slow down, but the francis drakes wouldn't work."

Frank & Pat – CHAT. (Origins; perhaps TV characters Frank and Pat Butcher from Eastenders)
1D. "Look, if you ever want to frank an' pat, I'm here for ye."

Frank Bough – OFF, (leave). (Origins; TV sports presenter)
2D. "I've been here too long, I'm gonna do the frank."

Frank Bough – SCOFF, (food). (Origins; TV sports presenter)
1D. "I'm hank an' lee, I'm going to get some frank bough before I expire."

Frank Skinner – DINNER. (Origins; UK comedian)
1D. "Let's get our frank skinner over our necks, then head to the rub a dub dub."

Frankie Dettori – STORY. (Origins; Italian jockey)
2D. "So what's the real frankie then? What happened?"

Frankie Howard – COWARD. (Origins; British actor/comedian)
1D. "At first signs of trouble, Jim legged it, he's such a frankie howard."

Frankie Vaughn – PAWN. (Origins; British singer)
2D. "I had to take me guitar to the frankie yesterday."

Frankie Vaughn – PORN. (Origins; British singer)
1D. "Have you got any frankie vaughn then, I'm dying on a good spanking."

Franz Klammer – HAMMER. (Origins; Austrian skier)
1D. "Pass me the franz klammer, and the dwang."

Frasier Crane – PAIN. (Origins; American fictional character)
1D. "Oh, that frazier crane in me back's returned with a vengeance."

Fray Bentos – NOSE. (Origins; UK maker of Steak & Kidney Pies)
1D. "Oh Jesus! Look at the fray bentos on that poor spank at the bar."

Frazer Nash – SLASH, (urinate). (Origins; brand of British sports car)
1D. "Gawd, I wish me bladder was bigger, I have to have a frazer nash again."

Fred Astaire – CHAIR. (Origins; American actor/dancer)
1D. "Pull up a fred astaire, me old china, let's have a rabbit about me soapies."

Fred Astaire – HAIR. (Origins; American actor/dancer)
2D. "Graham's gone an' dyed his fred again. Feckin' blue this time."

Fred MacMurray – CURRY. (Origins; American actor)
1D. "You know, no surprise here, but I fancy a fred macmurray."

Fred MacMurrays – WORRIES. (Origins; American actor)
2D. "Six pints of nelson will soon wash away any freds in me crust."

Fred West – PEST. (Origins; British mass murderer)
1D. "Watch out, eyes left, here comes that fred west yet again."

French Plait – FLAT. (Origins; type of hair braiding)
1D. "Her bristol an' west's are as french plait as the mountains in 'Olland!"

Friar Tuck – F*CK. (Origins; fictional character in Robin Hood)
2D. "You are a dozy friar, you should have just apologized."

Friar Tuck – LUCK. (Origins; fictional character in Robin Hood)
1D. He had another gee-gee's win, he always had a bit of friar tuck."

Fridge Freezer – GEEZER.
2D. "He tries to act the fridge, but he's nowhere near it."

Frog and Toad – ROAD.
2D. "I told you before, you don't ride your bike on the frog!"
3D. " He took off down the kermit like the devil himself was after him.".

Fromage Frais – GAY. (Origins; French cheese)
1D. "Oh look at the la-di-da's that just walked in, how fromage frais!"

Front Wheel Skid – YID, (Jew).

2D. "Did you know that Willie's went and turned full front wheel?"

Fruit Gum – CHUM, (friend, mate). (Origins; British chewy fruit candy)
1D. "Hows yer doing, my old fruit gum?"

Fruit & Nuts – GUTS. (Origins; Cadbury's chocolate bar)
1D. "It was 'orrible. His fruit an' nuts were all over the frog."

Frying Pan – FAN.
1D. "I've been a frying pan of the 'ammers since I can remember."

Frying Pan – OLD MAN, (father or husband).
1D. "I tried to haggle with the frying pan, but he wouldn't listen."

Funk Soul Brother – LOVER.
1D. "Oh come on, I'm a funk soul brother, not a read an' writer."

Fur Rugs – DRUGS.
1D. "I'm droppin' the fur rugs for a bit; they're clouding me head."

Furry Boots – WHERE ABOUTS?
1D. "You fell and hit your head? Furry boots?"
(A Scottish one for sure. The rhyme is a colloquialism of 'bout', to 'aboot', and is probably related to the definition directly below.)

Furry Muff – FAIR ENOUGH.
1D. "She said he wanted to split, an' I just froze, an' said furry muff."

Fuzzy Duck – F*CK. (Origins; British rock band)
2D. "I don't give a flying fuzzy what you do, I'm off."

G

Gamble & Procter – DOCTOR. (Origins; American conglomerate)
2D. "We just got news from the gamble; Debby's had a baby girl."

Gamma Ray – STRAY.
1D. "Gina? Oh, she's just a gamma ray we picked up on the way."

Gang & Mob – GOB, (mouth).
2D. "He's got a big gang for such a small fridge."

Garden Fence – DENSE, (stupid).
2D. "Don't ask Derek anything, he's a bit on the garden side."

Garden Gate – 8ᵗʰ OF COKE.
1D. "I'm off to score a garden gate, I need something to take the pain away."

Garden Gate – MAGISTRATE.
2D. "I got done for pickpocketing last week. I'm up in front of the garden."
(OLD; Included in Hotten's 1858 Rhyming Slang Glossary)

Garden Gate – MATE.
1D. "Hi mum, this is Colin, he's an old garden gate from school."

Garden Hose – NOSE.
2D. "I gave him a belt on the garden, that soon shut him up."

Garden Tool – FOOL.
1D. "You'd be a garden tool to think Wigan could get promotion."

Gareth Gates – MATES. (Origins; English singer/songwriter)

1D. "I'm having a birthday bash at the cruiser, gonna invite all me gareth gates."

Gareth Hunt – C*NT. (origins; English actor)
2D. "Albert tried to build 'is own kitchen; made a right gareth out of it."

Garry Abblett – TABLET, (pill). (Origins; English footballer)
1D. "Gawd, Frank was off his nuts on some kind of Gary Abletts."

Gary Glitter – BITTER, (beer). (Origins; English glam rock star)
1D. "Three pints of gary glitter please!"

Gary Glitter – SHITTER, (anus). (Origins; English glam rock star)
2D. "Me gary's been playing me up something rotten since that curry on Friday."

Gary Neville – LEVEL. (Origins; English footballer)
1D. "I don't how to take Phil, I never know if he's on the gary neville."

Gary Player – ALL DAYER, (drinking session). (Origins; golfer)
2D. "Great day yesterday, off on a gary, all around town."

Gates of Rome – HOME.
2D. "At last we reach the gates of, I'm ready to put me plates up."

Gawd's Truth – ROOF.
1D. "I hate heights, but I gotta fix the gawds truth."

Gay & Frisky – WHISKY.
2D. "Hey barman! Three pints of gary, two mother's ruins, and a gay for the jock!"

Gay Gordon – PARKING WARDEN. (Origins; Scottish dance)
1D. "Ooh, watcha mate, the gay gordons are out today."

Gay and Hearty – PARTY.
1D. "Hey, we're having a gay and hearty on Saturday, wanna come?"

Geoff Hoon – BABOON. (Origins; British politician)
1D. "Okay, I get it, there's no need to act like a geoff hoon about it."

Geoff Hurst – BURST. (Origins; English footballer)
1D. "I cheered so loud, I thought I'd geoff hurst."

Geoff Hurst – FIRST CLASS UNI DEGREE. (Origins; English footballer)
2D. "Colin's pleased; his daughter got a geoff with honours from Cambridge."

Geoff Hurst – THIRST. (Origins; English footballer)
1D. "I can't seem to slake this geoff hurst, another beer please!"

Geoffrey Chaucer – SAUCER. (Origins; English writer)
2D. "Hey, use a geoffrey for that jay z, don't mark the clark gable."

George & Zippy – NIPPY, (cold). (Origins; TV puppets from Rainbow)
1D. "It's a bit George an' zippy today, think I'll wrap up."

George Best – CHEST. (Origins; Northern Ireland footballer)
1D. "Look at Bertie, all proud, puffed out George best and everything."

George Bush – MUSH, (face). (Origins; American President)
1D. "She's got a george bush like a bag of franz klammers."

George Cole – DOLE, (welfare). (Origins; British cockney actor)
1D. "I'm off down the george cole, it's me interview day."

George Martin – FARTING. (Origins; Beatles manager)
1D. "Charlie's a pig, george martin everywhere."

George Michael – CYCLE, (menstrual). (Origins; British singer)
1D. "Give Sarah a body swerve for the next week, she's on her george michael."

George Raft – DRAUGHT. (Origins; American actor)
2D. "Shut the door, Geoff! There's a bit of a george in here!"

Georgie Bests – BREASTS.
1D. "Oh, look at the georgie bests behind the counter."

Georgio Armani – SARNIE, (sandwich). (Origins; Italian fashion designer)
1D. "Got me packed lunch, georgio armani with chees an' pickle."

German Bands – HANDS.
2D. "She took her german and slapped his kisser."

German Beer – ENGINEER.
1D. "The central heating's out, we're waiting on a german beer to turn up."

German Cruiser – BOOZER, (pub).
1D. "Things got chaotic at the german cruiser last night, fists and glasses flying."

German Fighter – LIGHTER.
"Hey, Donny! Toss me your german fighter."

German Flutes – PAIR OF BOOTS.
1D. "There was a dead guy in the alley. I got his german flutes!"
(OLD; Included in Hotten's 1858 Rhyming Slang Glossary)

Gert & Daisy – CRAZY.
2D. "Jane's all over gert right now, complete nutcase."

Gertie Gitana – BANANA. (Origins; British music hall star)
2D. "Go on mum, I like a gertie on my cornflakes."

Gianluca Vialli – CHARLIE, (cocaine). (Origins; Italian footballer/manager)
2D. "I need some Gianluca, any ideas?"

Giggle & Titter – BITTER, (beer).
2D. "Two giggles, and one frisky, please, barman."

Gilly Mint – BINT, (girl, woman).
1D. "Oh look at the gilly mint on Andrew's arm. What a cracker."

Ginger Ale – JAIL.
2D. "Colin's doing half a stretch in the ginger."

Ginger Beer – ENGINEER.
2D. "Listen to him, that ginger knows his stuff."

Ginger Beer – QUEER, (gay).
2D. "He's a bit ginger, but not in your face."

Ginger Beer – QUEER, (strange).
1D. "I don't know about that Global Warming, sounds a bit ginger beer to me."

Gipsy's Warning – MORNING.
1D. "Six! What time of the gipsy's warning do you call this?"

Giraffe – LAUGH.
1D. "You're havin' a bit of a giraffe, aren't you, mate?"
3D. "You're having a neck stretch on that one."

Girl And Boy – SAVELOY, (penny sausage).
1D. "The town crier's got girl an' boy on the barbeque."
(OLD; Included in Hotten's 1858 Rhyming Slang Glossary)

Glasgow Rangers – STRANGERS. (Origins; Scottish football club)
1D. ""Bunch of glasgow rangers in tonight, is there footy in town?"

Glass of Plonk – CONK, (Nose). (Origins; plonk is champagne)
1D. "Cor, look at the conan on Jimmy's glass of plonk."

Glass of Water – QUARTER.
1D. "Give's a glass of water of the black stuff, mate."

Glen Campbell – GAMBLE. (Origins; American singer)
2D. "You asked Jimmy? You're taking a glen, aren't you?"

Glenn Hoddle – DODDLE, (easy). (Origins; English footballer/manager)
1D. "Started my new job, it's a bit of a glenn hoddle really."

Gloria Gaynors – TRAINERS, (sneakers). (Origins; American singer)
2D. "That's a nice pair of gloria's that Dave's wearing."

Glorious Sinner – DINNER.
1D. "We had a great glorious sinner last night, as much as we could eat."
(OLD; Included in Hotten's 1858 Rhyming Slang Glossary)

Gobstopper – CHOPPER, (Penis).
1D. "Blow me, that's some gobstopper in 'is 'trousers!"

Goddess Diana – TANNER, (sixpence).
2D. "I found a goddess last night, five pints, an' thruppence left over."
(OLD; Included in Hotten's 1858 Rhyming Slang Glossary)

God Forbids – KIDS, (children).
2D. "Went to the war museum, school day out, bloody godfor's."

Godforsaken – BACON.
1D. "Godforsaken sarnie and brown sauce... yummy."

God's Glory – GORY.
1D. "We watched Private Ryan last night, it's a bit god's glory at the start!"

Gold Watch – SCOTCH, (whisky).
2D. "I think I'll have a nip of gold tonight, something special."

Goldie Hawn – PORN. (Origins; American actress)
2D. "Have you got any good goldie? I've running a stag night next week."

Goldie Locks – SOCKS.
2D. "You seen me football goldies anywhere?"

Gooseberry Puddin' – WOMAN.
1D. "I think that's a gooseberry puddin' over there, but I'm not sure."
(OLD; Included in Hotten's 1858 Rhyming Slang Glossary)

Goose's Neck – CHEQUE, (check).
2D. "Don't trust Charlie, he just paid his bill with a bouncy goose."

Gordon & Gotch – WATCH. (Origins Australian newspaper group)
2D. "Oi, mate what's the numbers on your Gordon?"
(Probably another rhyme from down under)

Gordon Brown – CLOWN. (Origins; British politician)
1D. "Watch up, Martin's playing the Gordon brown again."

Gorky Park – DARK. (Origins; park in the middle of Moscow)
2D. "Gor Blimey, it's a little gorky in here, an' no mistake."

Granny Flat – TWAT.
1D. "I like Raymond, but he can be a right granny flat around the ladies."

Grant Hackett – JACKET. (Origins; Australian swimmer)
1D. "Where's me grant hackett? Taxi's outside!"

Grass in the Park – NARK, (whistle blower).

139

2D. "Okay, we have to admit it; we have a grass in the organisation."

Grasshopper – COPPER.
1D. "Hear the news? Nobby got nabbed by the grasshoppers."

Gravy Lumps – DUMPS.
2D. "What's wrong, Harry? You look all down in the gravy."

Grease and Grime – TIME.
1D. "What's the grease an' grime Tony? Game starts soon."

Greatly Missed – PISSED.
1D. "I was greatly missed again last night."

Green Eggs & Ham – EXAM. (Origins; children's book by Doctor Seuss)
2D. "I'll not be around for a week or two, green eggs time."

Greengages – WAGES. (Origins; fruit like a plum)
1D. "I've went an' blown me greengages down at the dog track."

Gregory Peck – CHEQUE, (check). (Origins; American Actor)
2D. "I never 'ad any bread on me, so I 'ad to pay with a gregory."

Gregory Peck – NECK. (Origins; American Actor)
2D. "What a brass gregory! He scrounges tea, then pisses off."

Gregory Pecks – SPECS, (spectacles, glasses). (Origins; American Actor)
1D. "I found me gregory pecks; they were on me head."

Grey Mare – FARE.
2D. "I had to hoof it, didn't have the bread for the grey."

Grumble & Grunt – C*NT.
2D. "You know Neil, he's only after a bit of your grumble."

Gunga Din – CHIN. (Origins; Rudyard Kipling character)

140

1D. "Oh come on, I've never seen a gunga din that long before."

Gypsy Nell (gyp) – HELL.
2D. "My elbow is giving me pure gyp today."

Gypsy's Kiss – PISS.
2D. "I'm off out the back for a quick gypsy."

H

Habitual Knitter – BITTER, (beer).
2D. "Hey Brian, your round; I'll have a habitual."

Hackney Marsh – GLASS. (Origins; wet London area)
2D. "Ay, bartender, get me a clean 'ackney, will ya. This one's all lipstick."

Hackney Wick – STICK. (Origins; area in Hackney, London)
1D. "I was driving up to Newcastle with Hector last week, he fairly gave it some hackney wick."

Haddock & Bloater – MOTOR, (car, vehicle). (Origins; types of fish)
2D. "Love a duck, I've gone and locked me keys in the haddock."

Hagen Daas – ASS. (Origins; maker of up-market Ice Cream)
2D. "Man, it's icy outside, just slipped an' fell on me hagen."

Haigs Dimple – SIMPLE.
2D. "Ah, Jimmy's always been a bit on the haigs side."
(Possibly a Scottish rhyming slang here, I've said it most of my life)

Hail & Rain – TRAIN.
1D. "I'm off to Edinburgh, taking the hail and rain for a change."

Hair Gel – BELL, (to call on phone).
1D. "Sorry, Charlie, can't talk right now, I'll give you a hair gel tonight."

Hairy Chest – VERY BEST.
1D. "Well, public speakin' ain't me forte, but I'll give it me 'airy chest."

142

Hairy Knees – PLEASE.
2D. "Oh mum I need this shirt ironed for tonight, hairy?"

Hairy Muff – FAIR ENOUGH.
1D. "I'll swap you two choccy bics for one digestive, hairy muff?"

Hairy Nips – CHIPS, (French fries).
2D. "A fish supper, and a bag of 'airies, mate."

Hairy Toes – NOSE.
1D. "Got into a scuffle last night, put me fist right through a fridge's hairy toes."

Hale & Hearty – PARTY.
2D. "There goes Ray on the microphone, the heart of the hale."

Hale & Pace – FACE. (Origins; British comedy duo)
1D. "Oh, you should have seen his hale and pace when he saw Sandra smoochin' wif' another fella'."

Half a Gross – DOSE.
1D. "Me bruvva caught the flu last week, an' decided to give me a half gross."

Half-Inch – PINCH, (steal).
1D. "Oh, who half-inched my socket set?"

Half Past Three – TEA.
2D. "Eleven o'clock, I needs me a cuppa arf past?"

Ham & Cheesy – EASY.
1D. "I'm on a diet, and the first six pounds were ham and cheesy."

Ham & Egger – BEGGAR.
2D. "There's another ham an' standing by the junction."

Ham & Eggs – LEGS.

143

2D. "O'h, take a look at linda; she's got a lovely set of hams."

Hammer & Tack – BACK.
1D. "Me 'ammer and tack's playing me up again, I need some garys."

Hammer & Tack – SMACK. (Origins; Australian & NZ Rhyming Slang)
2D. "Scored me some hammer at the Bridge last night; good stuff."

Hampden Roar – SCORE, (jist, news, what's going on). (Origins; Scottish national football ground)
2D. "What's the hampden? I've been asleep all day."

Hampstead Heath – TEETH.
2D. Keith never sees a dentist; his hampsteads are a crime."

Hampton Wick – PRICK, (penis).
1D. "He's a bit of an 'ampton wick, always an ass, never a gentleman."

Ham Shanks – BANKS.
1D. "Doesn't matter what you do, the ham shanks will always win."

Ham Shanks – WANKS.
1D. "Look how skinny 'e is. There's hardly a ham shank in 'im."

Ham Shanks – YANKS.
1D. "Typical 'am shank tourists, all glitta' and no trousers!"

Hang Bluff – SNUFF.
1D. "I tried the hang bluff, but it made me sneeze real bad."
(OLD; Included in Hotten's 1858 Rhyming Slang Glossary)

Hank & Lee – STARVING. (Origins; Hank Marvin, English guitarist, and Lee Marvin, American actor)
1D. "Oi'm hank an' lee, bloody starvin'.

Hank Marvin – STARVING. (Origins; guitarist with English band, The Shadows)
2D. "My guts are makin' noises like blazes, I'm dead hank."

Hans Blix – FIX. (Origins; Swedish politician)
1D. "Me motor's done this time, even the mechanic can't hans blix it."

Hansel & Gretel – KETTLE. (Origins; children's nursery story)
2D. "Hey mum, stick the hansel on for a nice cup of rosy."

Happy Feed – WEED, (dope, drugs).
2D. "Hey Bert, got any happy on yer? I'm totally out."

Harold Wilsons – STILSONS, (pipe wrench). (Origins; British Prime Minister in the 70's)
2D. "Here, Tommy, 'and me the harolds, this nuts rusted on tight."

Harpers & Queens – JEANS, (denims). (Origins; Harpers and Queen is a woman's magazine)
2D. "Cor, look at Andy, he's gone and got 'imself a new pair of 'arpers."

Harris Tweed – SPEED. (Origins; Scottish woven fabric)
1D. "Can yer get me some harris tweed in town? I'm new."

Harris Tweed – WEED. (Origins; Scottish woven fabric)
1D. "I'm off to the alley behind the pub, score me some harris tweed."

Harry & Billy – SILLY. (Origins; sons of Princess Diana)
1D. "Look at Dave after just three pints, actin' all 'arry an' billy."

Harry Dash – FLASH, (dapper).
2D. "That's a nice whistle, Conny. You always was a bit of an 'arry."

Harry Flint – SKINT, (broke).
1D. "I can't go out 'til Friday, I'm totally harry flint."

Harry Hill – PILL, (usually contraceptive). (Origins; British comedian)
1D. "I can't get keith cheggers, I'm on the harry hill."

Harry Holt – BOLT, (run away). (Origins; Welsh footballer)
2D. "No time to waste, rain's starting, make a bolt for home."

Harry Kewell – COOL. (Origins; Australian footballer)
2D. "I'm feeling particularly harry today with me new whistle."

Harry Lime – TIME. (Origins; a character in the movie, 'The Third Man')
3D. "I forgot me watch, what's the third man?"

Harry Lin – CHIN.
1D. "Brucie's harry lin is one of his best features."

Harry Monk – SPUNK, (sperm).
1D. "Little Annie never hangs back from a tackle; she's got some harry."

Harry Nash – CASH.
1D. "There's always a discount if you're paying with harry nash."

Harry Potter – SNOTTER, (nose snot).
1D. "One thing I hate is a toddler with a harry pottered nose."

Harry Randall – CANDLE.
2D. He's getting on… look at the Harry's on his cake!"

Harry Tate – STATE, (condition).
1D. "Look at the harry tate that Keith's got himself into."

Harry Worth – TURF. (Origins; British comedian)
1D. "Laying new harry worth today, same brand as West Ham."

Harry Wragg – FAG, (cigarette). (Origins; famous jockey)
2D. "Have you got any harrys on yer? I'm all out."

Harvey Nichols – PICKLES. (Origins; British upper class store)
2D. "Give me the Branston for me sarnie, mum. Can't have cheese without harvey."

Hat Rack – BACK.
1D. "Poor Dave, he fell off his alibi ike and knobbled his hat rack."

Hat & Scarf – LAUGH.
1D. "Don't tell me that, you're having a hat and scarf."

Hatti Jaques (Jakes) – SHAKES. (Origins; British comedienne)
1D. "Oh, just thinking about spiders gives me the hatti jaques!"

Hay Stack – BACK.
1D. "I can't stand the pain in me hay stack anymore; I'm off to the doc's."

Haywards Heath – TEETH.
2D. "Look at the number of haywards in his gob, what a mouthful."
(OLD; Included in Hotten's 1858 Rhyming Slang Glossary)

Heap of Coke – BLOKE, (guy).
1D. "Is that a new heap of coke that Valerie's with?"

Hearts of Oak – BROKE. (Origins; rousing English patriotic song)
2D. "I'm borassic, mate. Totally hearts."

Heavenly Bliss – KISS.
2D. "C'mon me turtle, give us an 'eavenly on me filters then."

Hedge & Ditch – PITCH, (market stand, stall).
2D. "Hey Henry! Look after me hedge for a bit, I have to do some business."

Helter-Skelter – AIR RAID SHELTER. (Origins; amusement park ride)
1D. "In the Blitz, we was down the 'elter skelter every night."

Henry Moore – DOOR. (Origins; possibly English artist)
2D. "They broke the flippin' 'enry down, and arrested 'im."

Henry Neville – DEVIL. (Origins; British nobleman)
2D. "Gotta manage your sins here, or the henry will get ye."

Henry the Eighth – EIGHTH, (of coke). (Origins; English king)
2D. "Cut me out an 'enry, will ya?"
(Not exactly a proper 'rhyme', but I included it anyway)

Herring Bone – PHONE.
1D. "Get us a joe on the old 'erring bone. Time to go 'ome."

Hey Diddle Diddle – FIDDLE.
1D. "I don't trust our manager, I think he's on the hey diddle diddle."

Hickory Docks – SOCKS. (Origins; nursery rhyme)
2D. "Hey Tad? Loose the hickory's when you wear sandals."

Hide and Seek – CHEEK.
1D. "Oh Cathy, so romantic, he kissed me on my hide and seek."

Highland Fling – RING. (Origins; Scottish dance)
1D. "I'm going to surprise 'er, got me a highland fling, asking her tonight."

Hilary Swank – WANK, (masturbate). (Origins; American actress)
2D. "I caught him in the toilet, having a bit of a hilary."

Hillman Hunters – PUNTERS. (Origins; 1960's British car)
2D. "Lots of hillmans in the line, I'm going to wait."

Hit List – PISSED, (angry).
1D. "I'm really hit list today, we lost again."

Hit & Miss – KISS.
1D. "How about a little hit and miss then, Sophie?"

Hit & Miss – PISS.
1D. "Wait! He's taking the hit an' miss outs me!"

Hobson's Choice – VOICE. (Origins; phrase meant 'no choice')
2D. "He's singing terrible; what's the matter with 'is 'obsons then?"

Hockey Puck – F*CK. (Origins; the small black 'disc' used in ice hockey)
"I don't give a hockey puck, I want him out tomorrow."

Hod of Mortar – POT OF PORTER. (Origins; hod was the square box on a stick to carry bricks and mortar)
2D. "Another Hod of that delectable brew! Please."
(OLD; Included in Hotten's 1858 Rhyming Slang Glossary)

Holborn Viaduct – F*CKED. (Origins; old bridge in London)
2D. "They've scored three in the first half, we're holborn, aren't we?"

Holler Boys Holler – COLLAR, (prosecuted, charged).
2D. "Looks like Jimmy got hollered for that bank job, silly bugger."
('Had his collar felt', meant being charged with a crime, literally the police grabbed perpetrator by the collar and threw him in jail.)

Holly Hox – POX. (Origins; 'Hollyhocks' is a variety of flowering plant)
1D. "Looks like she's going back in for treatment... the old holly hox returns."

Holly Wreath – TEETH.

149

2D. "Look at the front holly on her. Gor, Bugs Bunny doesn't have a look in."

Holy Friar – LIAR.
1D. "Watch what Jackie says, 'e's a bit of a holy friar for sure."

Holy Ghost – TOAST.
2D. "Can we get another round of 'oly over 'ere, love?"

Holy Grail – EMAIL. (Origins; Christ's chalice at the last supper)
1D. "Okay, I got it. Holy grail me with details."

Home & Away – GAY, (homosexual). (Origins; possibly Australian TV soap; see note below)
"Oh Jeremy's home an' away, and that's a fact!"
(This is another clever one. 'Home and Away' is a sporting term for playing a team once at your ground, and once at theirs. Playing 'home' would be having a man/woman relationship. 'Playing away' is now a well-used phrase for having an affair, either straight or gay)

Honey Bees – KEYS.
1D. "Throw me the honey bees, love. I'm late already."

Hong Kong Fooey – FLU-EY, (having flu symptoms). (Origins; British TV cartoon)
2D. "I'm not going in to work today, I feel a bit hong kong."

Hopping Pot – LOT, (a share, that's all you get).
1D. "Eat every bit on your plate, cause that's your hopping pot, mate."

Horace Bachelor – SPATULA.
2D. "Throw me the 'orace, Billy, me 'ands are full."

Horse & Carriage – MARRIAGE.
1D. "Ah well, that's Rodney finished; e's off to his 'orse and carriage."

Horse & Cart – FART.
1D. "Have you just horse & carted, Barbara?"

Horse & Cart – HEART.
1D. "Oh, have a horse an' cart, Maisie, she's only six."

Horse & Cart – TART.
"That slapper of george's is a real horse, isn't she?"

Horse & Trap – CRAP.
1D. "I don't care a horse an' trap about Liverpool, just as long as they beat Spurs."

Horse's Hoof – POOF, (male homosexual).
1D. "Yeah Tony's a horse's hoof, but he's a real good friend too."

Horse's Hoof – ROOF.
2D. "I got stuck up on the horse's for an hour yesterday."

Hot Cross Bun – NUN. (Origins; British sweet bread bun with a cross on top)
1D. "I saw a bunch of 'ot cross buns walking in ewan blair today."

Hotpoint Fridge – SEVERN BRIDGE, (road bridge between England and Wales).
2D. "Off to Cardiff tomorrow, going over the 'otpoint to save time."

Hot Potato ('Potater') – WAITER.
1D. "So which one of the penguins is our hot potater, then?"

Hounslow Heath – TEETH. (Origins; nature reserve in west London)
2D. "I'm off down the dentist tomorrow, get me 'oundslows looked at."
(OLD; Included in Hotten's 1858 Rhyming Slang Glossary)

House to Let – BET, (wager).

1D. "So what's your best house to let on the Grand National, then?"

Housemaid's Knee – SEA. (Origins; working woman's ailment)
2D. "We're having a weekend in Brighton, paddle in the old housemaids."

Housewives Choice – VOICE. (Origins; British radio show)
1D. "I think me cuddles 'as lost 'er 'ousewives choice. I'm not going to miss a minute."

How Do You Do's – SHOES.
1D. "Got me a new pair of how-do-you-do's up at the market, just an ayrton senna."

How's Your Father – LATHER. (Origins; 'how's your father' is a euphemism for sex)
1D. "You want a hand in there? I'll hows-your-father yur back."

Huckleberry Finn – PIN. (Origins; Mark Twain character)
2D. "What do you do when a blond throws an 'uckleberry at you? Run, she's 'olding the grenade."

Hugo Boss – DOSS, (sleep). (Origins; German fashion house)
2D. "Do you mind if I hugo at your drum for a couple of days?"

Hum & Song – PONG, (smell).
2D. "That new kebab place don't half hum in the morning."

Hurricane Lamp – TRAMP.
2D. "I dropped the hurricane a nicker this morning, felt flush."

Hydraulics – BOLLOCKS.
1D. "Oh, I seen it, kicked square in the hydraulics, he went down like a felled tree."

I

Ian Beale – REAL. (Origins; Eastenders soap opera character)
1D. "Oh God, Tim's slapped her. This thruppeny suddenly got ian beale."

Ian Rush – BRUSH. (Origins; Welsh footballer)
1D. "Sandra's hair could do with a look at an ian rush."

Ian Wright – SHITE. (Origins; English footballer)
1D. "I can't believe the final score. We played ian wright for most of the game."

Ice Cream Freezer – GEEZER, (guy).
2D. "I like Fred. For a step-dad he's not a bad ice cream."

Ice Rink – DRINK.
1D. "Fricking hot today, I need me an ice rink and quick."

I Desire – FIRE.
1D. "Get yer arse down near the I desire, it's going to be a cold one."
(OLD; Included in Hotten's 1858 Rhyming Slang Glossary)

Ille Nastase – KHAZI, (toilet). (Origins; Romanian tennis player)
1D. "I'm off to the ille nastase, no time to waste."

I'm Afloat – OVERCOAT.
1D. "Where's me i'm afloat? It's damn parky outside."
(OLD; Included in Hotten's 1858 Rhyming Slang Glossary)

In and Out – GOUT.
1D. "Oh, me in and out's playing me up again."

In and Out – SNOUT, (cigarette).
1D. "Hey, Martha? You seen my in and out?"

In and Out – KRAUT, (German).
1D. No Steinburg watch for me; I don't wear that in and out crap."

Inky Smudge – JUDGE.
2D. "I've got a date with the inky next week after that row in the boozer, Friday."

Insects & Ants – PANTS, (underwear).
2D. "No insects today, going commando."

Inspector Morse – SAUCE. (Origins; Fictional British detective)
2D. "Where's the inspector for me bacon sarnie?"

Inspector Taggart – FAGGOT, (homosexual). (Origins; Fictional Scottish detective)
1D. "Oh, he looks a bit pink on the outside, a bit inspector taggart."

InterCity – KITTY, (cash). (Origins; type of UK train)
1D. "You got a good bit of intercity on you? It's going to be a long session."

In the Nude – FOOD.
1D. "I need some in the mood pronto; I'm hank an' lee."

Irish Jig – WIG.
1D. "Oh, look at the irish jig on that one at the bar; terrible syrup."

Irish Rose – NOSE.
2D. "He gave me a hard one, right on me Irish."

Iron Hoof – POOF, (homosexual).
1D. "Look at that bloke with Harvey, he's a right iron hoof, and no mistake."

Iron Horse – TOSS, (a care).
2D. "I don't give an Iron, mate, he means nothing to me."

Iron Lung – TONGUE.
2D. "You watch your iron when you talk to me, me lad."

Iron Tank – BANK.
1D. "Stick your cash in the iron tank, me son. It'll never go wrong there."

Iron Tank – WANK.
2D. "I'm off indoors for a quick iron."

Isabella – UMBERELLA.
1D. "You grab her isabella, an' when she's turnin' I'll grab her money pouch."
(OLD; Included in Hotten's 1858 Rhyming Slang Glossary)

Isle of France – A DANCE.
1D. "I got an invite to the Duchess's isle o' france, next Saturday."
(OLD; Included in Hotten's 1858 Rhyming Slang Glossary)

Isle of Skye – PIE. (Origins; Island off the west coast of Scotland)
1D. "My favorite, mum; shepherds isle of skye."

Isle of Wight – LIGHT, (beer). (Origins; Island off the south coast of England)
1D. "Two isle of wights, and a ruin for the trouble."

Isle of Wight – RIGHT.
2D. "MacDonalds? Go down the to the traffic lights and make an isle."

I Suppose – NOSE.
1D. "I'll have to get a handkie; me flipping I suppose is running."

Itchy Ring – BURGER KING. (Origins; hamburger fast food)

2D. "I don't fancy a curry tonight, think I'll try an itchy instead."

Itchy Teeth – BEEF.
2D. "My wife's got some itchy stew for tonight's dinner, so I'm off early."

Ivory Band – HAND.
2D. "Oy, Tony, give us an ivory for a minute! I've only got two."

J

J. Arthur Rank – BANK. (Origins; film magnate in the 60's)
1D. "I'm off down the j. edgar rank to deposit some bees an' honey."

J. Arthur Rank – SHANK. (Origin; golf term, a badly struck shot)
2D. "Ooh. RIGHT! Dang, I j. arthured that one."

J. Arthur Rank – WANK. (Origins; film magnate in the 60's)
2D. "Oh he's a right j. Arthur, always on the make."

Jabba the Hutt – SHUT. (Origins; Star Wars baddie)
"Oh, Jamesie! Tell no one; jabba yer gob."

Jack & Dandy – HANDY.
1D. "Oh scratch me back, up a bit, right there, oh, that's jack and dandy."

Jack & Danny – FANNY, (Backside).
1D. "Marge? She's at home on her Jack and Danny."

Jack & Jill – BILL. (Origins; nursery rhyme)
2D. "Waitress? Can we have the jack please, we're in a hurry."

Jack & Jill – CONTRACEPTIVE PILL. (Origins; nursery rhyme)
1D. "It's alright love, no worries on me. I'm on the jack 'n' jill, ain't I?"

Jack & Jill – HILL. (Origins; nursery rhyme)
2D. "Come on lads, put a bit of effort in; there's a pub at the top o' the jack."

Jack & Jill – TILL, (Cash Register). (Origins; nursery rhyme)

1D. "'E got nicked... 'is 'ands in the old jack and jill an' no mistake."

Jackanory – STORY. (Origins; BBC Kids program)
1D. "I don't believe a flippin' word, tell us another jackanory."

Jack Dash – SLASH, (urinate).
2D. "Tell 'em to hold the bus, dave, I've got to have a quick jack."

Jackdaw – JAW, (talk, blether).
1D. "Tell the missus I'll be home late, we're having a right jackdaw here."

Jackdaw And Rook – BOOK.
2D. "I'm reading a great jackdaw right now; a real political thriller."

Jack Dee – CUP OF TEA. (Origins; British comedian)
1D. "Hey Maisie? Fancy a cup of jack dee?"

Jack Randle – CANDLE. (Origins; either a noted pugilist or footballer),
1D. "Where do you keep the jack randles? The power's out!"
(OLD; Included in Hotten's 1858 Rhyming Slang Glossary)

Jackie Chan – CAN, (beer). (Origins; movie star)
2D. "Hey Terry? Fancy a tiddley tonight? I got a few jackies in the fridge."

Jackie Chan – PLAN. (Origins; movie star)
1D. "Surprise party for April? Cool. What's the jackie chan then?"

Jackie Danny – FANNY (vagina).
2D. "I'm itching for it. I'm going out to get some Jackie tonight."

Jack Flash – Hash, (drugs).
1D. "I'm going down the park, see if I can score a jack flash."

Jackie Flint – SKINT, (broke).

158

1D. "Sorry mate, stuck at home tonight, jackie flint, ain't I."

Jack Joner – LONER. (Origins; see next entry)
1D. "See him at the bar, never talks, he's a real jack joner."

Jack Jones – ALONE, (on your own). (Origins; This one is actually worth a story. Before the First World War, well-known Cockney music hall singer, Gus Elen, sung a song entitled *'E dunno where 'e are.* The song tells the story of a man called Jack Jones, who came into money, and thought of himself as too good for his former friends. The lyrics go thus…
When he's up at Covint Gardin you can see 'im a standin' all alone,
Won't join in a quiet little Tommy Dodd, drinking Scotch and Soda on 'is own.
'E 'as the cheek and impudence to call 'is muvver 'is Ma,
Since Jack Jones came into a little bit o' splosh, well 'e dunno where 'e are.
(A Tommy Dodd was a half-pint of beer).

Jack McGraw – DRAW, (cannabis).
1D. "I'm skint; can't even afford some jack mcgraw."

Jack Palance – DANCE. (Origins; American actor)
2D. "Come on Connie, get on yer plates. Me an' you is gonna 'ave a little jack."

Jack Straw – DRAW, (cannabis).
2D. "I'm off down the market, see if I can score me some jack."

Jack Tar – BAR. (Origins; an old term for a sailor in the Royal navy)
1D. "I'm off to the jack tar, mum, don't wait up."

Jack's Alive – FIVE.
1D. "I'm getting sloshed tonight, I've got nice blue jack's alive in me rocket."

Jackson Pollocks – BOLLOCKS, (testicles). (Origins; off the wall artist)

2D. "I just don't get it. Modern art's a load of old Jackson."

Jack (the) Dandy – BRANDY.
1D. "Staying in with the missus tonight, got a nice jack the dandy to surprise her."
(OLD; Included in Hotten's 1858 Rhyming Slang Glossary)

Jack the Ripper – KIPPER, (smoked haddock). (Origins, a Victorian serial killer)
1D. "Oh, I love me jack the ripper with a knob of butter on top."

Jack the Ripper - STRIPPER. (Origins, a Victorian serial killer)
1D. "Oh, great jack the ripper down the boozer last night."

Jack the Ripper – SLIPPER. (Origins, a Victorian serial killer)
2D. "Oh, it's cold outside tonight. You got me jacks by the fire?"

Jacobs Crackers – KNACKERS, (testicles). (Origins; wafer bread)
2D. "That slapper kicked me in the Jacobs an' legged it."

Jaffa Cake – MISTAKE. (Origins; a orangey biscuit)
2D. Second wife? Yup, I made a right Jaffa there, mate".

Jah Rule – SCHOOL. (Origins; this may be a modern term, Ja Rule is an American rapper)
2D. "Off to jah, another day nearer freedom."

Jakki Brambles – SHAMBLES. (origins; UK disc jockey)
2D. "Did you see United in the second half? What a jakki."

James Blunt – C*NT. (Origins; British singer/songwriter)
1D. "Sorry love, I got drunk last night, an' made a complete james blunt of me'self."

Jammed Brown – FROWN.
1D. "Look at the groom's mother. She can't keep the jammed brown from her face."

James Dean – KEEN. (Origins; American actor)
1D. "Look at him push the defense; I like him, he's james dean."

James Dean – OBSCENE. (Origins; American actor)
2D. "Listen to the words coming out of her north, pure james."

James Hunt – C*NT. (Origins; British Formula 1 champion)
1D. "Oh dear, she's only gone and slapped his face, what a james hunt."

Jam Butty – NUTTY (crazy). (Origins, a sandwich and jam (US jelly))
1D. "Tonya dumped him last night, and he went jam butty."

Jamie Redknapp – CRAP. (Origins; Liverpool football player)
1D. "I give up on football. The team's jamie redknapp, the whole lot of 'em."

Jam Jar – CAR.
2D. "The flipping jam is playing up again, transmission this time."

Jam Roll – ARSEHOLE.
1D. "Oh, look at that jam roll trying to push his car uphill."

Jam Roll – DOLE.
2D. "Sign on day at the jam, better wear me peckham."

Jam Roll – POLE, (from Poland).
1D. "Ronnie's a jam roll, came over as a pilot during the war."

Jam Tart – FART.
1D. "Sitting in the doctor's office, I dropped a huge jam tart."

Jam Tart – HEART. (Hearts are an Edinburgh football team, nicknamed, 'The Jam Tarts')
2D. "Oh, me jam's beating outa me george this mornin'."

Jan Leeming – STEAMING, (very drunk). (origins; British newscaster)
1D. "Oh I was jan leeming last night, had maybe three or four too many."

Jane Fonda – WANDER.
1D. "I think I'll take a jane fonda over to the supermarket today, I fancy kippers."

Janet Street-Porter – QUARTER, (a weight of drugs).
2D. "I need to score me a janet today, an' no mistake."

Jay Kay – TAKE AWAY, (order of food to go). (Origins, initials of Jonathan King, UK TV personality)
1D. "Don't cook tonight, love, we'll have a jay kay instead."

Jay Z – CUP OF TEA. (Origins; American rapper)
1D. "Put the kettle on, love, I fancy a nice jay z."

Jazz Bands – HANDS.
2D. "Oh, get yer jazz's off me! I know my rights!"

Jean & Norma – CHICKEN KORMA, (mild Indian Curry). (Origins; Marilyn Monroe's real name backwards)
1D. "I fancy a nice jean an' norma tonight, what about you?"

Jean Claude van Damme – SPAM, (processed tinned meat). (Origins; Belgian actor)
2D. "I need me some fried jean claude tonight, on toast!"

Jedi Knight – SHITE. (Origins; Star Wars character)
2D. "Where's the khazi? I need a jedi, and fast."

Jeff Beck – CHECK. (Origins; British rock guitarist)
1D. "I'll write you a jeff beck, is that okay?"

Jeff Beck – NECK. (Origins; British rock guitarist)
2D. "Gor, he's got a brass jeff, hasn't he?"

Jeffrey Dahmer – CHARMER. (Origins; American serial killer)
1D. "Look at her drool. Bob's a Jeffrey Dahmer an' no mistake."

Jekyll & Hyde – SNIDE, (fake, forgery). (Origins; R.L. Stevenson character)
1D. "Lenny's all jekyll an' hyde, not a blade of truth in 'im."

Jekyll & Hydes – STRIDES, (trousers). (Origins; R.L. Stevenson character)
1D. "I love a good pair of jekyll an' hydes, makes me feel great."

Jellied Eel – DEAL. (Origins; English delicacy)
1D. "Only ten bob? You got yourself a jellied eel, mate."

Jellied Eel – FEEL. (Origins; English delicacy)
1D. "I don't care how you jellied eel; you're going to school."

Jellied Eel – SQUEAL. (Origins; English delicacy)
2D. "Then she gave out a jellied, an' ran off cryin'."

Jelly Bone – PHONE.
2D. "Give me a call on the jelly nearer the date, firm up the time."

Jelly Roll Blues – NEWS, (paper).
2D. "So what's in the jelly roll today then? Who's on the front page?"

Jelly Tot – SPOT, (pluke). (Origins; British fruity confectionery)
1D. "Just before me big date, I got a jelly tot on me I suppose, typical."

Jem Mace – FACE. (Origins; boxer in the late 19th century)
2D. "Wipe that look off your jem, you're in for a hidin'."

Jenny Lee – FLEA. (Origins; either American or British actress)
1D. "Their drum got fumigated, bad case of jenny lees."

Jenny Linder – WINDER, (widow).
1D. "I lost me honeys, had to climb in the jenny linder."

163

(OLD; Included in Hotten's 1858 Rhyming Slang Glossary)

Jennie Powell – TROWEL.
1D. "There she was, kneeling in the garden, jennie powell in hand."

Jenson Button – MUTTON. (Origins; Formula 1 driver)
2D. "Good pie. That butcher sells the best jenson in town."

Jeremiah – FIRE.
1D. "He come running so fast, I asked him where the jeremiah was."

Jeremy Beadle – NEEDLE. (Origins; English TV presenter)
2D. "Spurs lost again on Saturday, let's go give Davie some jeremy."

Jeremy Hunt – C*NT. (Origins; British politician)
2D. "Watch out for Maisie's temper, she can be a real Jeremy sometimes."

Jeremy Kyles – PILES. (Origins; English TV presenter)
1D. "Oh, that curry didn't half bring me jeremy kiles on."

Jerry Cottle – BOTTLE, (courage). (Origins; possibly a circus venue)
1D. "I wanted to ask her out, but didn't have the jerry cottle."

Jerry O'Gorman – MORMON.
1D. "A bunch of jerry o'gormans have moved in next door; I don't know what to say."

Jerry Springer – MINGER, (ugly woman). (Origins; American TV presenter)
1D. "That bird's such a jerry springer, she'd make an ugly man!"

Jet Fighter – ALL NIGHTER.
1D. "Barman's just locked the door. Looks like we're going to have a jet fighter."

Jet Lag – FAG (gay).
1D. "Must be a jet lag convention in town, they're everywhere."

Jet Li – PEE. (Origins; Chinese actor)
1D. "I'm having a last jet li before we go, then we're off."

Jethro Tull – SKULL. (Origin; Scottish rock musician)
2D. "When will you get it thru your thick jethro! I'm not going out!"

Jim Bob Babs – CRABS, (std).
1D. "I heard that Janie's got a case of the jim bob babs."

Jim Fenner – TENNER, (ten pound note).
1D. "Can you lend me a jim fenner until Tuesday?

Jimi Hendrix – APPENDIX. (Origins; American rock musician)
1D. "I heard Susie's in hospital to get her jimmy Hendrix looked at."

Jiminy Cricket – TICKET. (Origins; Disney cartoon character)
2D. "Have you got the jiminy's? Don't forget them!"

Jimmy Boyle – FOIL, (drug paraphernalia). (Origins; Scottish crime lord)
1D. "Hey Davy? You got any jimmy doyle on yer?"

Jimmy Choo's – SHOES. (Origins; Malaysian fashion mogul)
1D. "Whad'ya think of the new jimmy choos? Snazzy right?"

Jimmy Cliff – WHIFF, (smell). (Origins; Jamaican singer)
1D. "I shook his hand, and got a jimmy cliff of his cologne, terrible!"

Jimmy Connors – HONOURS. (Origins; American tennis player)
1D. "Yup, she got her degree from Oxford, full jimmy connors too."

Jimmy Giraffe – LAUGH. (Origins; cartoon character)
1D. "Oh come on, Leeds get promoted? You're having a jimmy giraffe."

Jimmy Greaves – THIEVES. (Origins; English footballer/TV pundit)
1D. "Gotta watch those gypo's, bunch of jimmy greaves, the lot of 'em."

Jimmy Hill – BILL. (Origins; English footballer/TV pundit)
1D. "Dad? Have we paid the jimmy hill yet?"

Jimmy Hill – PILL. (Origins; English footballer/TV pundit)
1D. "No more panics, I'm on the jimmy hill now."

Jimmy Nail – EMAIL. (Origins; British actor/singer)
1D. "What's your jimmy nail? I'll send you the file."

Jimmy Nail – HAIL. (Origins; British actor/singer)
2D. "Real heavy andy, maybe with a touch of jimmy too."

Jimmy Nail – JAIL. (Origins; British actor/singer)
1D. "Victor's off to jimmy nail for a month; he's been busy."

Jimmy O'Goblin – SOVEREIGN.
1D. "I wouldn't give you a jimmy goblin for your chances."

Jimmy Riddle – PIDDLE, (widdle, pee, wee).
2D. "Gor, I'm dying on a jimmy right now. Where's the nearest cabin?"

Jimmy Shand – HAND. (Origins; Scottish accordionist)
1D. "Hey, do you want a jimmy shand moving that Joanna?"

Jimmy White – SHITE. (Origins; English snooker player)
1D. "Tommy? he's just a wee jimmy white anyway."

Jim Skinner – DINNER.
2D. "Mum? Is my Jim ready yet?"

Joanna – PIANO, (pronounced pee-ann-a).
1D. "Man, listen to Deirdre. She sure does well on the old Joanna."

Jo Blunt – C*NT.
1D. "Wow, being a gynecologist, looking at jo blunts all day long."

Jockey Whip – CHIP, (French fry).
2D. "I'll have a large portion of jockey's, loads of brown sauce."

Jockey Whip – KIP, (sleep).
1D. "I'm off home for a quick jockey whip before tonight's bash."

Jodie Marsh – HARSH. (Origins; English beauty/TV star)
1D. "Oh, a foul, yes, but a penalty is a bit jodie marsh."

Jodrell Bank – WANK, (masturbate). (Origins; Manchester astronomy facility)
2D. "I'm just off home for a quick wash and jodrell."

Joe Baksi – TAXI. (Origins; American heavyweight boxer)
2D. "Right folks, the joe's here, everyone outside who's going."

Joe Blake – CAKE. (Origins; English footballer)
2D. "Oh take a look at the wedding joe in the corner, isn't it cool?"

Joe Blake – SNAKE. (Origins; English footballer)
1D. "I can't stand him, he's a total joe blake."

Joe Blake – STEAK. (Origins; English footballer)
1D. "Joe blake an' jockeys please, mushy peas an' gravy."

Joe Brown – TOWN. (Origins; English singer, father of Sam Brown)
1D. "I'm taking a trip to the joe brown today, concert tonight."

Joe Daki – PAKI, (Pakistani).

1D. "There's a new newsagent on the high street, joe daki, of course."

Joe Goss – BOSS. (Origins; British boxer)
1D. "We've got a new joe goss at the shovel, things gonna change."

Joe Hart – FART. (Origins; English footballer)
1D. "I dropped a joe hart at the doctors today, I thought I'd die."

Joe Hook – BOOK.
1D. "I love getting my corned beef into a good joe hook."

Joe Hoppers – COPPERS, (police).
1D. "The joe hoppers were out in force on Saturday, Chelsea v Spurs."

Joe Rook – CROOK.
1D. "If you want anything, ask Eddie; his dad's a joe rook."

Joe Savage – CABBAGE.
1D. "Mum's making corn beef an' joe savage today, I ain't missin' it!"
(OLD; Included in Hotten's 1858 Rhyming Slang Glossary)

Joey Ramone – PHONE. (Origins; American rock musician)
1D. "Crap, I think I left my joey ramone in the cabin cruiser."

John Cleese – CHEESE. (Origins; British comedian/actor)
1/2D. Hey, I wonder if there's any john in the john cleese shop?"

John Cleese – KEYS. (Origins; British comedian/actor)
2D. "Luv a duck, 'ave you seen me jam johns anywhere?"

John Cleese – PEAS. (Origins; British comedian/actor)
1D. "Good old mushy john cleese; the stuff of legend."

John Deut – BEAUT. (Origins; possibly linked to John Denver, American singer, whose real name was Henry John Deutschendorf Jr)
1D. "Look at Henry's new bird, she's a john deut."

John Dillon – SHILLING, (pronounced shillin'). (Origins; too many to choose from)
1D. "Roll up, get your jelly roll here, just a john dillon."

John Hop – COP.
1D. "There's a new john hop on the manor, ginger, 'e is."

Johnny Horner – CORNER. (Origins; probably the children's nursery rhyme)
2D. "Don't let on you saw me, I'll meet you around the johnnie."

Johnny Rutter – BUTTER.
1D. "You just can't beat jockeys on brown with a little johnny rutter."

Johnny Cash – HASH, (cannabis). (Origins; American singer)
1D. "Oh you just can't beat a bit of johnny cash to take the edge off."

Johnny Cash – SLASH, (pee). (Origins; American singer)
2D. "I'm burstin' on a johnny. Where's the cadburys?"

Johnny Vaughn – PORN. (Origins; British comedian/TV presenter)
1D. "We caught young Neddy looking at johnny vaughn last week."

John Major – PAGER. (Origins; British Prime Minister)
1D. "Call me at the office, they'll hit me john major."

John Major – WAGER. (Origins; British Prime Minister)
1D. "I'll john major you a tanner to a bob that Red Rum will win."

John McCain – INSANE. (Origins; American politician)

1D. "Oh that Hilary Clinton, she's just completely john mccain!"

John O'Groat – THROAT. (Origins; northernmost point of mainland UK.)
1D. "I grabbed 'im by the john o'groat, and shook him around."

John Selwyn Gummer – BUMMER, (drug trip). (Origins; British politician)
2D. "I dreamed a last minute goal beat us. What a john selwyn."

John Skinner – DINNER. (Origins; possibly the English cricketer)
1D. "We're having roast beef for our john skinner, it smells amazing."

John Wayne – TRAIN. (Origins; American actor)
1D. "I'm getting the john wayne up to Edinburgh at the weekend."

John West – VERY BEST. (Origins; British canning company)
1D. "John got himself a BMW; only the john west for him, huh?"

Jonathan King – RING. (Origins; British pop mogul)
1D. "Look, Sandy's wearing a new jonathan king. Does that mean what I think it does?"

Jonathan Ross – TOSS (care). (Origins; British TV presenter)
2D. "I don't give a jonathan about the rugby, I'm a footie chappie."

Jonathan Ross'ed – LOST. (Origins; British TV presenter)
1D. "Colin got jonathan rossed in Clapham at the weekend."

Jude Law– SCORE. (Origins; English actor)
1D. "I lost a jude law when West Ham lost to Chelsea."

Judge Jules – TOOLS. (Origins; British musician)
1D. "I'd like to fix the pipe myself, but I got no judge jules."

Judy Dench – BENCH. (Origins; British actress)
1D. "He only tied her to the judy dench and scarpered."

Judy Dench – STENCH. (Origins; British actress)
2D. "There's a heck of a judy coming from the new kebab shop."

Judy Dench – WRENCH. (Origins; British actress)
2D. "Pass me that judy will ya, the adjustable."

Julian Clairy – FAIRY. (Origins; British comedian/actor)
2D. "That fridge behind the bar's a freakin' julian, ain't he?"
(Another clever one, since Julian is SO openly gay)

Julian Ray – GAY, (homosexual).
1D. "There a new festival up town, some sort of julian ray thing."

Julius Caesar – GEEZER, (bloke). (Origins; Roman emperor)
2D. "Gor, lummie, look at the hampsteads on that Julius!"

Jumbo Jet – BET, (wager). (Origins; Boeing 747)
2D. "I'm having my first jumbo of the year on the National."

Jumping Jack – BACK.
1D. "Me jumpin' jack's playing me up again, too much gardening."

Jumping Jack Flash – CASH. (Origins; Rolling Stones song)
2D. "At last I got me germans on some jumpin', got a big treble yesterday."

Jungle Jim – TIM, (Catholic person).
1D. "She can't marry him; he's a jungle jim, a cow's lick!"

Jurassic Park – DARK. (Origins; Michael Creighton book/film)
2D. "Oh, she's left me in the jungle on that one. I got no idea."

K

K Y Jelly – TELLY, (television).
2D. "Is there anything interesting on the KY tonight?"

Kangaroo Pouch – COUCH, (sofa).
2D. "Come sit on the kangaroo with me, we'll have a mix an' muddle."

Kansas & Missouri – TANDOORI. (tandoori is a type of Indian Curry)
2D. "What curry's it going to be then? Kansas or Basil?"

Kareem Abdul Jabbar – CAR. (Origins; US basketball player)
2D. "Come on you lot, get in the kareem, we're late!"

Kat Slater – LATER, (as in, catch/see you later).
2D. "Okay, I'm off home. kats!"

Kate Carney – ARMY. (Origins; Kate was a true Cockney music hall comedienne and singer)
2D. "Never guess about Steve? He's off and joined the Kate."

Kate & Sidney – STEAK & KIDNEY.
1D. "I'm off home tonight, wife's doing her famous Kate and Sydney pie."

Kate Moss – TOSS, (a damn). (Origins; fashion model)
1D. "Art? Basically I couldn't give a Kate Moss."

Kate Mossed – LOST. (Origins; fashion model)
1D. "We've been driving round in circles for ages, we're officially kate mossed."

Kate Nash – GASH, (vagina). (Origins; British singer)

1D. "I have to get me some kate nash soon or I'm going to go nuts."

Kathy Burke – WORK. (Origins; British comedienne)
1D. "I've been on the brew so long, it good to get back to kathy burke."

Katy Price – NICE. (Origins; English TV personality, AKA Jordan)
1D. "Look at the blonde at the bar; now that's what I call katy price."

Keith Cheggers – PREGGERS, (pregnant). (Origins; Keith Chegwin, UK disc jockey)
2D. "Oh, look at Allie's belly, no one told me she was a bit keith."

Keith Deller – Stella, (Artois; Belgian lager). (Origins; British darts player)
1D. "Oh, it's Saturday night, six pints of Keith Deller, please."

Keith Vaz – WAZZ, (pee). (Origins; British Muslim MP)
1D. "Hold up boys, I'm off down this alley for a quick keith vaz."

Ken & Barbie's – STARBY'S, (Starbucks). (Origins; children's dolls)
2D. "I'm meeting Karen at ken's this afternoon."

Ken Dodd – ODD. (Origins; British comedian)
1D. "I never trusted Sue, there was always something ken dodd about her."

Ken Dodd – WAD. (Origins; British comedian)
2D. "Economy's great; I've never had me a bigger wad."

Ken Dodds – ODDS. (Origins; British comedian)
1D. "Tottenham won, what were the ken dodds?"

Ken Smee – PEE.
2D. "I'm bursting, where's the ken room?"

Kermit the Frog – BOG, (toilet). (Origins; Jim Henson puppet)
2D. "I need to take a jimmy, where's the Kermit?"

Kermit the Frog – WOG, (brown person). (Origins; Jim Henson puppet)
2D. "Another corner shop opened, kermits of course."

Kerry Katona – BONER, (erection). (Origins; English singer/TV presenter)
2D. "Oh man, I've got a kerry for the Man United line up this year."
(Clever one, Kerry was in the band, Atomic Kitten, and is very cute)

Kerry Packered – KNACKERED, (tired). (Origins; Australian media magnate)
2D. "I'm right Kerry'd after moving into a new place."

Kevin & Linda – WINDA, (window).
1D. "Oh shut the kevin an' linda! It's cold out there!"

Kevin Keegan – VEGAN. (Origins; English footballer/manager)
1D. "Heard about Harvey? He's only gone kevin keegan on us."

Khyber Pass – ARSE. (Origins; strategic pass in Pakistan)
2D. "Chelsea? Stick that right up your khyber."

Kick and Prance – DANCE.
1D. "Maisie's trying to get me to kick an' prance, no way!"

Kick Start – TART.
2D. "So, is this a boys night out, or are we taking the kicks?"

Kidney Punch – LUNCH.
1D. "It's been a long mornin', I can't wait 'til kidney punch time."

Kiki Dee – TEA. (Origins; English singer)
2D. "I'm off down the cheggers, we're out of kiki!"

Kilkenny – PENNY. (Origins; Irish county/town)
2D. "Go out? I'm boracic mate, not a kilkenny to my name."

Kilroy Silk – MILK. (Origins; English chat-show host)
2D. "Rosy? Sure, Kilroy and two sugars."

King Death – BREATH.
1D. "Hurt? He damn near knocked the king death out of me."

King Lear – BEER. (Origins; Shakespeare character)
1D. "I really fancy a king lear right now."

King Lear – EAR. (Origins; Shakespeare character)
1D. "He smacked me round the king lear, cheeky sod."

King Lear – GEAR, (drug paraphernalia). (Origins; Shakespeare character)
1D. "I lost my stuff; do you have spare king lear?"

King Lear – QUEER. (Origins; Shakespeare character)
1D. "I've looked at Ian and Linda, but there's something king lear going on there."

King Tut – GUT. (Origins; Egyptian Pharaoh, Tutankhamun)
1D. "When I punched him in the king tut, he went down like a sack of taters."

Kingdom Come – BUM.
2D. "He just sat on his kingdom all day. Drove me nuts."

Kirk Stevens – EVENS, (betting term). (Origins; Canadian snooker player)
1D. "Man United or Chelsea? That's a kirk stevens one, mate."

Kisses & Hugs – DRUGS.
1D. "I've never touched kisses an' hugs, just not my thing."

Kitchen Sink – CHINK, (Chinese, either person or food).

1D. "Man, there's no one can do a curry like a kitchen sink, man. Awesome."

Kitchen Sink – CLINK, (prison).
2D. "After that last debacle he'll be in the kitchen for a long time."

Kitchen Sink – DRINK.
1D. "Man I'm parched, I need a kitchen sink, and pronto."

Kitchen Tap – JAP, (Japanese person).
2D. "I fought the shermans, then the kitchens... and lived to tell the tale."

Kitty Litter – BITTER.
2D. "Four pints of kitty, please, barman!"

Knight Rider – CIDER.
2D. "Okay Stan, your round; three kitty's, one knight, one cinderella."

Knobbly Knees – KEYS.
2D. "Have you got your knobblies with you? Mine are in the car."

Knobbly Knees – PEAS.
2D. "Dinner? We're havin' sexton, knobblies and lots of army and navy."

Kornikova – (THE) ONCE OVER, (examine). (Origins; Russian tennis player)
1D. "Hey, did you kornikova that last deep sea you got in change?"

Kuala Lumpur – JUMPER, (sweater). (Origins; capital of Malasia)
2D. "I'm taking a kuala with me, might be parky later."

Kung-fu Fighter – LIGHTER.
1D. "Have you got a kung-fu fighter on yer? I needs a light."

Kuwaiti Tanker – WANKER.
2D. "Billy's a right Kuwaiti after a kitty or two."

Kylie Minogues – BROGUES, (patterned shoes). (Origins; Australian actress/singer)
2D. "I'm wearing my kylies with my kilt to the wedding."

Kym Marsh – HARSH. (Origins; English actress/singer)
1D. "Tart? Oh come on, that's a bit kym marsh."

L

La-Di-Da – CAR.
1D. "Oi! Get your hands off my la-di-da!"

La-Di-Da – CIGAR.
2D. "Is it okay if I light up a la-di in your taxi?"

La-Di-Da – STAR.
2D. "Dennis don't talk to us anymore, one little bit of acting and he thinks he's a a la-di."

Lady from Bristol – PISTOL.
1D. "Look at Jimmy's sky rocket. Is that a lady from bristol?"

Lady Godiva – FIVER, (five pounds).
2D. "Hey Terry, when are you going to pay me back that lady?"

Lady in Silk – MILK.
1D. "I love full cream lady in silk on me cornflakes."

Lady Mucked – F*CKED.
1D. "Six-nil; we were well and truly lady mucked before half time."

Lager & Lime – TIME.
2D. "Hey, Colin. What's the lager? Are we late yet?"

Lamb & Mint – SKINT, (broke).
1D. "No pub for me this weekend, I'm lamb an' mint."

Lamb to the Slaughter – DAUGHTER.
2D. "That blokes lamb is a real stunner an' no mistake."

Lanzarote – TOTTIE, (good-looking female talent). (Origins; Spanish vacation island)
1D. "Let's go up west tonight, see if we can find some lanzarote."

Lara Croft – SOFT, (puny). (Origins; game character)
2D. "'E won't stand a minute in the daft, he's far too lara."

Larry Flint – SKINT, (broke).
2D. "I'm taking a packed lunch; I'm larry until Friday."

Last Card in the Pack – SACK.
2D. "I blew it, boss gave me the last card."

Lath and Plaster – A MASTER.
1D. "Be on the best behavior, we're in front of the lath an' plaster."
(Old; Included In Hotten's 1858 Rhyming Slang Glossary)

Laugh – BATH.
1D. "I'm beat; off 'ome. I'm having a laugh, a queer, an' a gary."

Laugh and a Joke – SMOKE.
2D. "Break out the laughs, Barry. I'm bernie."

Laugh & Titter – BITTER, (beer).
1D. "I'm real thirsty; the first laugh an' titter won't touch the sides."

Lauren Riddle – PIDDLE, (pee).
1D. "Three pints, and I have to lauren riddle."

Lawn Mower – BLOWER, (telephone).
1D. "Promise me you'll give me a call on the lawn blower tomorrow."

Laying Hen – PEN.
2D. "Autograph? Have you got a laying on yer?"

Leamington Spa – CAR. (Origins; English spa town)

1D. "Come on kids, get into the leamington spa before I lose my temper."

Lean And Lurch – CHURCH.
2D. "Come on, it's five past nine, we'll be late for the lean at this rate."
(Old; Included In Hotten's 1858 Rhyming Slang Glossary)

Lee Marvin – STARVING. (Origins; American actor)
1D. "Dinner's ready? Great, I'm hank an' lee here."

Lee van Cleef – GRIEF. (Origins; American actor)
2D. "Oh, come on, don't give me any lee-van, I'm only human."

Left in the Lurch – CHURCH.
1D. "I hope she doesn't get jilted at the left in the lurch!"

Left Jab – CAB.
1D. "Go outside and hail a left jab, I'm almost ready."

Leg of Lamb – GRAMME, (small metric measurement).
2D. "Come on, give me a leg on tick 'til I get paid, please?

Lemon & Dash – SLASH, (pee).
2D. "Come on drink up, I'm away for a lemon, then we're off."

Lemon & Dash – FLASH.
1D. "Jesus, Stuart, don't act so lemon an' dash, and you'll pull better."

Lemon & Lime – CRIME.
2D. "It's been quiet, sarge. Not one lemon reported all day."

Lemon & Lime – TIME.
1D. "Hey fridge? What's the lemon & lime?"

Lemon Barley – CHARLIE, (cocaine). (Origins; summer drink)
1D. "Any idea where I can score some lemon barley?"

Lemon Curd – BIRD, (girl). (Origins; lemon flavored preserve)
1D. "I'm going out with the lemon curd tonight, going to the flicks."

Lemon Curd – TURD. (Origins; lemon flavored preserve)
2D. "Had me a huge lemon this morning; jalfrezi last night."

Lemon Curd – WORD. (Origins; lemon flavored preserve)
1D. "What's the lemon curd on the street then? Nothing doing?"

Lemon Squash – WASH.
1D. "I'll have a quick lemon squash, then we can leg it pronto to the rub-a."

Lemon Squeezy – EASY. (Origins; dish washing liquid)
1D. "Four shops in a lunch hour? Lemon squeezy!"

Lemon Squeezer – GEEZER, (guy).
2D. "There's that lemon we met in the rub-a-dub last night!"

Lemon Tart – SMART, (cheeky).
1D. "He thinks he's so lemon tart, butter wouldn't melt…"

Lemony Snicket – TICKET. (Origins; pen name of American novelist Daniel Handler)
2D. "Okay, this is it, one hour to go… have you got the lemonies?"

Leo Fender – BENDER, (gay). (Origins; inventor of the fender guitar)
2D. "You may be right. That bloke looks a bit of a leo after all."

Leo Sayer – ALL-DAYER, (drinking spree). (Origins; English singer)
1D. "Oh, I feel so good, I can feel a leo sayer coming on!"

Les Dennis – TENNIS. (Origins; British comedian)
1D. "Anyone for some les dennis? It's a nice day."

Lesley Crowthers – TROUSERS. (Origins; British comedian)

1D. "I'm nearly ready, just puttin' on me lesley crowthers."

Leslie Ash – SLASH, (pee). (Origins; English actress)
2D. "I've got to go for a quick leslie before we leave."

Lester Piggot – BIGOT. (Origins; English jockey)
2D. "Oh Jimmy? He's as big a lester as I've ever seen."

Liberty X – SEX. (Origins; British-Irish pop group)
2D. "I'm going to get some liberty tonight if it kills me!"

Life & Death – BREATH.
1D. "Slow down, I need to get me life an' death back."

Light & Bitter – SHITTER, (arse). (Origins; types of English beer)
1D. "Where's the light an' bitter? I need to go bad!"

Light & Dark – PARK.
1D. "I'm off to a concert in the light an' dark."

Lightning Ridge – FRIDGE. (Origins; town in Australia)
2D. "Help yourself to a beer, they're in the lightening."

Lilian Gish – FISH. (Origins; American actress)
2D. "I had a good day on the lake; got a nice brace of lilians."

Lilley & Skinner – BEGINNER. (Origins; British shoe brand)
2D. "Look at Tom, drunk before ten; he's a real lilley."

Lilley & Skinner – DINNER. (Origins; British shoe brand)
1D. "What's for lilly and skinner, honey?"

Lily the Pink – DRINK. (Origins; song by The Scaffold)
2D. "Fancy a lily tonight? I've got me a real drouth on."

Limehouse Link – CHINK, (Chinese). (Origins; tunnel in east London)

2D. "I'm going out with a lighthouse right now, by god she can cook."

Linda Lusardi – CARDY, (cardigan). (Origins; English model)
2D. "Oh my God! Look at that awful linda he's wearing."

Linen Draper – NEWSPAPER.
2D. "Did we get a linen delivered today, love?"
(Old; Included In Hotten's 1858 Rhyming Slang Glossary)

Ling and Linger – RING ON FINGER.
1D. "Did you hear about Stan? He's only gone and done a ling an' linger."

Lionel Bart – TART. (Origins; British songwriter/composer)
2D. "Sammy's a right lionel, she'll take drinks from anybody."

Lionel Blair – NIGHTMARE. (Origins; British actor/dancer)
2D. "United are havin' a right lionel today, three down in the first half."

Lionel Blairs – FLARES, (trousers). (Origins; British actor/dancer)
2D. "It's a 70's night, I've got me best lionels on for the evening."

Lionel Ritchie – BITCHY. (Origins; American singer)
1D. "Tammy's a bit lionel ritchie tonight, she on the rag?"

Lion's Lair – CHAIR.
2D. "Take the weight off. Have a lion's an' chew for a while."

Lisa Tarbuck's – STARBUCKS. (Origins; British actress/comedienne)
2D. "I'm off to Lisa to get me my morning chewy. Do you want one?"

Little & Large – MARGE, (margarine).
2D. "Not got any stammer? I hate little on me toast."

Little Critter – BULLSHITTER.
1D. "Don't trust a word, she's the world's biggest little critter."

Little Jack Horner – CORNER. (Origins; nursery rhyme)
2D. "Look at poor Davey, all alone in the little jack."

Live Eels – FIELDS.
1D. "Going to the country this week, get a look at some live eels for a change."
(Old; Included In Hotten's 1858 Rhyming Slang Glossary)

Liz Hurley – EARLY. (Origins; British actress)
2D. "There's plenty time, he's never gotten here liz on his life."

Liza Minelli – TELLY, (television). (Origins; American singer)
2D. "Anything special on the Liza tonight? There's footy at seven."

Load of Hay – DAY.
1D. "What a load of hay I've had! Trouble from nine to five."
(Old; Included In Hotten's 1858 Rhyming Slang Glossary)

Loaf of Bread – HEAD.
2D. "Figure out a solution... use your loaf."

Lollipop – SHOP.
1D. "Nip into the lollipop, and get me a long acre."

Lolly Lick – DICK/PRICK, (penis).
1D. "Off to Ibiza? Keep yur lolly lick in yer pants this time!"
Another clever one, albeit a bit salacious.

London Fog – DOG. (Origins; London had bad smog in the 1800's and 1900's)
1D. "The break-ins were so bad, I had to buy me'self a London fog!"

Long Acre – BAKER. (Origins; street in central London)

184

1D. "I'm nipping into the long acre, fancy a currant bun for a change."
(Old; Included In Hotten's 1858 Rhyming Slang Glossary)

Long Acre – NEWSPAPER. (Origins; street in central London)
1D. "Pass the long acre will you, let's see what gee gee's are running today."
(Old; Included In Hotten's 1858 Rhyming Slang Glossary)

Long & Flexy – SEXY.
1D. "Hi toots, you're looking long an' flexy tonight."

Longers & Lingers – FINGERS.
2D. "Oh, look at the new waitress. Can't wait to get my longers on that."

Looby Loo's – SHOES. (Origins; Children's TV character)
1D. "Sporting my new looby-loos, the finest Italian leather!"

Loop the Loop – SOUP. (Origins; Airplane maneuver)
1D. "Oh, just what we need on a cold day, a sizzling plate of loop the loop."

Lord John Russell – BUSTLE, (clothing pad behind the waist).
2D. "Blimey, her lord john's a bit big, don't you think?"
(Old; Included In Hotten's 1858 Rhyming Slang Glossary)

Lord Lovell – SHOVEL.
1D. "Pass the lord lovell, and let's get diggin'."
(Old; Included In Hotten's 1858 Rhyming Slang Glossary)

Lord Mayor – SWEAR, (curse).
1D. "You never hear me lord mayor, do you Sally?"

Lord of the Manor – TANNER, (sixpence).
1D. "I found a lord of the manor walking home today; I feel rich!"

Lords & Peers – EARS.

2D. "I grabbed him by the lords, an' threw him through the winda'."

Lorna Doone – SPOON. (Origins; classic novel & character)
2D. "Hand me a lorna, would ya? Can't eat this with a duke."

Lost & Found – POUND, (money).
1D. "Mum! Can I borrow a lost an' found 'til Friday?"

Louis the 16th – A SIXTEENTH OF AN OUNCE. (Origins; King of France, Louis the 16th)
2D. "Hi Jackie, cut me a louis, will ya. That should do me."
(Technically, 'not' actually a rhyme, but, whatever...)

Louise Wener – TENNER, (ten pounds). (Origins; English singer/novelist)
2D. "Dad?, Can you lend me a louise until payday?"

Lou Reed – SPEED. (Origins; American singer/musician)
1D. "I scored some real good lou reed. Want some?"

Love & Kisses – MISSUS, (wife, girlfriend).
1D. "Hey, Stan? Where did your love and kisses go?"

Love Me Tender – BENDER, (homosexual). (Origins; Elvis song)
2D. "Cor, that bloke at the bar is a flamin' love-me, an' no mistake."

Lucky Dip – KIP, (sleep).
1D. "Man, if I don't get some lucky dip tonight, I'm going to be useless tomorrow."

Lucy Locket – POCKET. (Origins; English nursery rhyme)
1D. "Gawd, it's cold out; I got me jazz bands deep in me lucy lockets."

Lump Of Coke – BLOKE, (man).

1D. "That's some size of lump of coke that just walked in. He's huge!"
(Old; Included In Hotten's 1858 Rhyming Slang Glossary)

Lump of Ice – ADVICE.
1D. "Mum, I need some lump of ice about Julie... she'd driving me nuts."

Lump of Lead – HEAD.
1D. "How much rubbish is rattling around in that lump of lead of yours?"
(Old; Included In Hotten's 1858 Rhyming Slang Glossary)

Lump of School – FOOL.
2D. "You're eighteen, Sonny? Are you taking me for a lump?"

M

Macaroni – PONY, (25 British pounds).
1D. "Hey, Kevin, lend me a macaroni 'til Friday."

Macaroni Cheese – KEYS.
2D. "Hey, Sandra, throw me my macaroni's, please."

Macca – CRAP, (shit). (Convoluted third degree, (If there ever 'was' a fourth degree, this is it) so this one needs an explanation. 1D; Pony & Trap is rhyme for 'crap'. 2D; Pony is the abbreviated form of Pony & Trap. 3D; Macaroni rhymes with pony. 4D? Macca is short for macaroni.)
4D. "Get the next round in, I'm off for a quick macca."

Mae West – BEST. (Origins; American actress)
1D. "I don't know if I can do it, but I'll give it me may west."

Maggie's Den – NUMBER 10. (Origins; Prime Minister's address, 10 Downing Street)
1D. "What's the door number? Maggie's den?"

Magic Wand – BLONDE.
1D. "I was on the town last night, pulled a top-class magic wand."

Magnus Pike – DYKE, (lesbian). (Origins British Scientist and TV personality)
2D. "Look at the chick in the corner, looks like a right Magnus."

Mahatma Ghandi – BRANDY. (Origins Indian activist against British rule)
1D. "I'll have a mahatma ghandi to begin, cold outside."

Mahatma Ghandi – SHANDY. (Origins Indian activist against British rule)

2D. "First drink's a mahatma, I gotta get rid of me thirst."

Maids a Dawning (maids adorning) – MORNING.
2D. "Gawd, is it maids already? I feel like I didn't sleep."
(OLD; Included in Hotten's 1858 Rhyming Slang Glossary)

Mailed and Sent – BENT, (homosexual).
1D. "I heard Davie was mailed and bent, is that right?"

Major Loda – SODA.
2D. "A gay and major, please, bartender."

Major Stevens – EVENS, (betting term).
1D. "I'm off for a john on England v Poland, it's major stevens."

Mal Maninga – FINGER. (Origins; Australian Rugby coach.)
1D. "I didn't hesitate, I just gave him the mal maninga, and scarpered."

Malcolm in the Middle – PIDDLE, (pee). (Origins; American TV comedy show.)
2D. "Boss, can I go for a malcolm? I just gotta go."

Malcolm X – TEXT, (message). (Origins; American activist)
1D. "If you want me, malcolm x me; best way."

Malky Fraser – RAZOR. (Origins; Australian Prime Minister)
2D. "I'm a steel malky man myself, can't stand those electric things."

Mammy's Smiles – PILES, (hemorrhoids).
"Me mammy's smiles are being a literal pain in the april right now."

Mandy Dingle – SINGLE. (Origins; Character in UK soap, Emmerdale)
1D. "Brenda and me split up at the weekend, I'm back mandy dingle again."

Mandy Dingles – SHINGLES. (Origins; Character in UK soap, Emmerdale)
2D. "Oh, these mandy's are sure giving me jip."

Manfred Mann – PLAN. (Origins; British 60's rock band)
1D. "Okay so we've got a surprise party for Bill; what's the manfred mann?"

Manchester Scally – RALLY.
2D. "Manchester the troops, we've got a meeting with the west end boys tonight."

Man From Cairo – GIRO, (dole payment).
1D. "I'll be rich on Tuesday, me man from cairo arrives."

Man on the Moon – SPOON.
1D. "I've got me duke of york, but I eat ice cream with a man on the moon."

Manhole Cover – BROTHER, (pronounced 'bruvva').
1D. "I'm going out for a beer with me manhole cover on Sunday."

Manky Snatcher – MAGGIE THATCHER. (Origins; British Prime Minister, stopped the free issue of milk at school, and was nick-named; "Maggie Thatcher, the school milk snatcher")
1D. "I don't like the new PM, he's even worse than manky snatcher."

Marbles and Conkers – BONKERS, (crazy/mad). (Origins; old-fashioned boys games. This rhyme is probably where the phrase 'losing his marbles' comes from.)
2D. "Craig was never the same after he come home from the war, totally marbles."

Marble Slabs – CRABS. (Origins; a mortuary table)
2D. "Too many loose women; he's got a nasty case of marbles."

Mariah Carey – SCARY. (Origins; American singer)

1D. "Oh, I wouldn't go out with Diane for a million quid, she's way too mariah carey."

Marie Correlli – TELLY, (television). (Origins; British writer)
2D. "Okay, we're having a night in. What's on the marie then?"

Marilyn Manson – HANDSOME. (Origins; American pop star)
1D. "I like the look of Tommy, he's marilyn manson in a big way."

Marilyn Monroes – TOES. (Origins; American film star)
1D. "Colin's done a runner, had it off on 'is marilyn monroes."

Market Stalls – BALLS, (testicles).
2D. "I knew he had the better of me, so I kicked him hard in the markets."

Mark Ramprakash – SLASH, (pee). (Origins; English cricketer)
1D. "I'm off for a quick mark ramprakash; get the drinks in."

Marquis de Sade – HARD, (erection). (Origins; historical sadist)
2D. "All your dirty talk 'as got me mars all marquis, an' no mistake."

Mars & Venus – PENIS.
1D. "Oh, I wouldn't mind giving the brunette at the bar some of me mars an' venus."

Mars Bar – SCAR. (Origins; British candy bar - same as US 'Milky Way')
1D. "I fell down drunk last year, hit my head and ended up with a mars bar!"

Marty Pellow – YELLOW. (Origins; Scottish singer from the band, Wet Wet Wet)
1D. "Oh, I don't like the new Chelsea 'away' strip, way too marty pellow!"

Martial Arts – DARTS, (pub game).

2D. "I got me arrows with me, how about a game of martials?"

Martin Kemp – HEMP, (drugs). (Origins; band member of Duran Duran)
2D. "Have you got any martin on yer, I'm dying for a laugh."

Martini – LAMBOURGHINI.
1D. "After 'is lottery win, he only bought a pink martini!"

Mary Jane – COCAINE.
1D. "Hey, I got a huge bag of mary jane, and need to thin it out a bit."
Please note that the term Mary Jane is usually associated with marijuana (the MJ connection). This entry is for the rhyming slang part only.

Mary Rose – NOSE. (Origins; Henry VIII's sunken ship)
1D. "You should have seen her, bopped him right on the mary rose!"

Master McGrath – BRA, (brassiere).
1D. "Oh, perhaps she needs an industrial master mcgrath, they're some size."

Matheson Lang – Cockney Rhyming Slang.
2D. "You've not been using Matheson long, 'ave yer?"

Matt le Tiss – PISS. (Origins; Matthew le Tissier, English footballer)
2D. "You're trying to extract the matt, aren't you?"

Matthew Kelly – BELLY. (Origins; British TV personality)
1D. "Oh I love bouncing my gradkid on me matthew kelly."

Matthew Kelly – TELLY. (Origins; British TV personality)
2D. "There's nothing on the matthew, fancy going to the flicks?"

Maurice Gibb – FIB. (Origins; band member of the Bee Gee's)
1D. "Honest, I saw the queen, would I tell you a maurice gibb?"

Mavis Fritter – Shitter, (toilet or rectum).
2D. "Quick, where's the mavis; I'm touching cloth!"

Me & You – MENU.
1D. "Okay then, where's the me an' you; I'm starving."

Mechanical Digger – NIGGER.
2D. "I gotta get outa this place... it's full of mechanicals."

Melody Lingers – FINGERS.
2D. "Man, her apple pie was so delicious I licked my melodies clean."

Melvyn Bragg – FAG. (Origins; British television presenter)
2D. "Hey mate? Can I scrounge a melvyn from you? I'm all out."

Melvyn Bragg – SHAG. (Origins; British television presenter)
1D. "We melvyn bragged the whole night, she's fantastic."

Merchant Banker – WANKER.
1D. "Tommy's such a merchant banker, it's a wonder he's gotten any friends left."

Merchant Navy – GRAVY.
2D. "Come on luv, more merchant for me mashed taters."

Merlyn Rees – PIECE, (sandwich). (Origins; British politician)
1D. "I'd like a merlyn rees with turkey an pickle, please."

Merry Go Round – POUND, (money).
2D. "I need a merry for me fags, any chance of a loan?"

Merryheart – TART.
1D. "Janie's such a merryheart, look at her, dressed to Donald."

Merry Old Soul – ARSEHOLE. (Origins; nursery rhyme, Old King Cole)
1D. "Danny's a bit of a merry old soul, but he's not mean with it."

Meryl Streep – CHEAP. (Origins; American actress)
2D. "Twenty quid for a bottle of Jack Daniels? That's meryl, an' no mistake."

Meryl Streep – SLEEP. (Origins; American actress)
1D. "I couldn't me get one wink of meryl streep last night."

Metal Mickey – SICKIE, (sick day). (Origins; kids robot TV character)
"Tell the boss I'm taking a mickey, mum. I can't even get me head off me aston.'"

Metric Miles – PILES, (hemorrhoids).
2D. "Charlie's off to the docs again, getting his metrics taken care of."

Mexican Wave – SHAVE. (Origins; rippling crowd wave)
1D. "I need a mexican wave before work, but I don't have time."
(Point of information; although American crowds had been doing the 'wave' for years, the first time a global audience were introduced to it was at World Cup 1986.)

Michael Caine – PAIN. (Origins; British actor with trad Cocney accent)
2D. "Well Doc, it started wif a michael in me back, and now it's pure murder."

Michael Caine – TRAIN. (Origins; British actor with trad Cocney accent)
1D. "I only went an' missed me Michael caine, didn't I. Weekend ruined."

Michael Miles – PILES, (hemorrhoids). (Origins; British TV presenter)
1D. "I hate the damp weather, bring's me michael miles out in spades."

194

Michael Schumachers – KNACKERS, (testicles). (Origins; German Formula 1 driver)
1D. "I was standing in the wall, free kick. Then gazza grabbed me Michael schumackers!"

Michael Winner – DINNER. (Origins; Film Director)
1D. "I got a huge Geoff. I could sure use a cold jackie wif me michael winner."

Mick Jagger – LAGER. (Origins; English singer with the Rolling Stones)
1D. "How about a couple of mick jaggers over here? An' a uri!"

Mickey Bliss – PISS, (derogatorily poking fun).
2D. "I gotta go take a mickey. Get the beers in."
This expression is the original form of 'taking the mickey' (derogatorily poking fun) at someone. It is shortened to 'taking the mick' and lengthened to 'extracting the michael'. The original use of 'piss' for this use is probably the characterization of a self-important blusterer as 'all piss and wind'.

Mickey Duff – PUFF, (of marijuana). (Origins; Polish born British boxer)
1D. "I'm off outside for a bit. Got to have me a little mickey duff."

Mickey Monk – DRUNK. (Origins; probably the character, Mickey Monkey, in the kids comic, The Topper)
1D. "Last beer. Not getting mickey monk tonight; I'm on a promise."

Mickey Most – TOAST. (Origins; British record producer)
1D. "Best breakfast, sausage an' bacon on mickey most. Fantastic."

Mickey Mouse – HOUSE.
1D. "Barney's bought a new mickey mouse. A flash drum, up near Clackton."

Mickey Mouse – SCOUSE, (coming from Liverpool).

1D. "Jackie's got herself a new bloke. Some mickey mouser called Trevor."

Mickey Rourke – PORK. (Origins; American actor)
1D. "I do like me a bit of mickey rourke, barbeque sauce, onions."

Micro Chip – NIP, (Japanese person).
1D. "A camera in a ring? What will those micro-chips think of next?"

Midland Bank – WANK, (masturbate). (Origins; large banking chain in the UK)
2D. "What a midland banker Tommy is. Pure thoroughbred."

Mikkel Becks – SPECS, (spectacles, glasses). (Origins; Danish footballer)
2D. "Pass over me mikkels, luv. Oi can't read the small print."

Milky Way – GAY, (homosexual).
2D. "O come on. Harry's as milky as a pink fiver!"

Millwall in Riot – PIRATE.
2D. "Did you hear the latest about those Somali millwalls? Bastards."

Milton Keynes – JEANS, (denims). (Origins; 'New Town' in England)
2D. "Oi'm getting a new pair of miltons at the weekend, probably Levis."

Mince Pies – EYES.
2D. "She's a bit thick, but she's got beautiful minces."

Minnie Driver – FIVER, (five pounds). (Origins; English actress)
2D. "Got a fake Rolex down the market, only cost me a minnie."

Missing Link – CHINK, (Chinese person).

1D. "Takeaway tonight? How about I call into the missing links on the way home?"

Mix And Muddle – CUDDLE.
1D. "Come on luv. Come over here and give us a nice mix and muddle."

Moby Dick – PRICK, (penis). (Origins; whale character in novel by Herman Melville)
1D. "I'd love to invite Kris to the party, but he's such a moby dick."

Moby Dick – SICK. (Origins; whale character in novel by Herman Melville)
2D. "I'm not coming today, boss. I'm right moby."

Mods & Rockers – KNOCKERS, (boobs, breasts). (Origins; gangs in 1960's England)
1D. "Cor Blimey! Look at the mods an' rockers on the new secretary!"

Molly Malone – PHONE. (Origins; Irish folk song character)
2D. "I'll give you a bell on the molly to firm up a time for Saturday."

Molly O'Morgan – ORGAN. (Origins; song on Wonder Woman soundtrack)
2D. "She don't look much, but when she gets a hold of yer molly!"

Molten Toffee – COFFEE.
1D. "Give us a cup of your strongest molten toffee, luv. I got me a head."

Money Pits – STRIPPER'S TITS.
1D. "Luv a duck! That barmaid's got some money pits on her."

Monkey Wrench – WENCH.
2D. "I'm off on holiday, not taking the monkey though... I want some fun."

(The adjustable spanner is known as 'gas grips' in the UK)

Monkey's Tails – NAILS.
2D. "Hand us over some of the inch'n'half monkeys, will yer?"

Monty's Army – BARMY, (crazy). (Origins; probably UK WW2 General Montgomery)
2D. "I'm not going to the Burnley game, their lads are totally monty!

Mop & Broom – FRUIT OF THE LOOM. (Origins; budget clothing manufacturer)
1D. "Nice gaff. Not exactly the place to wear mop an' broom. Is it?

Morecombe & Wise – FLIES. (Origins; British comedian duo)
2D. "Watch out Harry, your morecombe's are undone."

Moriarty – PARTY.
1D. "Got a good moriarty lined up for Saturday. Wanna come?"

Mork & Mindy – WINDY. (Origins; American sit-com)
1D. "Bloody Nora. It's a bit mork an' middy up here, an' no mistake."

Morning Glory – STORY.
1D. "I heard rumors, Stan. Come on. What's the real morning glory?"

Morris Minor – VAGINA. (Origins; 1960's British compact car)
1D. "Gawd, they're tight on 'er. You can see 'er morris minor!"

Mother & Daughter – QUARTER, (cocaine).
2D. "I've only got an apple core. Can you do me a mother? Can yer?"

Mother Goose – LOOSE. (Origins; imaginary author)
1D. "She's got her claws in, that one. Jimmy'll never get mother goose for years."

Mother Hubbard – CUPBOARD, (closet). (Origins; nursery rhyme character)
2D. "I fancied a fry-up, but there's nothing in the mother."

Mother of Pearl – GIRL.
1D. "Well, that is my kind of mother of pearl; she's got everything!"

Mother's Ruin (roo-in) – GIN.
2D. "Before I go pope in rome, another mothers would sit well."

Mountain Bike – DYKE, (lesbian). (Origins; type of bicycle)
1D. "Oops, ten o'clock high, couple of mountain bikes have just walked in."

Mozambique – KEEK, (peek, quick look).
1D. "Oh crap, I think Monica's just walked in. take a mozambique over my shoulder."

Mozart & Liszt – PISSED. (Origins; classical composers)
2D. "Gotta call a halt. Another round and I'm Mozart."
(Also often used as Brahms and Liszt)

Mozzle and brocha – ON THE KNOCKER. (Origins; Yiddish words)
2D. "Best of muzzle to yer, mate. See ya tonight."
Mozzle and Brocha are Yiddish words for good luck and good health respectively. They refer mostly to the occupation of door-to-door salesman. From old sources, there are six requirements for the success of such a person; good luck, good health, good looks, good temper, good voice and good manners.

Mrs Chant – AUNT.
1D. "Hey, don't look at Cloe like that, she's my flippin' mrs chant!"

Mrs Duckett – BUCKET.
1D. "I think I'm gonna throw up. Where's the missus duckett?"

Muff Diver – FIVER, five pounds. (Origins; a person performing cunnilingus)
2D. "Lend us a muff 'til Friday. Go on, be a mate."

Mum & Dad – MAD.
1D. "Third time in drunk, and they went a bit mum an; dad at me."

Mumbly Pegs – LEGS. (Origins; a game played with pocket knives)
2D. "I'm leavin home this month. Gotta stand on me own mumbleys for a change."

Murray Mint – SKINT, (broke). (Origins; British creamy hard mint)
2D. "Sorry, no weekend for me, I'm totally murray 'til the end of the month."

Murray Walker – TALKER. (Origins; British TV Sports commentator)
2D. "The new girl? She's a real murray; I can't get her to shut up!"
(Clever one, as anyone who has heard Murray's commentary knows he talks a hundred words a minute)

Mushy Peas – KEYS. (Origins; English fast food side-dish)
1D. "I can't find my mushy peas. Any ideas?"

Muswell Hill – BILL. (Origins; district in north London)
1D. "Oh I can't wait for the muswell hill, we drank like fishes!"

Mutt and Jeff – DEAF. (Origins; American newspaper strip cartoon)
2D. "You'll have to shout, Donnie's a bit mutt, poor bugger."

Mutter & Stutter – BUTTER.
1D. "Got no marge? I can't stand mutter an' stutter."

Myleen Klass – ARSE. (Origins; British singer)

2D. "Gawd struth! Look at the tight myleen on the redhead!"

Mystic Megs – LEGS. (Origins; British TV personality)
1D. "Not just her bristols either, look at those mystic megs!"

N

Nose-My – BACKY, (tobacco).
1D. "Hey frank, you got any nose-my? I've got papers."
(OLD; Included in Hotten's 1858 Rhyming Slang Glossary)

Nails & Tacks – FAX.
2D. "E-mail? No, we're still in the stone-age, nail me."

Nanny Goat – BOAT.
2D. "Going across to south London by nanny."

Nanny Goat – COAT.
1D. "I'm wearing me nanny goat; it's going to be cold later."

Nanny Goat – THROAT.
2D. "Get that down your nanny, great ginger and no mistake."

Naomi Campbell – GAMBLE. (Origins; fashion model/actress)
2D. "I'm going to have a naomi on the National, first in ages."

Native New Yorker – PORKER, (fat person).
1D. "Oh, look at his gut, a real native new Yorker."

Nat King Cole – DOLE, (welfare). (Origins; American singer)
2D. "I'm off to sign on the old Nat King."

Nat King Cole – HOLE, (sex). (Origins; American singer)
1D. "Did you get your nat king cole last night?"

Near & Far – BAR.
1D. "I'm off to the near and far; see you later."

Near & Far – CAR.

2D. "I'm taking the near today, you'll have to get the bus."

Needle & Pin – GIN.
2D. "I'll have a large needle and tonic; it's been a long day."

Neil Sedaka – PARKA, (jacket). (Origins; American singer)
1D. "I'm taking my neil sedaka; it's going to be cold."

Nelly Duff – LIFE.
2D. "Lend you a tenner? Not on your nelly, mate."

Nelson Mandela – STELLA, (Artois, beer).
2D. "I'm drinking nelson's tonight; I can already taste it."

Nelson Eddy's – READIES, (cash money). (Origins; American singer)
2D. "Look at Henry, 'e's got a big wad of nelsons!"

Nervo & Knox – GOGGLE BOX, (television). (Origins; original 'Crazy Gang' members)
1D. "What's on the nervo an'knox tonight? Is it the footie!"

Nervo & Knox – POX. (Origins; original 'Crazy Gang' members)
2D. "Poor Nigel's off to the 'ospital with a real bad dose of nervo."

Nervous Wreck – CHEQUE, (US, check).
2D. "No cash, just write me a nervous, it'll be okay."

New Delhi – BELLY.
1D. "They have great steak here son, get it down your new delhi."

Newgate Jail – TALE. (Origins; prison in London)
2D. "Oh, that's a long newgate, an' no mistake."

Newington Butts – GUTS. (Origins; London area now known as the Elephant and Castle)

2D. "Bad curry last night, me newingtons are playing me up something rotten."

Niagara Falls – BALLS, (testicles). (Origins; waterfalls in USA/Canada)
2D. "He went down like a sack of potatoes; I got him right in the niagara's."

Nick Cotton – ROTTEN. (Origins; BBC Eastenders soap character)
1D. "Oh, look at those apples. They've all turned nick cotton on me."

Nicky Lauder – POWDER, (cocaine). (Origins; formula 1 champion)
2D. "Come on, Georgy, get it out, I know you got some good nicky on yer."

Nifty – FIFTY.
1D. "Nigel, gives a lend of a nifty until payday."

Nigel Benn – TEN, (pounds). (Origins; British politician)
2D. "Man, if you can't afford a nifty, how's about a nigel?"

Nigel Mansell – CANCEL. (Origins; British Formula 1 driver)
1D. "Sorry mate, I'll have to nigel mansell on yer, something's come up."

Nightboat to Cairo – GIRO, (unemployment cheque).
2D. "No drink 'til Tuesday, after me nightboat, I'm shiny."

Nina Simone – PHONE. (Origins; American singer)
1D. "I think I left me nina simone down the boozer last night.

Noah's Ark – PARK.
2D. "Watch where you noah, there's yellow lines everywhere."
3D. "I'm off down the two-by-two to see a man about some charlie."

Noah's Ark – SHARK.
1D. "Don't take money from Sid, he's a real bad noah's ark."

Nobby Stiles – PILES, (hemorrhoids). (Origins; English footballer)
2D. "I can't even sit on those hard chairs, me nobby's are bad this week."

Noddy Holders – SHOULDERS. (Origins; lead singer in glam rock band, Slade)
2D. "'Ere you go love, get up on me noddys, you'll see the stage no problem."

No Hope – SOAP.
1D. "Always the same in boozers bogs, crappy no hope."

North & South – MOUTH.
2D. "You better watch your north, old son, you're lippy an' no mistake."

Nose & Chin – GIN.
1D. "I think I'll have a snifter of nose and chin."

No Surrenders – SUSPENDERS.
1D. "Just what I like, frilly alan wickers and matching no surrenders."

Nuclear Sub – PUB.
2D. "We had a great time down the nuclear on Saturday."

Nuns & Habits – RABBITS.
1D. "Ain't seen Tony since he got married, he's still be at it like nuns an' rabbits."

Nuremburg Trials – PILES, (hemorrhoids).
2D. "Me Nuremberg's are really playing me up this week."

Nutmegs – LEGS. (Origins; a football term... the attacker kicks the ball between an opponent's legs)

1D. "Look at the length o' the nutmegs on Davie's new bird."

O

Oats & Barley – CHARLIE, (cocaine).
1D. "Any idea where I'd get me 'ands on some oats an' barley?"
(OLD; Included in Hotten's 1858 Rhyming Slang Glossary)

Oats And Chaff – FOOTPATH.
1D. "Thank goodness there's an oats an' chaff; I'd have got lost otherwise."
(OLD; Included in Hotten's 1858 Rhyming Slang Glossary)

Obediah – FIRE. (Origins; Biblical name, 'servant of God')
1D. "Terrible obediah down the market last week."

Obi Wan Kenobi – MOBI, (mobile/cell phone). (Origins; Star Wars character)
2D. "I can't fine me obi wan anywhere!"

Obie Trice – NICE. (Origins; American rapper)
1D. "At last Neil seems to have found a girl that falls into the obie trice category."

Ocean-Going Squid – QUID, (British pound).
2D. "Hey bud, lend me an ocean-going 'til Thursday."

Ocean Pearl – GIRL.
1D. "Oh, take a look at the new barmaid. Now that's what I call a real ocean pearl."

Ocean Wave – SHAVE.
1D. "Crap, I forgot to ocean wave this morning, the boss'll give me hell."

Oedipus Rex – SEX. (Origins; ancient Greek play)

2D. "New barmaid; I wouldn't mind having me some Oedipus with that."

Ogden Nash – SLASH, (pee). (Origins; American poet)
2D. "Can hardly wait to get to the pub, dying on an ogden."

Oil Lamp – TRAMP.
1D. "So many oil lamps these days, and they all have dogs!"

Oil Rig – WIG.
1D. "Ooh… look at the well dodgy oil rig at the end of the bar."

Oil Tanker – WANKER.
1D. "I don't associate with Clive anymore, he's turned into a real oil tanker."

Oily Rag – FAG, (cigarette).
2D. "Come on Steve, hand me an oily since you got your pack handy."

Old King Cole – DOLE, (unemployment benefit). (Origins; nursery rhyme)
1D. "I got kicked off the old king cole; got caught moonlighting, didn't I."

Old Mother Hubbard – CUPBOARD. (Origins; nursery rhyme)
2D. "No dinner? What we got in the old mother then?"

Oliver Hardy – LARDY, (fat). (Origins; American actor)
2D. "Henry's got real lardy since he got married."

Oliver Reed – WEED. (Origins; English actor)
1D. "Has anyone got any oliver reed? I'm getting kinda antsy."

Oliver Twist – FIST. (Origins; Charles Dickens book)
2D. "One minute we was talking, next he's got his oliver in my face."

Oliver Twist – PISSED, (drunk). (Origins; Charles Dickens book)
1D. "Me trouble was oliver twist last night, fell asleep on the couch."

Omar Sharif – GRIEF. (Origins; Egyptian Actor)
1D. "Good omar sharif! What are you standing on the table for?"

Omer Riza – PIZZA. (Origins; English footballer)
2D. "Fancy an omer tonight, I'll pick it up."

Once a Week – BEAK (magistrate).
1D. "Looks like I'm up in front of the once a week; too much fun on Saturday night."

Once a Week – CHEEK.
2D. "She slapped me right across the once-a."

One and the Other – BROTHER.
1D. "So what's me one and the other doing recently, mum?"

Ones & Twos – SHOES.
1D. "New pair of ones and twos, classy brogues; I love 'em."

One Time Looker – HOOKER.
2D. "Check out the bird at the end of the bar; a one time, and no messing."

Onion Bagi – SARGY, (sergeant). (Origins; Indian starter)
2D. "I got caught by the onion, he marched me for four hours solid."

On the Floor – POOR.
1D. "I'm on the floor this week, I'll catch up later."

On Your Knees – PLEASE.
2D. "Give us a cup o' rosie, on yer."

Optic Nerve – PERV.

2D. "Look at the way he looks at kids; I swear he's an optic."

Orange & Pear – SWEAR, (curse).
1D. "Listen to 'er gob, orange and pearin' all the time."

Orange Peel – FEEL.
2D. "I wouldn't mind copping an orange of her Bristols!"

Orchestra Stalls – BALLS, (testicles).
2D. "When he touched her, she kicked him in the orchestra!"

Orinoko (orinoker) – POKER. (Origins; South American river)
1D. "Pass the orinoker, will ya. This fire needs some tlc."
(OLD; Included in Hotten's 1858 Rhyming Slang Glossary)

Orson Cart – FART. (Origins; comic character... also short for 'Horse 'n' Cart')
2D. "He dropped an orson in the doctor's office."

Osama Bin Laden – PARDON. (Origins; Al-Qaeda founder)
2D. "The beak let him off with an Osama."

Oscar Asche – CASH. (Origins; Australian actor and producer)
2D. "No rub a dub for me for a while, I've got no Oscar."

Oscar Wilde – MILD (beer). (Origins; Irish poet/playwright)
1D. "Two pints of gary glitter, and two of oscar wilde."

Otis Reading – HEAD IN, (being annoyed). (Origins American musician/singer)
1D. "Oh stop it about pokemon! You're doing me otis reading."

Otis Reading – WEDDING. (Origins American musician/singer)
2D. "Did you get an invite to the royal otis? Thought not."

Outings & Festivals – TESTICLES.
1D. "Loose shorts... plenty of room for me outings and festivals."

Oven Mitts – TITS, (breasts).

2D. "She's as flat as a pancake; no ovens at all."

Over the Stile – SENT FOR TRIAL.
1D. "He's in big trouble, he's been charged and over the stile."
(OLD; Included in Hotten's 1858 Rhyming Slang Glossary)

Owen Nares – CHAIRS. (Origins; British actor)
2D. "Come on, the game's starting, pull up your owens."

Oxford Punt – C*NT. (Origins; college boat)
2D. "I made a total oxford of me'self last night. I'm sorry."

Oxford Scholar – COLLAR. (Origins; English University)
"Copper grabbed him by the oxford scholar, lifted him right into the van."
('Had his collar felt', meant being charged with a crime, literally the police grabbed perpetrator by the collar and threw him in jail.)

Oxford Scholar – DOLLAR. (Origins; English University)
2D. "Hey Bob, lend me an oxford until Friday?"

Oxo Cube – TUBE, (idiot). (Origins; British gravy cube)
1D. "Come on Sidney, don't be an oxo cube; he's bram stoking!"

Oyster Bay – GAY, (homosexual).
2D. "Look at Nigel's new friend, looks a bit oyster to me."

P

Paddy Quick – STICK. (Origins; Irish have often been called 'Paddys')
1D. "I've had to use this paddy quick since I sprained my ankle last week."
(OLD; Included in Hotten's 1858 Rhyming Slang Glossary)

Paddy Quick – THICK. (Origins; Irish have often been called 'Paddys')
2D. "Oh for God's sake, don't be so paddy. Of course I was joking."
(This may be intentionally satirical. In UK comedy, the Irish are often the butt of the joke, being seen as stupid or thick. (Much as the Americans beat up the Polish (Polack's) in USA humour.)
(OLD; Included in Hotten's 1858 Rhyming Slang Glossary)

Pam Shriver – FIVER, (five pounds). (Origins; American tennis player)
1D. "Harry? Here's that pam shriver I owe you."

Pants and Vest – CHEST.
1D. "This cough is really killing me pants and vest."

Paper Hat – PRAT, (arse).
1D. "And don't drink too much; you'll just make a paper hat of yourself as always."

Paper Plate – MATE.
1D. "This is the life! Out on the fields with me paper plates."

Paraffin Lamp – TRAMP, (hobo).
2D. "Money? I gave me last godiva to that old paraffin."

Paraffin Oil – BOIL.

2D. "Oi! Get the hansel on the paraffin, an' make some rosy!"

Park Benches – FRENCHIES.
1D. "Bloody rugby, look at all the park benches in the cabin cruisers."

Pat & Mick – SICK.
1D. "I've been pat an' mick all week."

Pat Cash – SLASH, (pee). (Origins; Australian tennis player)
1D. "Pause the film, I gotta go for a pat cash."

Pat Malone – ALONE.
1D. "Hey Jimmy? No missus, all pat Malone tonight?"

Patrick McNee – PEE. (Origins; British actor)
2D. "I'm off for a quick patrick, they'll probably score."

Patrick Swayze – CRAZY. (Origins; American actor)
1D. "I just kissed 'er, an' she went all patrick swayze on me."

Patrick Swayze – LAZY. (Origins; American actor)
2D. "I feel like a real Patrick day today, watching Wimbledon all day."

Patsy Cline – LINE, (of cocaine). (Origins; American singer)
2D. "Katy caught me doing a patsy last night; she's not talkin'."

Paul Dickov – KICK OFF. (Origins; Scottish footballer)
1D. "Scotland v Engerland… when's the paul dickov?"

Paul McKenna – TENNER, (ten pounds). (Origins; Scottish hypnotist)
1D. "Sorry mate, I'm down to me last paul mckenna."

Paul Weller – STELLA, (beer). (Origins; member of rock band, The Jam)
1D. "Six pints of paul weller, and I'm anybody's."

Pauline Fowler – GROWLER, (vagina). (Origins; BBC soap Eastenders character)
2D. "She just flashed her Pauline at me!"

Peanut Butter – NUTTER.
1D. "I've dropped Phil from my friends list, he's such a peanut butter."

Pear Halved – STARVED.
1D. "I can't wait for frank skinner, I'm pear halved already."

Pearl Diver – FIVER.
1D. "I found a pearl diver outside the battle cruiser last night."

Pearl Diver – SKIVER.
2D. "That new guy, Robbie; he's such a pearl, so he is."

Pearly Queen – SEEN.
2D. "Shit, there's my ex. Has she pearlied me yet?"

Peas & Gravy – NAVY.
1D. "Gawd. Johnny's only gone and joined the bloody peas an' gravy!"

Pea Shooter – HOOTER, (nose).
1D. "Blood went everywhere, his pea shooter crumbled."

Peas in the Pot – HOT.
2D. "Don't touch that alexander just yet - it's bloody peasy."

Pebble-Dashed – SMASHED, (drunk). (Origins; outer wall covering)
1D. "Oh, man, I was wasted last night; completely pebble dashed."

Peckham Rye – TIE. (Origins; park in London)
2D. "I'm putting on me best whistle and me new peckham for the wedding."

Pedal & Crank – BANK.
1D. "I'm off to the pedal an' crank to see about a loan."

Pedal & Crank – WANK.
2D. "I can't get peace an' quiet to have a quick pedal."

Pen and Ink – STINK.
1D. "Oh Gawd, get a whiff of the pen and in in here!"
(OLD; Included in Hotten's 1858 Rhyming Slang Glossary)

Penelope Cruz – BOOZE. (Origins; Spanish actress)
2D. "I'm off to the offie to stock up on me penelope for the new year."

Penelope Keith – TEETH. (Origins; British actress)
1D. "Look at the penelope keith inside that gang an' mob."
Clever use here, the actress Penelope Keith had a pronounced set of teeth!

Penny a Pound – GROUND.
2D. "There was so much turbulence, I was glad to get me feet back on the penny!"

Penny-Come-Quick – TRICK, (a con).
1D. "I just watched the guy shuffle cards, I knew it was a penny-come-quick."
Again, clever use, as it described a trick of confidence made for easy money.

Peppermint – SKINT, (broke).
1D. "I've never been so peppermint; nothing coming in for weeks."

Percy Thrower – BLOWER, (telephone). (Origins; TV personality/gardener)
2D. "Get Reggie on the percy, I need to talk this through."

Percy Thrower – MOWER. (Origins; TV personality/gardener)

1D. "Must get me percy thrower out this weekend, me ernie's up to me chips!"
Clever, remembering Percy's gardening show.

Perpetual Loser – BOOZER, (pub).
2D. "We're meeting at the perpetual, then off to the terry."

Perry Como – HOMO. (Origins; American singer)
1D. "I heard that Gordon's a bit of a perry como. Do you think that's right?"

Persian Rugs – DRUGS.
2D. "So I said, "'ere mate. Got any persians?" I laughed so hard."

Pete Tong – WRONG. (Origins; British disc jockey)
1D. "Then he called Gerry a tin roof to his face; it was all so pete tong."
Mentioned in the movie "It's All Gone Pete Tong" (2004).

Peter Crouch – GROUCH. (Origins; English footballer)
1D. "I don't like to sit with Bill; he's such a peter crouch."

Peter Kay – GAY. (Origins; English comedian)
1D. "I can't believe you didn't realize that Rik was peter kay!"

Peter Pan – OLD MAN, (father). (Origins; J. M. Barrie novel character)
1D. "I had to have words with the peter pan last night; that was awkward."

Peter Pan – TAN. (Origins; J. M. Barrie novel character)
2D. "Hey honey? I'm off to the pool to top up me peter."

Peter Purves – NERVOUS. (Origins; Children's TV presenter)
1D. "I must admit to being a bit peter purves about this interview."

Petrol Pump – HUMP, (moodiness).
1D. "I just said he looked bigger, an' he got the petrol pump!"

Petrol Tanks – YANKS.
2D. "City's full of petrols this month; US fares must be cheap."

Phil Babb – KEBAB. (Origins; English footballer)
2D. "Blimey, I'm proper olivered - anyone fancy a phil?"

Philharmonic – GIN & TONIC.
1D. "Two pints of Uri, and a philharmonic, please."

Piccadilly – SILLY. (Origins; area in London)
1D. "The whole plate fell on him; he looked pretty piccadilly, I can tell you."

Piccadilly Percy – MERCY. (Origins; London baronet)
1D. "When I took my dicky dirt off, she was at my piccadilly percy!"

Piccolo & Flute – SUIT.
2D. "I went round the charity shops, got me a great piccolo for an ayrton!"

Pick & Mix – STICKS, (in the countryside).
1D. "Charlie's got a new gaff , but it's in the pick'n'mix; not for me."

Pie & Liquor – VICAR.
1D. "We had the old pie an' liquor round for rosie lee the other night."

Pie & Mash – CASH. (Origins; English delicacy)
1D. "Hold on, there's an ATM, I'll get some pie an' mash for tonight."

Pie & Mash – SLASH, (pee). (Origins; English delicacy)
2D. "Keep a look out, I'm going for a quick pie in that doorway."

Pieces of Eight – WEIGHT. (Origins; Old money, Spanish gold)
1D. "Cor, that's a heavy watch, feel the pieces of eight on this."

Pied Piper – HYPER. (Origins; folklore character from Germany)
1D. "Typical Gerry, he's had three, an' he's all pied piper."

Pig and Roast – TOAST.
1D. "What's for brekkie, mum? Don't tell me, burnt pig an' roast?"
Another clever one, a cynical reference to an everyday food, while referring it to a high menu item.

Pig's Ear – BEER.
2D. "Can I buy you a pig, Dad? It's my round."

Pillar & Post – GHOST.
2D. "Rod's face is white. Looks like he's seen a pillar!"

Pillar & Post – HOST.
1D. "Who's the pillar and post for the next poker night?"

Pimple & Blotch – SCOTCH, (whisky).
2D. "Drink? I'll have a double pimple if you're buying."
Clever, because a long indulgence with whisky can have a considerable detrimental effect upon the skin.

Pineapple – CHAPEL.
1D. "We're off to the pineapple for the last rehearsal before the otis."

Pineapple Chunk – BUNK.
2D. "I'm exhausted; could use a couple of hours in me pineapple."

Pineapple Chunk – DRUNK.
1D. "Man, I was pineapple chunked last Saturday; it's a total blank."

Ping Pong – STRONG. (Origins; common name for table tennis)
1D. "Oh, that curry smell's a bit ping pong; I'm hungry now."

Pinky & Perky– TURKEY. (Origins; British 60's children's TV puppets)
2D. "Can't wait for xmas dinner, I love me pinky an' stuffin'."

Pins & Pegs – LEGS.
1D. "Crikey, look at Bertie go down, his pin pegs just gave way under him."

Pipe in Your Eye – CRY.
1D. "I hate funerals, everybody trying hard not to pipe in your eye."

Pirate Booty – FOOTIE, (football).
1D. "Going to get some pirate booty on Saturday, Leeds at home!"
3D. "Pieces of eight time! Kick off, three o'clock!"

Pirate Ship – FULL OF SHIT.
1D. "When he'd finished talking, I reckoned he was all pirate ship, an' no mistake."

Pirates of Penzance – PANTS.
"When that jack the ripper pulled down Brandon's pirates, I lost it."

Pistol & Shooter – COMPUTER.
2D. "I'm doing a person search on the pistol. I know I've seen him before."

Pitch & Fill – BILL.
1D. "Gawd, they're drinking like fish. How much will the pitch an' fill be?"
(OLD; Included in Hotten's 1858 Rhyming Slang Glossary)

Pitch & Toss – BOSS. (Origins; old game throwing coins)
2D. "I need to find a new job. My bloody pitch kept me late again."

Pittsburg Steelers – PEELERS, (policemen). (Origins; US American Football team)
2D. "Looks like we're playing Arsenal. Pittsburgs are out in force."

Plate of Meat – STREET.
2D. "If I don't see ya in the cabin, I'll se ya on the plate."
(OLD; Included in Hotten's 1858 Rhyming Slang Glossary)

Plates & Dishes – MISSUS.
2D. "So, how's you and the plates getting on these days then?"

Plates of Meat – FEET.
1D. "Young man! Get your plates of meat off the table!"

Pleasure & Pain – RAIN.
2D. "I can't take it. Any more pleasure and we'll be swimming home."

Plimsole Mark – PARK.
1D. "We're off down the plimsole mark for a wee game of footie."

Plough the Deep – GO TO SLEEP. (Origins; from 'Arran Maid', Scottish folk song)
1D. "I'm done, off upstairs to plough the deep. Goodnight all."
(OLD; Included in Hotten's 1858 Rhyming Slang Glossary)

Plymouth Argyles – PILES, (hemorrhoids). (Origins; English football team)
1D. "No, I'll stand, thanks. Me plymouth argyles are flaring."

Plymouth Sound – POUND. (Origins; Bay in Plymouth, England)
2D. "I got this Rolex down the market. Only a plymouth."

Pocket Watch – SCOTCH, (whisky).
1D. "Pint? Nah, I'll hit the shorts. Get me a pocket watch instead."

Polo Mint – BINT, (girl, woman). (Origins; British mint shaped like an o)
1D. "Come on, there's a busload of polo mints just arrived from the sticks!"

Polo Mint – SKINT, (broke). (Origins; British mint shaped like an o)
2D. "I'll be hanging out at home for a bit, I'm a little polo right now."

Pontius Pilate – TOILET. (Origins; Biblical character)
1D. "Damn, I just can't get my aristotle off the pontius pilate today!"

Pony and Trap – CRAP, (shit).
2D. "Give's a minute, mate. Just gotta have a pony before we go."

Poor Man's Gruel – LIVERPOOL.
2D. "We're off to poor man's at the weekend, West Ham away game."

Pope in Rome – HOME.
2D. "Jimmy's not allowed out? Let's pop 'round his pope and fetch him."

Poppy Red – BREAD, (Money). (Origins; Flower in the trenches after WW1)
2D. "I'll need some poppy soon, my jam's on the way out."

Porcupine – WINE.
1D. "Where's the porcupine waiter? He's taking his damn time."

Pork & Cheese – PORTUGUESE.
1D. "Ronaldo's pork an; cheese, isn't he? Or is he Spanish?"

Pork Pies – LIES.
2D. "Blimey, Chas gets two pigs in him and he starts spouting porkies."

221

Porno Mag – SLAG, (loose woman). (Origins; pornographic magazine)
1D. "I love Sandra, she may be a bit of a porno mag, but she's solid."

Porridge Knife – LIFE, (prison sentence).
2D. "Word came down, they've only given him porridge; 25 years."

Posh & Becks – DECKS, (turntables). (Origins; nicknames for Posh Spice and David Beckham)
2D. "Look at the skill of that DJ, he owns those poshes."

Posh & Becks – SEX. (Origins; nicknames for Posh Spice and David Beckham)
1D. "I love having our own drum, posh an' becks anytime we like."

Posh & Becks – SPECS, (spectacles, glasses). (Origins; nicknames for Posh Spice and David Beckham)
2D. "How do like me new poshes then? Bifocals."

Postage Stamp – TRAMP.
1D. "London's going downhill. Postage stamps in every doorway."

Postman Pat – FAT. (Origins; UK children's TV program)
1D. "Hold on Jimmy, you're getting a bit postman pat, aren't you?"

Pot & Pan – OLD MAN, (father).
2D. "I saw me pot just yesterday. He's looking more like me every day."

Pot of Glue – CLUE.
1D. "Don't talk to Frankie about fottie; 'e hasn't got a pot of glue."

Potatoes in the Mould – COLD.

2D. "Blimey, you better wrap up; it's taters out there, an' no mistake."

Pots & Dishes – WISHES.
2D. "Okay, you got three pots; what's top of your list?"

Prince's Trust – BUST, (boobs). (Origins; Prince Charles musical charity)
1D. "Look! Girl in the white sweater. A prince's trust to be proud of."

Private Dancer – CANCER. (Origins; Tina Turner song)
1D. "Both me mum an' dad got taken by the private dancer. Tragic."

Puddings and Pies – EYES.
Look at Sandy; Oh man, I could lose myself in those puddings."
(OLD; Included in Hotten's 1858 Rhyming Slang Glossary)

Puff and Dart – START.
2D. "The flippin' jam won't puff. Too flippin' taters out there."

Pull Down The Shutter – BUTTER.
2D. "The perfect breakfast, toast, pull down, marmalade, an' jacks to finish."

Punch & Judy – MOODY. (Origins; old street puppet theatre/characters)
1D. "Don't talk to Maisie tonight; she's a bit punch an' judy."
This is a subtle one; the character of Punch is always being beaten up by his wife, Judy, who always seems to be in a bad mood.

Push & Shove – LOVE.
1D. "I push an' shove my job. I get to drive fast cars for a living."

Push in the Truck – F*CK.
1D. "God, I'd give that one a good push in the truck."

223

Put in the Boot – SHOOT. (Origins; probably a football term) 1D. "This is worse than terrible, the forwards don't want to put in the boot!"

Q

Quaker Oat – COAT.
2D. "Take your quaker with you, it's cold out there."

Queen Mum – BUM. (Origins; slang term for the Queen Mother)
1D. "Look at the size of the queen mum on the new barmaid."

Queens Park Ranger – STRANGER. (Origins; London football club)
2D. "Who's the queen's park at the checkout? Not noticed him before."

Quentin Crisp – LISP. (Origins; English writer)
2D. "Your mate Harry's got a bit of a quentin, hasn't he?"

Quentin Tarantino – VINO, (wine).
3D. "My missus drinks reservoir dogs, nothing else."

R

Rabbit & Pork – TALK.
(This is another one so entrenched in the British vocabulary, we often forget where the phrase originated. Chas & Dave had a song, 'Rabbit', in which they sing… "She's got more Rabbit than Sainsbury's")
1D. "She won't shut up; full of rabbit and pork."
2D. "He's always rabbiting on about something or other."
3D. "Sandra gets on my nerves; she's got far too much bunny for my liking."

Rabbit Hutch – CRUTCH, (crotch).
1D. "He got kicked in the rabbit hutch; oh, that's nasty."

Rabbit in a Hat – TWAT, (vagina).
2D. "Shelly looks a right rabbit in that silly dress."

Radio Rental – MENTAL, (disturbed). (Origins; British TV rental outlet)
2D. "Watch out for Frankie, he's a bit radio."

Radio Transmitter – SHITTER, (arsehole).
2D. "I've got the runs so bad, me radio's on fire."

Railway Timetable – FABLE.
1D. "Oh he told me a wild tale, a flipping railway timetable."

Rainbow Trout – KRAUT, (German).
2D. "Those bloody rainbows beat us 2-1 last night!"

Raleigh Bike – DYKE, (Lesbian). (Origins; British bike maker)
2D. "She's a right Raleigh, an' no mistake, mate."

Randolph Scott – SPOT. (Origins; American actor)

1D. "Look at the randolph scott's on his coupon."

Rank and Riches – BREECHES.
2D. "He's going to the stables, got his thruppeny's and ranks on."

Rant & Rave – SHAVE.
1D. "Oh, me shadow's coming on strong; I need a good rant an' rave."

Raquel Welch – BELCH. (Origins; American actress)
2D. "Drank that last one too quick, I need a good old rachel."

Raspberry Ripple – CRIPPLE.
1D. "That car crash turn poor Fred into a raspberry ripple."

Raspberry Ripple – NIPPLE.
2D. "Oh God, look at the thruppneys on her; raspberries like cigar buts!"

Raspberry Tart – FART.
(This is another phrase so well-imbedded in our vocabulary, few people recognize it as Cockney Rhyming Slang at all.)
2D. "He blew a raspberry at me, the cheeky sod."

Raspberry Tart – HEART.
1D. "That was a steep hill, me raspberry tart's beating like wildfire."

Rat & Mouse – HOUSE.
1D. "I'm off to me rat an' mouse before I get into trouble."

Rats & Mice – DICE.
1D. "I'm going to try my hand at the rats an' mice at the casino tonight."

Rattle and Clank – BANK.
2D. "Made a deposit in the rattle this morning, saving are go!"

Rattle and Clank – TANK.

1D. "Listen to his truck, it sounds like a flipping rattle an' clank."

Rattle & Hum – COME.
1D. "Man, when she rattle an' hums, she sure squeals!"

Ravi Shankar – WANKER. (Origins; Indian musician)
2D. "That referee is a right Ravi, that was a sure-fire penalty."

Ray Mears – BEERS. (Origins; English survivalist TV presenter)
1D. "Three beers when you're at the bar, it's your round."

Razor – BLAZER.
1D. "I'm off in razor and callards; this is a posh do."

Read Of Tripe – TRANSPORTED FOR LIFE.
1D. "Poor Frankie, he got read of tripe, and just cos he stole a shillin'."
(Old; Included In Hotten's 1858 Rhyming Slang Glossary)

Read And Write – FIGHT.
2D. "Jimmy's a mess; he'd rather read than run away."
(Old; Included In Hotten's 1858 Rhyming Slang Glossary)

Read And Write – FLIGHT.
1D. "Jimmy's got to learn the art of reading an' writing."
(Old; Included In Hotten's 1858 Rhyming Slang Glossary)

Real Madrid – QUID, (pound). (Origins; Spanish football club)
1D. "Hey Harry, can you lend me a real madrid; I got no fags 'til Friday."

Red 'n' Yella – UMBRELLA.
1D. "Don't forget yer red an' yella today; rains on the forecast."

Red Red Rubies – BOOBIES.
2D. "Wow. I don't think I've seen better red red's in my entire life."

Red Rose – NOSE.

1D. "Gawd, that red rose came straight from Julius Ceasar!"

Reels of Cotton – ROTTEN.
1D. "Their management is reels of cotton to the very core."

Reg Varney – PAKISTANI. (Origins; 1960's TV comedian)
2D. "Can you adam an' eve it? Martin's new bird's a reg, no kiddin'."

Reg Varney – SARNIE, (sandwich). (Origins; 1960's TV comedian)
1D. "I gotta find a bakers; I'm dying on a cheese an' ham reg varney."

Reggie Blinker – STINKER, (bad game). (Origins; Surinamese footballer)
2D. "He's top class, cost millions, but he played a total reggie today."

Rex Mossop – GOSSIP. (Origins; Australian sports commentator]
2D. "What's the latest rex about Sid and Nancy, love?"

Rhubarb Crumble – GRUMBLE.
1D. "Yeah, I know we're mid-table, but I do like me a good rhubarb crumble!"

Rhubarb Hill – PILL.
2D. "I got our Shirley on the rhubarb this week, she's sixteen!"

Rhythm & Blues – SHOES. (Origins; musical style/genre)
1D. "Come on! Get your rhythm and blues on, it's time to hit the street."

Riccardo Patrese – HAZY. (Origins; Formula 1 racing driver)
2D. "I'm not exactly sure what I saw; Saturday night was a bit riccardo."

Richard & Judy – MOODY. (Origins; husband & wife TV presenters)
1D. "The divorce is affecting Chuck; he's been richard and judy for weeks."

Richard Burtons – CURTAINS. (Origins; Welsh actor)
2D. "Come on! Shut the richards - I'm trying to get some shut-eye."

Richard Gere – BEER. (Origins; American actor)
1D. "Hey Frank, do ya fancy a richard gere tonight, I got a drouth from last night."

Richard the Third – BIRD, (girl). (Origins; English 'hunchback' king)
2D. "Look what that bloody richard's done to my freakin' life!"

Richard the Third – TURD. (Origins; English 'hunchback' king)
1D. "Oh crap! Literally! I just stood on a richard the third."

Rick Whitter – SHITTER, (arsehole). (Origins; English singer/songwriter)
1D. "My rick whitter is still stinging after that ruby last night."

Ricky Lake – FAKE. (Origins; American TV presenter)
1D. "Oh listen to that Cockney accent! It's so ricky lake it's terrible!"

Ricky & Bianca – WANKER. (Origins; character couple on BBC's Eastenders)
2D. "Stan is such a ricky; he never knows when to stop."

Ricky Gervais – FACE. (Origins; English actor/comedian)
1D. "Well she slapped his ricky gervais so hard, he fell down."

Riddick Bowe – B.O., (body odor). (Origins; American boxer)
1D. "Can you give Derek a bar of soap as a gift? He's got real bad riddick."

Riff Raff – CAFÉ, (pronounced 'caff'). (Origins; derogatory for the great unwashed)
1D. "Tell mum I'm off to the riff raff. I'll meet her there."

Rifle Range – CHANGE, coins.
2D. "Have you got pound coins? I've got no rifle for the bus."

Right Said Fred – BREAD. (Origins; British band, 'I'm too Sexy')
1D. "Have you got any spare right said fred? I'm pennyless right now."

Right Said Fred – DEAD. (Origins; British band, 'I'm too Sexy')
3D. "I can't believe it. One minute he's here, the next he's gone; too sexy."

Rigobert Song – THONG. (Origins; Cameroonian footballer)
2D. "Look, her skirt's so tight, you can see the line of her rigobert!"

Ringo Starr – BAR. (Origins; English drummer/singer)
2D. "I'll meet you at the railway station ringo. Have a couple before we get aboard."
Trivia; as far as I know, Ringo is the only Beatle to have a rhyming slang.

Rink a Dink – CHINK, (Chinese).
2D. "We're going to get rinky take-away. Sweet an' sour chicken for me."

Rio Ferdinand – GRAND, (£1000). (Origins; English footballer)
2D. "Some git's hit me car with a shopping trolley! That just cost me a Rio".

River Lea – TEA. (Origins; Irish river)
1D. "Hey mum, Lennie's coming over later, so can you get the river lea on?"
(Old; Included In Hotten's 1858 Rhyming Slang Glossary)

River Nile – DENIAL. (Origins; African river)

1D. "Colin still thinks Jenny'll come back. He's in serious river nile."

River Ouse – BOOZE. (Origins; English river)
1D. "I'm going to hit the river ouse tonight, I can feel it in my water."

Roast Pork – FORK.
2D. "I've always preferred fork an' apple sauce to charlie an' mint anyway."

Robbie Fowler – HOWLER. (Origins; Liverpool football player)

2D. "I dropped a right robbie, called my wife by the wrong name."

Rob Roy – BOY. (Origins; Scottish historical character)
1D. "We got news from the hospital! Janie's just dropped a rob roy!"

Robin Hood – GOOD. (Origins; English fictional legend)
2D. "That sounds like it's robin jelly roll, I'm so happy for you."

Robinson & Cleaver – FEVER. (Origins; possible a Monserrat politician)
2D. "Harry's down wif a robinson. He might not make it."

Robinson Crusoe – DO SO. (Origins; Daniel Defoe novel character)
1D. "Look, if you promised you would, then robinson crusoe!"

Rock & Roll – DOLE, (unemployment benefit). (Origins; music style/genre)
1D. Herbert hasn't worked a day in 'is life; always on the rock and roll."

Rockford Files – PILES, (hemorrhoids). (Origins; James Garner TV series)
"F*ckin' damp weather! Me jim rockford's are giving me gip!"

Rock of Ages – WAGES.
1D. "Thank God it's Friday; rock of ages today, cabin tonight."

Rocking Horse – SAUCE. (Origins; children's toy)
2D. "Pass the rocking, dad. Can't do mash without me HP."

Rod and Reel – STEAL. (Origins; fishing gear)
1D. "If I can't afford a new watch by Xmas, I'm going to rod an' reel one."

Rodney Marsh – HARSH. (Origins; English footballer)
1D. "A yellow card for that? That was a bit rodney marsh, wasn't it?"

Roger Mellie – TELLY, (television). (Origins; cartoon from Viz magazine)
1D. "A night in front of the roger mellie. All me soaps, and footie at eight!"

Roger Moore – DOOR. (Origins; English actor)
2D. "Open that roger, will yer! I burnt the biscuits!"

Roger Starling – CARLING, (Black Label, lager).
1D. "Drink? Me? I'll have a pint of roger starling, please."

Rogue and Villain – SHILLIN', (shilling).
1D. "Oi found a rogue an' villain in the street, Friday. Made moi week."
(Old; Included In Hotten's 1858 Rhyming Slang Glossary)

Roland Rat – TWAT. (Origins; kids TV puppet character)
1D. "Oh I can't stand Jim's friends, roland rats, every one."

Rolf Harris – ARRIS (arse; short for Aristotle). (Origins; Australian singer/TV personality)
2D. "She kicked him in the Rolf, right onto the field!"

Roll and Butter – NUTTER.

1D. "That bloke at the bar's a bloody roll-and-butter. He'll be out soon."

Roller Coaster – POSTER. (Origins; funfair ride)
1D. "Did you see the roller coaster. It says they'll be in London in March!"

Roller Coaster – TOASTER. (Origins; funfair ride)
2D. "Come on mum; get the uncle into the roller. I gotta go!"

Rolls Royce – CHOICE. (Origins; British engineering/car company)
1D. "I didn't have much of a rolls royce, luv. It was go for a beer or sit outside."

Roman Candles – SANDLES. (Origins; type of firework)
1D. "It's June; time to get the kids some roman candles for the beach."

Ronald de Boer – SCORE. (Origins; Dutch footballer)
2D. "So did you see the ronald? West Ham's three up!"
Nice one, doing a football rhyme with a football player.

Ronald Riches – BITCHES.
1D. "I'm going off women, a bunch of ronald riches. Ooh. New barmaid!"

Ronan Keating – CHEATING. (Origins; Irish singer)
1D. "Oi! You can't pick up two cards! That's ronan keating!"

Ronan Keating – MEETING. (Origins; Irish singer)
2D. "Look, I was at the ronan, I know what was said!"

Ronnie & Reggie – VEGGIE. (Origins; British crime lords)
1D. "Give us a ronnie an' reggie burger please, luv. With cheese."

Ronnie Barker – MARKER, (pen). (Origins; English Comedian/actor)

1D. "Pass that ronnie barker, Kevin. I need to mark the calendar."

Great for Ronnie to have his own rhyming slang. His comedy skits and his show, Porridge, are all well worth a look (Ronnie plays a Londoner from Muswell Hill). Look up 'Two Ronnies Four Candles' on YouTube for an IMMENSE skit (lesson) on the British accent. After one short 4 min skit, you'll be hooked.

Ronnie Corbett – ORBIT. (Origins; English Comedian/actor)
1D. "She kicked his arris so freakin; hard, she nearly put him in ronnie corbett!"

Again, great for Ronnie to have his own rhyming slang. Ronnie Corbett is the other half of the Two Ronnies, comedy duo. Look up 'Two Ronnies Four Candles' on YouTube for an IMMENSE skit (lesson) on the British accent. After one short 4 min skit, you'll be hooked.

Ronson Lighter – SHITER, (toilet). (Origins; lighter manufacturer)
2D. "Where's the ronson in this place? I could piss like a racehorse!"

Roof Rack – BACK.
1D. "You want me to carry you? Okay, get up on me old roof rack then."

Roof Tile – SMILE.
1D. "Of course I thought the joke was funny. Can't you see my roof tile?"

Rory McGrath – LAUGH. (Origins; English comedian/TV personality)
1D. "What, me wear a kilt? You're having a rory mcgrath!"
Clever, using a comedian's name to be the rhyme of laughing.

Rory O'Moore – DOOR. (Origins; Irish lord/rebel)
1D. "Come on, shut the rory o'moore, there's a draught!"
(Old; Included In Hotten's 1858 Rhyming Slang Glossary)

Rory O'Moore – FLOOR. (Origins; Irish lord/rebel)
2D. "I ended up sleeping on the rory, never got to me bed."
(Old; Included In Hotten's 1858 Rhyming Slang Glossary)

Rosie Lea – TEA.
2D. "Come on in, luv. I've just put the rosy on."

Round the Houses – TROUSERS.
1D. "Went up town, got meself a new pair of round the houses."
(Old; Included In Hotten's 1858 Rhyming Slang Glossary)

Royal Navy – GRAVY.
1D. "Pass the royal navy, dad. Love me my taters an' bernards."

Roy Hudd – BLOOD. (Origins; English actor/comedian)
1D. "You should have seen Jack; covered in roy hudd from head to toe."

Roy Hudd's – SPUDS, (potatoes). (Origins; English actor/comedian)
1D. "Got me a job in the sticks picking roy hudds!"

Rub a Dub – PUB.
1D. "Bye mum, I'm off down the rub a dub, meeting Chris and the empires."

Rub a Dub – SUB, (submarine).
1D. "When we went to Plymouth, we got a tour round a rub a dub. Kinda scary."

Rubber Duck – F*CK.
1D. "Hello darlin', how would you like to be me rubber duck for tonight?"

Rubber Glove – LOVE.
1D. "Look at Helen tonight. I wouldn't mind giving her some rubber glovin."
Clever and risqué. Rubber gloves and a lubricant are well known male masturbatory aids.

Rubber Gregory – BOUNCING CHEQUE. (Origins; American actor)
1D. "Cheeky sod took a £500 johnathan, an' left me with a rubber Gregory."
Adapted from the original rhyme using 'Gregory Peck' for a cheque/check.

Rubik's Cube – PUBE, (pubic hair). (Origins; 1980's puzzle/toy)
2D. "And when she took her alans off, she'd got no rubiks!"

Rubik's Cube – TUBE, (idiot). (Origins; 1980's puzzle/toy)
1D. "I always thought of Henry as a bit of a rubik's cube."

Ruby Murray – CURRY. (Origins; Irish singer)
2D. "What's for dinner, darlin'? Rinky ruby? Great!"
Trivia; in March, 1955, Ruby achieved the rare feat of having five songs in the UK Top 20 in a single week.

Rum & Coke – JOKE.
1D. "Go on then, tell us another rum and coke; you're on a roll."

Runner Bean – QUEEN.
1D. "I'm off to the Palace, maybe I'll see the runner bean."

Runner Beans – JEANS, (denims).
2D. "Hey Jerry, how do you like me new runners then?"

Russell Crowe – DOUGH, (money). (Origins; New Zealand actor)
2D. "How much russell have yer got on yer, dad? I could do with new shoes."

Russell Harty – PARTY. (Origins; English TV presenter)
1D. "I'm going to a russell harty on Saturday, wanna come?"

Rusty Bucket – F*CK IT.
1D. "Oh, rusty bucket! I'm off home, this game's shite!"

Rusty Lee – PEE. (Origins; Jamaican TV chef/personality)
1D. "Take my shots at the pool table, I'm off for a rusty lee."

Rusty Lee – WEE. (Origins; Jamaican TV chef/personality)Rusty Nail – 'jail'.
2D. "Get me a whisky, just a rusty one."

Rusty Spike – DYKE, lesbian.
1D. "Look at Sandy, she makes no bones that she's a bit of a rusty spike."

Ruud Hullit – GULLET. (Origins; Dutch footballer)
1D. "Look at that seal eat the fish; straight down the ruud hullit."

S

Saddam Hussein – INSANE. (Origins; Iraqi despot)
2D. "I'm never going out with sherry again, she's completely saddam."
Clever.. cos he was a bit of a barmy onion if you ask me.

Sage & Onion – BUNION.
1D. "My sage an' onions are doing me jip this morning."

Salvador Dali – CHARLIE, (cocaine). (Origins; Spanish painter)
1D. "I'm off the salvador dali for good; cold turkey."

Salford Docks – ROCKS.
"Mother's ruin an' salford for the trouble, Harry."

Salisbury Crag – SKAG, (heroin). (Origins; rock formation in Edinburgh, Scotland)
2D. "Hey, Henry? Got any Salisbury crag? I'm gaggin'!"
My home town, Edinburgh, was once known as the capital of Heroin, giving rise to a film drug culture, Trainspotting, etc.

Salmon & Trout – GROUT.
1D. "Me missus 'as got me doing salmon an' trout in the bathroom."

Salmon Trout – MOUTH.
Get that steak in yer salmon trout. Yer won't get a better chance!"
(OLD; Included in Hotten's 1858 Rhyming Slang Glossary)

Salmon & Trout – SNOUT.
2D. "Hey Nicky, got any salmon on yer, love?"

Salmon & Trout – STOUT.

239

2D. "I'll have a pint of that dark salmon, please."

Salt Lake City – TITTY, (breast). (Origins; city in Utah, USA)
2D. "Come on, yer ain't seen a better pair of salt lakes than those!"

Salvation Army – BARMY.
1D. "Villa supporters are all salvation army, every one."

Samantha Mumba – NUMBER. (Origins; Irish singer/actress)
1D. "I pity Roger, his girl did a real samantha mumba on him, an' no mistake."

Samba Brazilian – CIVILIAN.
2D. "Those cops are doing good, as long as no sambas get hurt."

San Bruno – PRUNO, (prison alcohol).
1D. "God, that whisky's rotgut; worse than san Bruno."

Sandy Lyle – SMILE. (Origins; Scottish golfer)
1D. "Look at Jimmy, you couldn't wipe the sandy lyle from his face with sandpaper."

Sandy Lyle – STYLE. (Origins; Scottish golfer)
2D. "Oh, that Janie's got sandy; but she doesn't get it from 'er mum."

Sandy McNabs – CRABS, (STD).
1D. "I hear Geoff's got a bad case of sandy mcnabs."

Santas Grotto – BLOTTO, (drunk).
1D. "She had to put me to bed last night, I was absolutely santas grotto."

Sara Cox – SOCKS. (Origins; English DJ and fashion model)
2D. "Look, it's warm enough for vandals and no saras!"

Satin and Silk – MILK.
1D. "You left the satin and silk out of the fridge again!"

240

Saucepan Handle – CANDLE.
1D. "Damn power's went off again, where are the saucepan handles?"

Saucepan Lid – KID.
1D. The saucepan lids grow so quick, I'm forever buy clothes for them."

Saucepan Lid – QUID, (pound).
2D. "Can you lend me a couple of saucepans until Friday, just to get me salmon?"

Sausage & Mash – CASH. (origins; famous English dinner)
2D. "I haven't got sausage right now, totally bernie."

Sausage & Mash – CRASH. (origins; famous English dinner)
1D. "He was in a terrible sausage and mash last month."

Sausage & Mash – SLASH, (pee). (origins; famous English dinner)
2D. "I gotta go for a sausage, keep your eye on me handbag."

Sausage Roll – DOLE, (welfare). (Origins; British pastry-covered sausage)
2D. "Frankie? He ain't worked in years; he's on the sausage."

Sausage Roll – GOAL. (Origins; British pastry-covered sausage)
1D. "What a sausage roll! That must have been thirty yards out!"

Sausage Sarnie – PAKISTANI. (Origins; British delicacy; sausage on a sandwich)
1D. "There's a new store opened on the corner, run by sausage sarnies, of course."

Scapa Flow – GO. (Origins; Anchorage in Shetland Islands)
1D. "Shit, I hear sirens, scapa flow! Everyone!"

Scapa Flow is the harbor in the Shetlands where the WW1 German fleet was scuttled. The rhyming slang phrase gave birth to the word... scarper.

Schindler's List – PISSED. (Origins; movie starring Liam Neeson)
2D. "Oh man, I was schindler's on Friday night... totally smashed."

Schindler's List – WRIST. (Origins; movie starring Liam Neeson)
1D. "Well, she grabbed me by the schindler's list and dragged me all over town."

Scooby Doo – CLUE. (Origins; cartoon character)
2D. "See how gormless he is around women; he's not got a Scooby!"

Scooby-Doo – SUBARU. (Origins; cartoon character)
1D. "Go on then, give us a drive in yer new scooby-doo."

Scooby Doos – SHOES. (Origins; cartoon character)
1D. "These new Scooby doos don't half hurt my feet righ now."

Scotch Eggs – LEGS. (Origins; Scottish egg delicacy)
1D. "Ouch. Check out the scotch eggs on the blond playing darts."

Scotch Mist – PISSED, (drunk). (Origins Scottish phrase meaning 'nothing')
1D. "Sharon dumped me; I'm getting scotch mist tonight, an' no mistake."

Scotch Pegs – LEGS.
2D. "Come on in. Sit down and take a load off your pegs."
Probably a local variant of 'clothes pegs'.

Scott Gibbs – FIBS, (little lies). (Origins; Welsh rugby player)
2D. "Don't listen to Steve about Barbara, he's been telling scotts again."

Scott Mills – PILLS. (Origins; British DJ)
1D. "I need some scott mills right now, me back's doing my head in."

Scratch & Itch – RICH.
2D. "I don't trust 'im. He got scratch too damn quick."

Scratch 'n' Sniff – SPLIFF.
2D. "Hey, pass the scratch, don't hog it mate."

Scratch Yer Head – BED.
1D. "Go on, get to yer scratch yer head; you look shattered."
For many years, a common acceptance as 'bed' is the single word, scratcher. Not everyone knows the rhyming slang as its source.

Screaming Alice – CRYSTAL PALACE FC, (London football team).
1D. "We've got screamin' alice this weekend, at home. Shoe in!"

Screaming Lord Such – CRUTCH. (Origins; UK singer/crank politician)
2D. "She kneed him in the screaming, and poured his beer over his head."

Sean Bean – MEAN. (Origins; English actor)
1D. "I didn't know me dad had a sean bean side to him."

Sean Ryder – CIDER. (English musician)
1D. "Can't wait to get to Somerset, get some sean ryder in me."

Sebastian Coes – (on my) TOES, (running fast). (Origins; British athlete)
2D. "I wasn't hanging about. I was off on me sebastians before the fight started."
Clever, Seb Coe was a world champion middle distance runner.

Second Hand Merc – TURK. (Origins; used Mercedes car)

2D. "I'm off down the second hand, got to get me a shish kebab."

Selina Scott – SPOT. (Origins; TV news presenter)
1D. "I can't go out like this! I got a selina scott on the tip of me nose!"

Septic Tank – WANK.
2D. "Charlie's a real septic when he's pissed."

Septic Tank – YANK, (American).
1D. "Typical London summer, septic tanks everywhere."
2D. "I love a chat with a septic from time to time. Makes me feel superior."
2D+. "Albert don't like tourists; he's especially anti-septic."
3D. "Dad remembers the septics from the war, he's totally listerine."
(Listerine being a brand of anti-septic.)

Sexton Blake – CAKE. (Origins; comic strip character)
2D. "Hi mum, how about a nice slice of that new cream sexton?"

Sexton Blake – FAKE. (Origins; comic strip character)
1D. "He wears a watch that says Cartier but it's a sexton blake."

Sexton Blake – STEAK. (Origins; comic strip character)
2D. "Gotta love me a good sexton, army, and mashed taters."

Shake & Shiver – RIVER.
1D. "It was so hot, she jumped right into the shake 'n' shiver, clothes on, the lot!"

Shaken Not Stirred – BIRD.
2D. "Ooh. Take a look at Stan's new shaken not... a bit classy, huh?"

Shakin Stevens – EVENS, (equal odds). (Origins; Welsh singer)
1D. "Oh-oh. Jake an' Harry are facing up. I call it shakin' stevens money."

Sharon Stone – PHONE. (Origins; American actress)
2D. "Get yer Sharon out, call us a left jab. We need to scarper."

Shawshank Redemption – PENSION. (Origins; Steven King book/film)
2D. "I'll be sixty-seven next month, I've already claimed me shawshank."

Sheffield United – EXCITED. (Origins; English football team)
1D. "Oh, I'm all sheffield united; I haven't seen Billy Joel before."

Shepherd's Plaid – BAD.
2D. "Kenny dumped her for his secretary, now that was a bit shepherds of him."

Sherbet Dab – CAB, (taxi). (Origins; sherbet dipping confectionary)
2D. "Oh he's an old hand; been on the sherbet for five years.

Sherbet Dip – KIP, (sleep). (Origins; sherbet dipping confectionary)
1D. "I'm going to have a quick hour's sherbet dip before I go out; been a long day."

Shereen Nanjiani – FANNY, (vagina, sex). (Origins English TV newsreader)
2D. "Jimmy's all togged up; he's out looking for some shereen, an' no mistake."

Sherman Tank – WANK, (masturbate). (Origins; American tank in WW2)
1D. "I hate old man Hill; he's such a sherman tanker most of the time."

Shetland Isles – PILES, (hemorrhoids). (Origins; islands to north of Scotland)
2D. "Doc gave me new cream for me shetlands; it's doing the trick!"

Ship in Full Sail – POT OF ALE.
1D. "I'll have a ship, barman, full sail, laugh an' titter."
(OLD; Included in Hotten's 1858 Rhyming Slang Glossary)

Ship's Anchor – WANKER.
1D. "Oh don't be a ship's anchor, Jimmy. Get down from the lamppost."

Shirley Bassey – CHASSIS. (Origins; Welsh singer)
1D. "Hey Bert, look at the shirley bassey on the redhead waitress."

Shirt Front – C*NT.
1D. "Yup, Tommy's done it again; made a total shirt front of himself."

Shit in a Hurry – CURRY.
1D. "What's after hours tonight? Are we going for a shit in a hurry?"
Clever... if any of you have had 'one in a hurry' after sampling the local Indian, you'll know exactly what I mean.

Shop Front – C*NT.
1D. "Frank's an obnoxious shop front most of the time, but after ten beers..."

Short of a Sheet – ON THE STREET.
1D. "Gail threw him out. I guess he's short of a sheet for a bit."
Clever... Implying a situation of poverty and hence the lack of a bed.

Short & Stout – KRAUT, (German).
1D. "Come on! Gotta beat those short an' stouts to the pool."
Trivia; supposedly the name, Kraut, was first used in the 1700's, but came into mainstream in 1914, and came from the Germans' love of sauerkraut.

Shovel & Pick – THE NICK, (prison).

2D. "What's up with George? He's spending a bit of time in the shovel."

Shovel & Spade – BLADE, (knife).
2D. "This could go south. You tooled? I got a shovel with me."

Shredded Wheat – CHEAT. (Origins; breakfast cereal)
1D. "Don't play cards with wee Michael; he's a shredded wheat, and a good 'un"

Sieg Heils – PILES, (hemorrhoids). (Origins; Nazi salute in WW2)
1D. "I'll stand if you don't mind - me sieg heils are acting up again.

Sigourney Weaver – BEAVER, (vagina hair area). (Origins; American actress)
1D. "That bikini hides nuthin'! There's a huge sigourney in there!"
Very clever; I love this. Anyone who remembers her hiding in the spacesuit rack in the movie, Alien, will know what I'm talking about.

Silvery Moon – COON, (black person). (Origins; song "By The Light of the Silvery Moon")
2D. "He's a silvery alright, dark as pitch, but by God he can sing."
Back in the days of the British Empire, Brits were very particular when it came to the origins of people of color... Coons and Nignogs were 'black', (people of African descent), and Wogs, on the other hand, were 'brown', of Indian or Asian descent).

Silvery Spoon – COON, (black person).
1D. "I see Harriet's got herself a new bloke; a silvery spoon from Muswell Hill."
Back in the days of the British Empire, Brits were very particular when it came to the origins of people of color... Coons and Nignogs were 'black', (people of African descent), and Wogs, on the other hand, were 'brown', of Indian or Asian descent).

Simon Said – DEAD. (Origins; children's game)
1D. "God, did you hear about Donald; simon said. Just dropped in the street."

Simon Cowell – TROWEL. (Origins; TV personality)
1D. "Here, Carenza, pass me my simon cowel, I think there's a wall here."
(Just my little in-house "Time Team" joke (Channel 4 archaeology programme))

Simon Schamas – PYJAMAS. (Origins; British historian/TV presenter)
1D. "Ah, freshly ironed simon schamas; I could go to heaven."

Sinbad the Sailor – TAILOR. (Origins; character in Arabian tale)
2D. "Gotta run, got an appointment with me Sinbad at two."

Single Fish – PISH, (pee, urinate/urination).
1D. "Get the pints in, Raymond. I'm off for a single fish."
In the UK chip shops, an individual item, such as a fish, black pudding or pie, is ordered as 'a single' (to denote no added chips/fries). Most orders include chips/fries, and the main dish/chip combination is termed a 'supper'. Fish supper, or pie supper... etc.

Sir Arthur Bliss – PISS, (pee). (Origins; British composer)
2D. "Oh I hope the bus gets there quickly; I'm dying on a sir arthur."

Sir Walter Scott – A POT, (of beer). (Origins; Scottish writer)
2D. "A sir walter of porter, please maestro! I found a sparsy!"
(OLD; Included in Hotten's 1858 Rhyming Slang Glossary)

Sistine Chapel – APPLE. (Origins; Pope's residence)
1D. "Oh, and get a pound of sistine chapels, I'm making an isle of skye."

Six & Eight – STATE, (condition). (Origins; British money, six shillings and eightpence)
1D. "Look at the six an' eight John's got himself into. Order a joe baxi."

Skein of Thread – BED. (Origins; Scottish weaving term)
2D. "I'm off to my skein, got a huge day tomorrow."

Skin & Blister – SISTER.
1D. "I'm going out with my skin an' blister tonight, gotta meet her new squeeze."

Sky Diver – FIVER, (five pounds).
1D. "Here's that sky diver back I owe ye, thanks mate."

Sky Rocket – POCKET.
1D. "They cost how much? Hold on, I'll check me sky rockets."

Sky the Wipe – HYPE, (needle/hypodermic, drug paraphernalia).
1D. "Okay, you wanna do this? I got clean sky the wipes."

Slander & Libel – BIBLE.
2D. "Mysterious ways. That's what it says in the slander. Go check."

Slay 'em in the Ailes – PILES, (hemorrhoids).
2D. "My slay-em's are busting my ass today."

Slap Dash – CASH. (Origins; quick low quality job)
2D. "Sorry mate, I haven't gotten any slap on me."

Slice Pan – VAN. (Origins; type of bread)
1D. "Okay, let's get in the slice pan, and get out of this concrete jungle."

Slippery Slope – DOPE.
2D. "Charlie? Do you know anyone with access to a bit of slippery?"

Clever... dope being a gateway drug to so many more.

Slits in a Dress – MESS.
2D. "Oh you should have seen the slits; there was roy hudd everywhere."

Sloop Of War – WHORE. (Origins; small fighting ship)
1D. "There they are, on the corner like sloops of war."
(OLD; Included in Hotten's 1858 Rhyming Slang Glossary)

Small Geezers – MALTESERS, (British chocolate/malt confection).
1D. "Come on, the film's started. Get the small geezers out."

Smash & Grab – CAB. (Origins; quick hit and run crime)
1D. "I'm drinking late; let's look for a smash and grab to go uptown."

Smoke Screen – QUEEN.
1D. "I hear the smoke screen's opening a new building opposite."

Snake In The Grass – LOOKING GLASS, (mirror).
1D. "Take a look in the snake in the grass, who's prettier now?"
(OLD; Included in Hotten's 1858 Rhyming Slang Glossary)

Snake's Hiss – KISS.
2D. "Come on darlin', give an old man a snake's."

Snake's Hiss – PISS.
1D. "I'm off to the khazi to have a snake's hiss."

Snow & Slush – FLUSH, (to temporarily have money).
1D. "I'm snow an' slush this week, drinks are on me."

Sock & Blister – SISTER.
1D. "It's me sock an' blister's birthday this week, gotta get a pressie."

Sol Campbell – GAMBLE. (Origins; English footballer)

1D. "I think I might have a wee sol campbell on the Chelsea game."

Sol Campbell – RAMBLE. (Origins; English footballer)
2D. "Gerry's lost the plot, sol'in all over the place. Focus man!"

Soldiers Bold – COLD.
1D. "Remember to wrap up well; it's soldiers bold out there."

Son & Daughtered – SLAUGHTERED, (drunk).
1D. "Wow I've got me a head; I was son an' daughtered last night."

Sooty & Sweep – SLEEP. (Origins; British Children's TV puppets)
2D. "I've got to get to me scratcher, I need me some sooty, pronto."

Sorrowful Tale – THREE MONTHS IN JAIL.
1D. "Jimmy was up before the beak yesterday; sorrowful tail, not out 'til Christmas."
(OLD; Included in Hotten's 1858 Rhyming Slang Glossary)
A classic rhyme with original meaning alluded to.

Sorry & Sad – BAD.
2D. "That dinner was a bit on the sorry side."

So Say All Of Us – BUS, (coach). (Origins; from the song 'For He's a Jolly Good Fellow'.)
2D. "Come on, hurry! The so-say's here!"

Soup & Gravy – NAVY.
1D. "I heard young cousin Nigel's off to join the soup an' gravy."

Space Hopper – COPPER, (police). (Origins; kids bouncy inflatable toy)
1D. "Scarper lads, the do-no will have the space hoppers here in no time."

Spade & Bucket – F*CK IT.
1D. "Spade an' bucket, I've heard enough of Tom's lip, I'm gonna smack him down."

Spaghetti Junction – FUNCTION. (Origins; section of twisting highway)
2D. "No dinner for dad; he's got a spaghetti tonight."

Spanish Onion – BUNION.
1D. "Crap! She's only gone an' stepped on me spanish onions!"

Spanish Waiter – POTATO, ('potater').
2D. "Mashed spanish please, luv. Peas, an' buckets of army."

Spanish Waiter – SEE YA LATER.
1D. "That was a nice night lads, Spanish waiter to you all."

Spark and Smoulder – SHOULDER.
1D. "Darn it if me tennis elbow's mover to me spark an' smoulder."

Spark Plugs – DRUGS.
1D. "Hey Tim? I got me a party starting Saturday. Got any spark plugs? Mild stuff."

Sprarsy Anna – TANNER, (sixpence).
2D. "Mickey? Lend us a sprarsy - I wanna get some toe-rags."

Speckled Hen – TEN, (usually pounds).
2D. "Mum, can I borrow a deep sea, well, maybe a speckled 'til Friday?"

Spiders & Bugs – THUGS.
2D. "We can't even go up town at night; too many spiders hanging around."

Spider's Web – PLEB.
2D. "Man look at the low-life in here tonight; bunch of spiders an' no mistake."

The word, Pleb, is an impolite derogatory Roman term for normal people.

Spit & a Drag – FAG, (cigarette).
1D. "Make me up a spit an' drag, will ya? Me fingers are too cold."
Usually associated with home-made roll-ups.

Split Asunder – COSTERMONGER, (street seller).
2D. "Look at them splits on the corner. Raining like cats, and they're still workin'."
(OLD; Included in Hotten's 1858 Rhyming Slang Glossary)

Split Pea – TEA.
1D. "Go see Jenny, she's makin' a brew of good strong split pea."
(OLD; Included in Hotten's 1858 Rhyming Slang Glossary)

Sport And Win – JIN, (card game).
1D. "Come on Holly, get yer arse on a seat; playin' sport an' win."
(OLD; Included in Hotten's 1858 Rhyming Slang Glossary)

Sportsman's Bet – INTERNET.
2D. "Hansen never played for Chelsea. Look it up on the sportsmans."

Spotted Dick – SICK. (Origins; cake dessert with raisins)
2D. "We don't have a goalie this week, cos John's spotted."

Spotty Dog – BOG, (toilet).
1D. "I'm off to the spotty dog, can you order me a pint of mild?"

Squid – QUID, (pound).
1D. "Oh, here, Johnny. Here's the five squid I owe ye."

Squiddly Did – QUID, (pound).
2D. "I got a bonus this week, a whole twenty squiddleys."

Sri Lanker – WANKER. (Origins; person from Sri Lanka (Ceylon))
1D. "I can't stand John Barrymore; he's a complete sri lanker."

St Louis Blues – SHOES.
2D. "Whad ya think of me new st louis? Got them down the market."

St Martins-le-Grand – HAND. (Origins; area in London)
2D. "I can't believe it. I had it in my st. martins just a minute ago."
(OLD; Included in Hotten's 1858 Rhyming Slang Glossary)

Stamford Bridge – FRIDGE. (Origins; home ground of Chelsea FC)
1D. "Come on then, show us what beers you got in your stamford bridge."

Stammer & Stutter – BUTTER.
2D. "Mickey most? Sure; extra stammer for me."

Stand at Ease – CHEESE.
2D. "I wouldn't mind a bit of stand-at on top of me chili."

Standing Election – ERECTION
1D. "Looks like Roddy's holding a standing election in his trunks!"

Stand to Attention – PENSION, (usually soldier's).
1D. "I got me stand to attention diverted straight to me bank."

Stars & Garters – TOMATOES, (tomarters).
1D. "I planted me stars an' garters early this year."

Star's Nap – TAP, (borrow).
2D. "Can I stars you for a fiver 'til Monday?"

Starsky & Hutch – CLUTCH. (Origins; 70's US TV cop show)
"Gawd, I'm no mechanic, but it sounds like yur starsky's on the way out."

Steak & Kidney Pie – FLY. (Origins; British comfort food)

2D. "Got me a nice earner; I get paid cash on the steak an' kidney."

Steam Packet – JACKET. (Origins; steam ship cargo or package)
1D. "Better take your steam packet, looks like ache an' pain."
(OLD; Included in Hotten's 1858 Rhyming Slang Glossary)

Steam Tug – BUG.
2D. "Terrible night; the motel bed was full of steamers."

Steam Tug – MUG, (face, or chump/victim).
1D. "Look at the steam tug on the blonde; a bag o' hammers!"

Steely Dan – TAN. (Origins; American jazz/rock band)
1D. "Jim's back from Lanzarote; look at his steely dan."

Steffi Graf – BATH, (baff). (Origins; German tennis player)
2D. "I'm just going for a quick Steffi to ease me back."

Steffi Graf – LAUGH. (Origins; German tennis player)
"Leicester for the Premier title? You're havin' a steffi graf."

Steve Claridge – GARAGE. (Origins; English footballer)
2D. "I'm off down the steve; top up the jam for the trip."

Steve McQueens – JEANS. (Origins; American actor)
2D. "Lilly's new steves are a bit tight, huh?"

Stevey Bold – COLD.
1D. "Wrap up today, it's stevie bold outside, an no mistake."

Stevie Nicks – FLICKS, (pictures, cinema). (Origins; American singer)
1D. "We's off down the stevie nicks for the new Superman film."

Stevie Wonder – CHUNDER, (Aussie for be sick, throw up). (Origins; American pop star)
1D. "Looks like Billy's had enough; stevie wondering down the thunderbox."

Stewart Granger – DANGER, (both chance, and threat).
(Origins; English actor)
1D. "Any stewart granger of getting my mower back?"

Stewed Prune – TUNE. (Origins; dried plum delicacy)
1D. "Oh Gawd, he's awful. Couldn't hold a stewed prune in a bucket."

Stick of Glue – JEW.
1D. "Bunch of sticks of glue hanging round the corner on Leicester Square."

Sticks & Stones – BONES.
2D. "Oh these old sticks can't take the cold anymore."

Sticky Toffee – COFFEE.
2D. "It's past time for sticky, Henry. It's eight thirty."

Stinging Nettle – KETTLE.
2D. "Stick the stinging on, Nancy, get some rosie on the go."

Stirling Moss – TOSS, (care). (Origins; English racing driver)
1D. "I don't give a stirling moss, mate. Get out of the fountain."

Stock Market Crash – SLASH.
2D. "I'm off for a quick stock market. Meet you in the gadaffe in ten."

Stoke on Trent – BENT, (homosexual, illegal). (Origins; English town)
2D. "He's as stoke as a nine bob note."

Stop Thief – BEEF.
1D. "Dinner's great; I haven't has stop thief for ages."
(OLD; Included in Hotten's 1858 Rhyming Slang Glossary)

Stop yer Bitchin' – KITCHEN.

2D. "Come on through the stop-yer, see what beer's in the Stamford."

Strange & Weird – BEARD.
1D. "I don't like this craze of mountain men's strange an' weirds... it's unnerving."

Strawberry Split – GIT, (bad person).
2D. Tommy's a right strawberry when he's on the lily."

Strawberry Split – TWIT, (fool).
2D. "Xander's a classic old English strawberry, but he's harmless."

Strawberry Tart – HEART.
1D. "Oh come on, honey. You knows me strawberry tart belongs to you."

Street Fighter – LIGHTER.
1D. "Hand me your street fighter, Bill. Let's get these fireworks started."

String of Beads – LEEDS, (town in midlands England).
1D. "What a game! Hammer's six, string o' beads holborned from the third minute."

Struggle & Grunt – C*NT.
2D. "I don't mind her sister, but Rachel's a right struggle."

Sue Lawley – POORLY, (ill). (Origins; British newsreader)
1D. "Mary's not coming tonight, she's a bit sue lawley."

Sue Ryder – CIDER. (Origins; charity organization/chain of shops)
2D. "Give us a pint of Sue, mate, I'm feckin' parched."

Sugar and Honey – MONEY.
2D. "That's me last penny; I'm now officially sugarless."
(OLD; Included in Hotten's 1858 Rhyming Slang Glossary)

Sugar Basin – MARBLE MASON, (specialist stoneworker).
1D. "I was down the sugar basin last week, picking me new kitchen counter."
Clever... The appearance of rough white marble resembles a sugar lump and being a soft stone (when newly quarried) it is easy (ie; sweet) to work with.

Sugar Candy – BRANDY.
1D. "Pass the sugar candy, keep it going round."
(OLD; Included in Hotten's 1858 Rhyming Slang Glossary)

Sunday Roast – POST, (mail).
1D. "Has the sunday roast been yet? I'm expecting an elephant."

Sunny Dancer – CANCER.
1D. "Did you hear about old Frank passing? Sunny dancer. Need I say more?"

Supersonic – TONIC, (mineral drink).
1D. What yer drinking? How about a nice vera and supersonic, love?"

Surrey & Hants – PANTS, (knickers). (Origins; English counties (Hampshire))
2D. "Blimey! Mum! I got no clean surreys for school!"

Surrey Docks – POX. (Origins; part of London)
1D. "I'll give you a laugh! Gordon's only gone an' got the surrey docks!"
Maybe a clever one here, perhaps the Surrey Docks was a prostitute area? Perhaps every dock area had its own local rhyme.

Swanee River – LIVER.
2D. "Are we having swanee for dinner again, Mum?
Trivia; believe it or not, there is no Swanee River. The Sawannee River in Florida inspired the song.

Sweaty Sock – JOCK, (Scotsman, sometimes derogatory).
2D. "An Englishman, a tea caddy and a sweaty walk into a bar..."

Sweeney Todd – FLYING SQUAD, (fast acting police unit).
(Origins; the demon barber)
2D. "Here comes the sweeney, lights blazin'. Crooks hear 'em for miles!"
The Sweeney was one of my favorite cops an' robbers programs of the 1970's.

Syrup of Figs – WIG.
2D. "Oh my God, look at that syrup he's wearing!"

T

Take a Fright – NIGHT.
2D. "Come on, Jack, hurry up. Take-a's almost upon us."
(OLD; Included in Hotten's 1858 Rhyming Slang Glossary)

Talk & Mutter – BUTTER.
2D. "I'd like some talk on me toast, an' marmalade."

Tartan Banner – TANNER, (old sixpence coin).
1D. "I found a tartan banner outside the pub last night."

Tate & Lyles – PILES, (hemorrhoids). (Origins; east London sugar producer)
3D. "Cold weather doesn't do me sugars any good at all."

Taters in the Mould – COLD.
2D. "Grab a weasel, it's taters out there."

Taxi Driver – FIVER.
2D. "Remember, Hoggy, you owe me a taxi."

Tea Caddy – PADDY, (Irishman). (Origins; cover for tea pot)
1D. "Hey! Did you know young Kevin is a tea caddy?"

Tea Leaf – THIEF.
1D. "Peter's always been a bit of a tea leaf, now he's doing a stretch."

Tea Leafing – THIEVING.
1D. "What! My bag! Come back you little tea leafing bastard!"

Tea Pot Lid – KID.
2D. "I'm taking my teapots to the country this weekend."

Tea Pot Lid – QUID.
2D. "I hate playing brag with George; I'm down a teapot already."

Tea Pot Lid – YID, (Jew).
2D. "We're playing Israel tonight, expect a few tea pots after the game."

Tea, Two and a Bloater – MOTOR, (car).
2D. "Where did you park yer tea-two? It's going to rain."

Tear in a Bucket – F*CK IT.
1D. "I'm off home to get some shut-eye. Tear in a bucket!"

Ted Heath – TEETH. (Origins; British Prime Minister)
2D. "Gor blimey. Her teds hardly fit in her north!"
Clever, as Ted had a massive set of chewing irons.

Ted Ray – GAY, (homosexual). (Origins; English actor/comedian)
2D. "Jeremy's a bit too ted for my liking."

Teddington Lock – SOCK. (Origins; lock system on the Thames River in SW London)
2D. "I can't find me teddingtons. How can I go without them?"

Telecom Tower – SHOWER. (Origins; British Telecom tower in London)
2D. "I'm going to pop in the telecom before I hit me scratcher.

Ten Ounce Rump – DUMP, (a defecation).
2D. "Make way! I have to take an emergency ten ounce."

Ten Speed Gears – EARS. (Origins; bicycle gears)
2D. "Lummey! Look at the size of his ten speeds!"

Tennis Racquet – JACKET.
1D. "I bought a new tennis racquet on Carnaby Street on Saturday."

Terry Butcher – TAIL TOUCHER, (homosexual). (Origins; English footballer)
1D. "Lionel's a tail toucher, to be sure, but I think he's harmless."

Terry Nation – STATION. (Origins; Welsh TV writer)
1D. "Take the last michael caine to Clarksville, and I'll meet you at the terry nation."

Terry Waite – LATE. (Origins; British cleric and activist)
1D. "It's half past six! You're a bit terry waite for the early film."

Tex Ritter – BITTER, (beer). (Origins; American country star)
2D. "I've had enough tex, let's start on the gay an' frisky, huh?"

Thelonious Monk – SKUNK, (marijuana). (Origins; American jazz pianist)
2D. "Hey Charlie, got any Thelonious wi' yer?"

Thelonious Monk – SPUNK, (sperm). (Origins; American jazz pianist)
1D. "Oh man, it was a picture, there was Thelonious monk everywhere!"

Thick & Thin – GIN.
1D. "I enjoy a bit of thick and thin from time to time."

Thick & Thin – SKIN, (could be body skin or profit).
2D. "Ooh, that dress is showing way too much thick for my liking."

Thirteen Amp – TRAMP, (hobo). (Origins; UK standard electrical outlet rating)
1D. "How untidy! Look at that bunch of thirteen amps over there."

This & That – CAT.
2D. "Gawd, let the this'n in would yer? He's making a terrible racket."

Thomas Edison – MEDICINE. (Origins; American Inventor/tycoon)
2D. "Come on, open up. Take your Thomas like a man!"
(And that sentence could be interpreted in so many ways)

Thomas Moore – WHORE. (Origins; politician/advisor to Henry VIII)
1D. "Oh, that dress don't half make her look like a thomas moore."

Thomas Tank – WANK, (masturbate). (Origins; UK books/TV Children's program)
1D. "I caught our Harry the other night, thomas tankin' on 'is bed!"
(Probably with his 'fat controller')

Thomas Tilling – SHILLING. (Origins; name of UK bus group)
2D. "Here, dad? Lend me a thomas for me bus fare."

Thora Hird – TURD, (shite). (Origins; British actress/comedienne)
2D. "Oh, I gotta go upstairs, I feel a thora approaching."

Three Card Trick – DICK, (penis).
2D. "What a date! She couldn't keep her jazz's off my three card."

Three Quarters Of A Peck – NECK. (Origins; unit of measure)
2D. "Oh look at the swan three quarters on the girl selling flowers!"
(OLD; Included in Hotten's 1858 Rhyming Slang Glossary)
A peck is equivalent to 2 dry gallons, 8 dry quarts, 16 dry pints, or 9.09 liters. (Two pecks make a kenning, and four pecks make a bushel).
However, despite being widely accepted as the amount of pickled peppers that peter piper picked, it is also commonly known that pickled peppers are rarely sold by the peck.
So the re-researched tongue twister should read... "The possibility of peter piper picking a peck of pickled peppers is

particularly poor, as the punnet or poke provided was probably not peck pro-rated."

Three Wheel Trike – DYKE, (lesbian).
2D. "She must be a bit of a three wheeler, looks more like a man."

Throw Me In The Dirt - SHIRT.
2D. "I've wore the same throw-me for five days."
(OLD; Included in Hotten's 1858 Rhyming Slang Glossary)

Thruppeny Bits – TITS. (Origins; old UK 3d currency coin)
2D. "Here comes Ada; cor look at the Thruppeny's on her."

Tia Maria – DIARRHEA. (Origins; coffee liquer)
1D. "Oh I can't go into work today, real bad case of tia maria."

Tick Tack – RACE TRACK.
1D. "I'm off to the tick tack this weekend, Saturday meeting."
Trivia; the term now relates to the hand signals made by bookmakers to each other.

Tick Tock – CLOCK.
1D. "Are we late? What's the time on the mantelpiece tick tock?"

Tick Tock – KNOCK.
1D. "Tick tock on the bloody door; it's freezing out here."

Ticket to the Dance – REDUNDANCE, (redundancy).
1D. "Crap, we're all getting our tickets to the dance on Friday."

Tiddly Wink – CHINK, (Chinese food or person). (Origins; children's game)
2D. "I don't fink he's from around these parts. I fink e's a tiddley."

Tiddly Wink – DRINK. (Origins; children's game)
2D. "Just one more tiddle for the road and I'm off home."

Tijuana Brass – ARSE. (Origins; Herb Alpert's band)

1D. "Cheeky pup. Come back here so's I can kick your tijuana brass!"

Tilbury Docks – SOCKS. (Origins; dockland in London)
2D. I can't find me tilbury's anywhere. Me football ones!"

Tin Bath – LAUGH.
1D. "Go on. Streak across the park. Just for a tin bath."

Tin Lids – KIDS. (Origins; common military term for metal helmet)
1D. "I can't walk without stepping on one of the tin lids' toys!"

Tin Roof – POOF, (homosexual).
1D. "Take a look at the new guy. Tin roof, an' no mistake."

Tin Tack – THE SACK, (paid off, fired).
1D. "Frankie got the tin tack the other day; cheek to the boss."

Tin Tank – BANK.
1D. "I'm off down the tin tank, get some cash for tonight."

Tit For Tat (Tit-fer) – HAT.
2D. "That's a lovely tit-fer that Sandra's wearing."

Tit Willow – PILLOW.
2D. "I can't wait 'til me head hits the tit tonight, exhausted."

Toblerone – ALONE. (Origins; Swiss triangle chocolate confectionery)
1D. "Come on, let's sit wif Charlie, 'e's over there on his toblerone."

Toby Ale – RAIL. (Origins; beer from the Charrington Brewery)
2D. "Off to Edinburgh this weekend; traveling by toby."

Toby Jug – LUG, (ear). (Origins; ceramic mug of a sitting person)
2D. "Here. Let me bend your toby about this upcoming election."

Toby Jug – MUG, (face, or chump; pushover). (Origins; ceramic mug of a sitting person)
2D. "I'm sick fed up with people taking me for a complete toby."

Todd Carty – PARTY. (Origins; English Actor)
2D. "We're going to a posh todd this weekend; uptown address."

Todd Sloane – ALONE. (Origins; American jockey)
2D. "Michelle's at 'er mums'; looks like I'm on my todd tonight."
Clever rhyme; looks like this jockey had a tendency to race his horses at the front of the pack... all alone.

Toe Rag – FAG, (homosexual, or cigarette).
1D. "Lend us a sprarsy, will ya? I wanna get some toe-rags."

Tom, Dick & Harry – DICTIONARY.
2D. "I don' believe yer. I'll just check the meaning in the old tom."

Tom & Dick – SICK.
1D. "I only worked three shifts last bubble; off tom an' dick."

Tom & Huck – F*CK. (Origins; Mark Twain characters)
1D. "I don't give a tom an' huck. I'm not going."

Tom & Jerry – MERRY.
2D. "I like having Georgie around; he's a tommy bloke."

Tom Cruise – BOOZE. (Origins; American actor)
1D. ""Kerry can't take her tom cruise; she's all over the place."

Tom Cruise – BRUISE. (Origins; American actor)
1D. ""He grabbed me so hard, I still got the tom cruises on me arm."

Tom Cruise – LOSE. (Origins; American actor)
2D. "Oh sweet Chelsea, you're going to tom... so hard!

Tomfoolery – JEWELRY. (Origins; pranks, jokes)

2D. "Christine looks a bit flash tonight, look at all 'er tom."

Tom Hanks – THANKS. (Origins; American actor)
1D. "And at the end, you stand up, give the tom hanks, and we're done."

Tom Hanks – YANKS. (Origins; American actor)
1D. "Dad said it got real bad during the war, all the tom hanks around."

Tom Jones – BONES. (Origins; Lady Chatterley's Lover book character)
1D. "Going to rain tonight; I can feel it in me tom jones."

Tom Kite – SHITE. (Origins; American golfer)
1D. "Now Henry, you know what Mickey says is a lot of tom kite."

Tom Mix – FIX, (drugs). (Origins; American actor)
1D. "I need to get me a tom mix, an' pretty fecking smartish."

Tom Silk – MILK.
1D. "Cornflakes, cold tom silk, and a sprinkle of the sweet stuff."

Tom (Tommy) Tank – WANK, (masturbate). (Origins; UK books/TV Children's program)
1D. "I caught him last night, having a tom tank in the bath!"

Tom Thumb – BUM. (Origins; nursery rhyme/tale character)
2D. "So what ya gonna do? Sit un yer arse with yer finger up yer tom?"

Tom Thumb – DUMB. (Origins; nursery rhyme/tale character)
1D. "Jimmy's always been a bit on the tom thumb side."

Tom Thumb – RUM. (Origins; nursery rhyme/tale character)
2D. "It's late; I'll have a couple of toms and I'm off."

Tom Tit – SHIT. (Origins; pen name of caricaturist Arthur Good)

1D. "Ah! A khazi! I've needed a tom tit all afternoon!

Tom Tripe - PIPE.
1D. "I love the feeling of fresh bacca in me tom tripe."
(OLD; Included in Hotten's 1858 Rhyming Slang Glossary)

Tommy Hilfiger – NIGGER. (Origins; clothing manufacturer)
2D. "A couple of tommy's just realized they walked into the wrong bar."

Tommy O'Rann – SCRAN, ('vulgar' for food).
1D. "The smell of that tommy o'rann is wafting all over the camp."
(OLD; Included in Hotten's 1858 Rhyming Slang Glossary)

Tommy Trinder – WINDOW, (wind-er). (Origins; English stage/radio comedian)
1D. "I lost me knobbleys, Jimmy'll have to climb in the tommy trinder."

Tommy Tucker – F*CKER. (Origins; nursery rhyme character)
2D. "Look at that tommy run! Gawd, he's yards ahead."

Tommy Tucker – F*CK HER. (Origins; nursery rhyme character)
1D. "Listen, if the chick don't wanna know, then tommy tucker."

Tony Benn – TEN. (Origins; English politician)
1D. "I'll meet you at the Spire around tony benn."

Tony Blair – CHAIR. (Origins; British Prime Minister)
2D. "Pull up a tony, and we'll have a wee chew-the."

Tony Blair – HAIR. (Origins; British Prime Minister)
1D. "Wif this wind, me tony blair's a real mess."

Tony Slattery – BATTERY. (Origins; English comedian)
1D. "The bloody jam won't start; I've checked the tony slattery."

Tooting Bec – PECK, (of food). (Origins; area in south London)
1D. "Gawd, I'm so hungry I could throw a tooting bec over me neck."
Not sure what came first here, the rhyme or the slang; peckish… being slightly hungry. Now the measurement of a peck is 2 dry gallons, so that's a LOT to eat!

Top Hat – CHAT.
1D. "So you want to join the daft an', huh? Let's top hat about it."

Top Jint – PINT, (of beer). (Origins; vulgar pronunciation for joint, establishment)
2D. "I'm so thirsty, the first top ain't gonna touch the sides."
(OLD; Included in Hotten's 1858 Rhyming Slang Glossary)

Top of Rome – HOME.
1D. "When I hit the top of rome, I'm going straight into me scratcher."
(OLD; Included in Hotten's 1858 Rhyming Slang Glossary)

Topps Tiles – PILES, (hemorrhoids). (Origins; tile retailer in the UK)
1D. "This damp weather sure don't do me topps tiles any good."

Top Ten Hit – SHIT. (Origins; a hit record in the charts)
2D. "Gotta go an' have me a top ten real soon; it's touching cloth!"

Tord Gripps – NIPS, (nipples).
1D. "Cor blimey. Look at the tord gripps on the redhead!"

Torvill & Dean – KEEN. (Origins; British ice dancers)
2D. "Watch out for Suzie; she's a bit torvill on my eldest, Barry."

Torvill & Dean – QUEEN. (Origins; British ice dancers)
1D. "I love old Frank; he's a right old torvill an' dean, no mistake."

Touch Me on the Knob – BOB, (shilling).

2D. "Can I borrow a touch me? I'll pay back Friday."

Town Crier – LIAR. (Origins; town announcer of news)
1D. "Don't listen to Yorgi, he's a well-known town crier."
This one's clever, yet a contradiction; the Town Crier was meant to be reproachable, above lies and scandal, only reporting the truth.

Town Halls – BALLS, (testicles).
1D. "Don't worry about henry's blustering; he's not got the town halls to hurt anyone."

Tramp on a Bench – WENCH.
2D. "Have you seen Billy's new tramp? She's a corker."
Possibly the origin of the derogatory 'tramp' label for a loose woman.

Treacle Tart – SWEETHEART.
2D. "Oh come on Sadie, you know you're my treacle, no mistake."

Trevor Sinclair – NIGHTMARE. (Origins; English footballer)
2D. "Oh dear, they're having a trevor this afternoon; 3-0 at half time."

T-Rex – TEXT. (Origins; English glam/pop band)
2D. "Hey Sandy? T-Rex me the details; I'll be there."
3D. "Drop me a marc bolan, with the time and place."
Marc Bolan was the lead singer and guitarist.

Trombone – PHONE.
1D. "Here, Charlie? You dropped your trombone at the bar."

Trouble and Strife – WIFE.
2D. "I'm out on me todd tonight, trouble's at her mothers."
Clever, controversial, but oft-times true.

True 'Til Death – BREATH.
2D. "Gawd, I can't catch me true-til; those stair's will be the death of me."

The connection is so apt.

Tube of Glue – CLUE.
1D. "Look at Roger with the girls; he hasn't got a tube of glue how to act."
3D. "Gerry's funny when he plays darts; totally bostick-less."

Tufnell Park – LARK, (prank, fun). (Origins; area in north London)
2D. "Love a duck; I'm always up for a Tufnell or two."

Tumble Down the Sink – DRINK.
2D. "Hey Ginger? Fancy a tumble-down sometime, chew the fat?"

Tung Chee Hwa – BRA, (brassiere). (Origins; Chinese businessman)
2D. "I'm off to 'Arrods to buy a tung-chee for the trouble's birthday."

Tuppence a Pound – GROUND.
2D. "I came a cropper last night, fell, put me face right in the tuppence."

Turkish Bath – LAUGH.
2D. "Tottenham for the cup? He's 'avin' a turkish, aint he?"

Turkish Delight – SHITE. (Origins; sugary/jello delicacy)
1D. "West Ham's playing turkish delight this season, one win in six games."
This is a total lie; Turkish Delight is one of the best things you can put in your mouth!

Turtle Dove – LOVE.
2D. "All right me old turtle, grab your gladrags, we're going out on the town."

Turtle Doves – GLOVES.
2D. "Where's me white turtle's honey? I need them!"
(OLD; Included in Hotten's 1858 Rhyming Slang Glossary)

271

Tutti Frutti – BEAUTY. (Origins; many things, ice cream flavor)
1D. "Tony's new twist is a real tutti frutti, an no mistake."

Twist & Shout – GOUT. (Origins; 1961 pop song)
2D. "Twist's set into me real bad; I have to go to the docs."

Twist & Shout – KRAUT, (German). (Origins; 1961 pop song)
2D. "Did you see the twist's last night? Beat the bubbles 4-0."

Twist & Twirl – GIRL.
2D. "Kevin's new twist looks like a nice lass."
Clever, very visual rhyme.

Two & Eight – STATE. (Origins; amount of money)
1D. "Look at the two an' eight Donny's in! Looks like he fell in a puddle!"

Two & Six – FIX. (Origins; amount of money)
1D. "Got me a nice two an' six this morning; I feel top of the world."

Two Bob Bit – SHIT. (Origins; two shilling coin)
1D. "I'm bursting on a two bob bit. Where's the cadbury's log?"

Two Foot Rule – A FOOL.
1D. "Don't get involved with Spencer's schemes; he's a two foot rule."
(OLD; Included in Hotten's 1858 Rhyming Slang Glossary)

Two Thirty – DIRTY.
2D. "Blonde at the bar; she's got the mix of classy and two thirty."

Tyne & Wear – QUEER, (homosexual). (Origins; region in North England)
1D. "I'm not comfy with Jerry; he's tyne an'wear, an' creeps me out."

Typewriter – FIGHTER.
1D. "Hey, I'm a danny glover, not a typewriter."

U

Uncle Ben – TEN.
2D. "Go on my son, I've got an uncle on this race."

Uncle Bert – SHIRT.
1D. "I'd bet my uncle bert on City winning the cup."

Uncle Billy – CHILLY.
1D. "Grab yer quaker, it's kinda uncle billy out there today."

Uncle Bob – JOB.
1D. "I got me an uncle bob at the grocers, I start Friday!"

Uncle Bob – KNOB, (penis).
1D. "It's so cold, I think me uncle bob's going to fall off."

Uncle Buck – F*CK.
1D. "I don't give an uncle buck if you're tired, get it finished."

Uncle Dick – SICK.
1D. "I can't go in to work today; I'm a bit uncle dick."

Uncle Fester – CHILD MOLESTER. (Origins; character in the Addams Family, US TV)
1D. "I'd keep my minces on him, 'e's a bit of an Uncle Fester."

Uncle Fred – BREAD.
1D. "I like some uncle fred with my bangers 'n' mash."

Uncle Gus – BUS.
1D. "Car's in the garage, I have to take the uncle gus today."

Uncle Ned – BED.
1D. "I keep me valuables under me uncle ned."

Uncle Ned – HEAD.
1D. "I've got a real bad uncle ned this morning, too many last night."

Uncle Reg – VEG (vegetables).
1D. "I like me food traditional; meat an two uncle reg's."

Uncle Sam – HAM.
1D. "I like a big roast uncle sam at xmas."

Uncle Ted – BED.
1D. "I'm beat, off to me uncle ted."

Uncle Toby – MOBI, (mobile/cell phone).
1D. "I'll give you a call on the mobi when I'm ready."

Uncle Toms – Bombs.
1D. "London was a mess in the Blitz, all those uncle toms and such."

Uncle Willie – SILLY.
1D. "Giggs, playing at right back? That's just uncle willy."

Uncles & Aunts – PANTS, (underwear).
1D. "Remember to pack an extra pair of uncles and aunts, just in case."

Union Jack – BACK. (Origins; British Flag)
1D. "My old Union Jack's giving me some real bad pain these days."

Unscheduled Meeting – BEATING (assault).
1D. "Oh, it wasn't a fight, it was an unscheduled meeting an' no mistake."

Uri Geller – STELLA (artois, beer). (Origins; Israeli illusionist)
2D. "Three pints of uri, landlord!"

V

Vandals – SANDALS.
1D. "I can't find me vandals, mum, an' it's hot on the beach."

Vauxhall Cavalier – QUEER, (homosexual). (Origins; British Car)
2D. "I see Tony's going round with that vauxhall from Bromley."

Vauxhall Novas – JEHOVAH'S, (witness's). (Origins; British Car)
1D. "We've been getting a spate of vauxhall novas round the doors lately."

Vera Lynn – GIN. (Origins; British singer from the war years)
2D. "Give us two veras and tonic, mate."

Vera Lynn – HEROIN. (Origins; British singer from the war years)
1D. "I'm kinda getting' the urge to fix again, need me some vera lynn."
Trivia; Lyrics by David Gilmore, from Pink Floyd (The Wall); "Goodbye Vera Lynn I'm leaving you today.", meaning 'I'm giving up heroin'.

Vera Lynn – SKIN, (cigarette paper). (Origins; British singer from the war years)
1D. "Hey boss, you got any vera lynns? I'll trade yer."

Veronica Lake – BRAKE. (Origins; American actress)
2D. "I'm going to put the veronica's on this relationship."

Vicar's Daughter – QUARTER.
2D. "You wouldn't happen to have a spare vicars on ye?"

Vincent Price – ICE. (Origins; American actor)
1D. "Two shots of tequila, and a couple of dobs of vincent price."

Vincent van Gogh – COUGH. (Origins; Dutch painter)
2D. "That's a nasty vincent that Larry's got."

Vincent van Gogh – F*CK OFF. (Origins; Dutch painter)
1D. "Why don't you just van gogh and die!"

Vindaloo – CLUE. (Origins; Indian hot curry)
2D. "Look at Sid trying to pour a pint, he hasn't got a bloody vinda."

Virginia Wades – SHADES, (sunglasses). (Origins; British tennis player)
1D. "Rodney's wearing virginia wades cos he's gotten a shiner."

Vivien Leigh – KEY. (Origins; English Actress)
2D. "Where's me vivians for me jam jar?"

Von Trappe – CRAP. (Origins; surname from Sound of Music)
1D. "He's got so much von trappe, there's no room for his kids."

W

Wallace & Grommit – VOMIT. (Origins; British cartoon)
1D. "I love Sunday morning strolls, pavements covered in Wallace an' Grommit."

Wally Grout – SHOUT, (turn to buy drinks). (Origins; Australian cricketer)
2D. "It's your wally, Steve, I'll have a uri."

Wally's Scarf – LAUGH. (Origins; Cartoon character)
2D. "Leicester win the league? He's having a wally."

Walnut Whip – TRIP, (on drugs). (Origins; British confectionery)
1D. "I'm on the wagon for a while, Jim. Real bad walnut whip last time."

Walter Anchor – WANKER.
2D. "I made a complete walter of myself last week at the pub."

Walter Mitty – KITTY. (Origins; fictional character)
1D. "After Pingy died, I couldn't look at another walter mitty."

Walter Mitty – TITTY, (breast). (Origins; fictional character)
2D. "That new assistant's got a lovely set of walters."

Wankers Cramp – TRAMP, (hobo).
1D. "There's a new bunch of wankers cramps up town, I reckon they're jam rolls."

Watch & Chain – BRAIN.
1D. "Look at the whole team, not a watch an' chain between 'em."

Watford Gap – CRAP. (Origins; area in England)
1D. "What a bunch of watford gap. 'Ammers haven't won in four weeks."

Wayne Rooney – LOONY. (Origins; English footballer)
2D. "Don't give Dave another drink; he'll go all wayne on me."

Weakest Link – DRINK. (Origins; TV game show)
3D. "I'm going for an Anne Robinson on Saturday, not been out all week." (the UK host)

Weasel & Stoat – COAT.
2D. "Damn, I left my weasel in the pub last night."

Weasel & Stoat – THROAT.
1D. "Too much shouting at the footy, got a sore weasel and stoat this morning."

Weaver's Chair – PRAYER.
2D. "Look at Alec an' the barmaid; he hasn't got a weaver's of getting into her alans."

Weeping Willow – PILLOW.
2D. "I need a new weeping, this one's falling apart."

West End Thespian – LESBIAN, (gay).
2D. "She's a gorgeous girl but she is west end, an' no mistake."

West Ham Reserves – NERVES. (Origins; West Ham football Club, right smack in the middle of Cockney territory)
2D. "Look at 'is 'ands shake; 'e's got a bad case of the west 'am's."

Westminster Abbey – SHABBY. (Origins; Britian's biggest abbey)
1D. "London's looking a bit westminster abbey since the Olympics."

Westminster Bank – WANK, (masturbate).
2D. "Do I Westminster? Of course I do, everybody does."

Weston Super-Mare – NIGHTMARE. (Origins; seaside resort in North Somerset)
2D. I went for a job interview last week; it was a total weston super."

Wet & Wild – CHILD.
1D. "Look at that wet 'n' wild, I'd give him a spank if I were 'is dad."

Wet & Damp – TRAMP.
2D. "I felt sorry for the wet on the pub doorstep, gave him a godiva."

Whisky & Soda – SKODA, (Russian cheap car).
1D. "He drives a whisky an' soda, so he's probably better off by bus."

Whisky & Soda – VODA, (brand of mobile phone).
2D. "I don't like whisky at all, their customer service is totally pony."

Whistle & Flute – SUIT.
2D. "What do ye think of the new whistle; made to measure up town."

White Mice – ICE.
1D. "Stick a dod of white mice in, will ya, kinda hot out here."

Widow Twanky – HANKY. (Origins; pantomime character)
2D. "Pass me a widow, this films getting to me."

William Pitt – SHIT. (Origins; British Prime Minister)
2D. "Country's all went to william since they opened the chunnel."

Willy Wonka – PLONKER, (idiot). (Origins; Roald Dahl character)
2D. "Don't be a willy, Rodney."

Wilson Picket – TICKET. (Origins; American singer)
2D. "I'd love to travel to Australia, but I can't afford the wilsons."

Wind & Kite – WEB SITE.
1D. "Got meself a wind an' kite for me model airplane hobby."

Wind Do Twirl – FINE GIRL.
2D. "Oh, look at that wind-do; she's a cracker."
(OLD; Included in Hotten's 1858 Rhyming Slang Glossary)

Windjammer – HAMMER.
1D. "I'd love to fix the door, love, but I can't find me windjammer."

Winnie the Pooh – SHOE. (Origins; A. E. Milne character)
2D. "Where's me winnies, love? The brown ones."

Winona Ryder – CIDER. (Origins; American actress)
2D. "Hey Barney? Can I get three pints of winona please?"

Wobbly Jelly – TELLY, (television).
2D. "Hand me the Radio Times so I see what's on the wobbly."

Wooden Pews – NEWS. (Origins; church seats)
1D. "Did you see the riots on the wooden pews yesterday?"

Wooden Plank – YANK.
2D. "Look at all the wooden tourists; you can spot them a mile off."

Wooly Hat & Scarf – LAUGH.
2D. "Oh, you gotta see him live; we wooly hatted all night."

Wooly Woofter – POOFTER, (homosexual).
2D. "You didn't know Sid was a wooly? Where you been?"

Wormwood Scrubs – PUB. (Origins; London Prison)
2D. "I'm off down the wormwood, catch you later."

Worzel Gummidge – RUMMAGE. (Origins; kids TV character)
1D. "I'm going into the attic for a worzel gummidge; I want to find the old photos."

Worzel Gummidge – SCRUMMAGE, (rugby melee). (Origins; kids TV character)
2D. "Oh it ended up in a big worzel; peelers called, the lot."

Wrigley's Gum – BUM.
1D. "Would you look at the wrigleys gum on that bird at the bar."

Wyatt Earp – BURP. (Origins; American wild west character)
1D. "And then I wyatt earped in front of the vicar!"

Y

Yarmouth Bloater – MOTOR, (car). (Origins; a species of fish)
2D. "I got meself a new yarmouth yesterday, lovely jubbly."

Veronica Lake – BRAKE.
2D. "Honestly officer, I tried to stop, but the veronicas failed."

Yogi Bear – HAIR. (Origins; cartoon character)
2D. "Going uptown to get me yogi trimmed, big day on Saturday."

You & Me – TEA.
1D. "Good to see ya, Colin. Fancy a cup o' you and me?"

You Must – CRUST.
1D. "Best bit of the bread, the you musts!"

YoYo Ma – CAR. (Origins; American cellist)
1D. "I'm off to Brighton in me new yo yo ma."

Yul Brynner – DINNER. (Origins; Russian actor)
1D. "I'm hank and lee, can't wait for me yul brynner."

Z

Zachary Scotts – TROTS, (diarrhea). (Origins; American actor)
1D. "Bad curry last night, got me a case of the zachary scotts."

Zig & Zag – SHAG. (Origins; TV puppets)
1D. "Oh, I'm gaggin' on a zig 'n' zag, it's been months!"

Zippy & Bungle – JUNGLE. (Origins; TV puppets)
1D. "Watch how you go in the city, Elaine, it's a zippy an' bungle out there."

PART TWO: ENGLISH TO COCKNEY

NUMBERS

1st (Uni degree)	Geoff Hurst
2nd (Uni degree)	Desmond Tutu
2:2 (Uni degree)	Desmond Tutu
3rd (Uni degree)	Dickie Bird
3rd (Uni degree)	Douglas Hurd
8th (of coke)	Garden Gate
16th (of coke)	Louis the 16th
22	Dinky Do
66	Clickety Click

A

Advice	Lump of Ice
Aids	Ace of Spades
Aids	Bucket & Spades
Air Raid Shelter	Helter-Skelter
Alarm	Do No Harm
All Dayer	Leo Sayer
All Dayer	Gary Player
All Nighter	Jet Fighter
Alone	Jack Jones
Alone	Pat Malone
Alone	Toblerone
Alone	Todd Sloan
Appendix	Jimmy Hendrix
Apple	Sistine Chapel
Arc (theater light)	Finsbury Park
Arm	Chalk Farm
Army	Daft and Barmy
Army	Kate Carney
Arris (arse)	Rolf Harris
Arrow	Cock Sparrow
Arse	April in Paris
Arse	Aristotle
Arse	Blade of Grass
Arse	Bottle and Glass
Arse	Khyber Pass
Arse	Myleen Klass
Arse (Arris)	Rolf Harris
Arse	Tijuana Brass
Arsehole	Elephant & Castle
Arsehole	Jam Roll
Arsehole	Merry Old Soul
Ass	Hagen Daas
Aunt	Mrs. Chant

B

Baboon	Geoff Hoon
Baby	Basin of Gravy
Bacon	Godforsaken
Back	Cadburys Snack
Back	Cilla Black
Back	Fleetwood Mac
Back	Hammer and Tack
Back	Hat Rack
Back	Hay Stack
Back	Jumping Jack
Back	Roof Rack
Back	Union Jack
Backy (tobacco)	Nose-My
Bad	Alan Ladd
Bad	Shepherd's Plaid
Bad	Sorry and Sad
Badger	Dennis & Gnasher
Bad House	Flea and Louise
Baker	Long Acre
Bald	Bertie Auld
Ball	Egyptian Hall
Balls (testicles)	Albert Hall's
Balls (testicles)	Berlin Walls
Balls (testicles)	Cobbler's Awls
Balls (testicles)	Coffee Stalls
Balls (testicles)	Davina McCalls
Balls (testicles)	Market Stalls
Balls (testicles)	Niagara Falls
Balls (testicles)	Orchestra Stalls
Balls (testicles)	Town Halls
Balti (curry)	Basil Fawlty
Banana	Gertie Gitana
Banger (sausage)	Bernard Langer

Bank	Armitage Shank
Bank	Cab Rank
Bank	Iron Tank
Bank	J. Arthur Rank
Bank	Pedal & Crank
Bank	Rattle and Clank
Bank	Sherman Tank
Bank	Tin Tank
Bank	Tommy Tank
Banks	Ham Shanks
Bar (pub)	Bazaar
Bar (pub)	Jack Tar
Bar (pub)	Near and Far
Bar (pub)	Ringo Starr
Barber	Dover Harbour
Barmy	Dad's Army
Barmy	Montey's Army
Barmy	Salvation Army
Barnet	Alf Garnet
Barrow	Bow & Arrow
Barrow	Cock Sparrow
Bath	Laugh
Bath	Steffi Graf
Battery	Charm & Flattery
Battery	Tony Slattery
Beak	Bubble and Squeak
Beak (magistrate)	Once a Week
Beard	Strange & Weird
Beast	Bag of Yeast
Beating (assault)	Unscheduled Meeting
Beaut	John Deut
Beauty	Tutti Frutti
Beaver (vaginal hair)	Sigourney Weaver
Bed	Fakey Ned
Bed	Scratch Yer Head
Bed	Skein of Thread
Bed	Uncle Ned
Bed	Uncle Ted
Beef	Itchy Teeth

Beef	Stop Thief
Beer	King Lear
Beer	Pig's Ear
Beer	Richard Gere
Beers	Brittney Spears
Beers	Ray Mears
Beggar	Ewan McGregor
Beggar	Ham & Egger
Beginner	Lilley & Skinner
Belch	Raquel Welch
Believe	Adam and Eve
Believe	Christmas Eve
Bell	Aunt Nell
Bell (to call)	Hair Gel
Belly	Auntie Nellie
Belly	Derby Kelly
Belly	Matthew Kelly
Belly	New Delhi
Bench	Judy Dench
Bender (homosexual)	Leo Fender
Bender (homosexual)	Love Me Tender
Bent (criminal)	Stoke on Trent
Bent (homosexual)	Behind with the Rent
Bent (homosexual)	Clark Kent
Bent (homosexual)	Duke of Kent
Bent (homosexual)	Mailed and Sent
Bent (homosexual)	Stoke on Trent
Best	Mae West
Bet (wager)	House to Let
Bet (wager)	Jumbo Jet
Beverage	Dame Edna Everage
Beverage	Edna Everage
Bevvy (drink)	Don Revie
Bible	Slander & Libel
Biggun	Barry McGuigan
Bigot	Lester Piggot
Bike	Alibi Ike
Bike	Clever Mike
Bike	Dick Van Dyke

Bill (statement)	Beecham's Pill
Bill (statement)	Jack and Jill
Bill (statement)	Jimmy Hill
Bill (statement)	Muswell Hill
Bill (statement)	Pitch & Fill
Bint (girl, woman)	Gilly Mint
Bird (girl, woman)	Lemon Curd
Bird (girl, woman)	Shaken Not Stirred
Bint (girl, woman)	Polo Mint
Bird (girl, woman)	Richard the Third
Bitches	Ronald Riches
Bitchy	Lionel Ritchie
Bitter (beer)	Apple Fritter
Bitter (beer)	Gary Glitter
Bitter (beer)	Giggle and Titter
Bitter (beer)	Habitual Knitter
Bitter (beer)	Kitty Litter
Bitter (beer)	Laugh & Titter
Bitter (beer)	Tex Ritter
Blade	Shovel & Spade
Blazer	Razor
Blind	All Behind
Blind	Bacon Rind
Bloke	Heap of Coke
Bloke	Lump Of Coke
Blonde	Magic Wand
Blood	Roy Hudd
Blotto	Santas Grotto
Blower (telephone)	Lawn Mower
Blower (telephone)	Percy Thrower
Blowy	David Bowie
B.O. (body odor)	Riddick Bowe
Boat	Nanny Goat
Bob (shilling)	Touch Me on the Knob
Bog	Boss Hogg
Bog	Cadbury's Log
Bog	Cat & Dog
Bog (toilet)	Kermit the Frog
Bog	Spotty Dog

Boil	Arthur Conan Doyle
Boil	Can of Oil
Boil	Conan Doyle
Boil	Paraffin Oil
Bollocks	Flowers & Frolics
Bollocks	Hydraulics
Bollocks	Jackson Pollock
Bolt (run away)	Harry Holt
Bombs	Derry and Toms
Bombs	Uncle Toms
Boner (erection)	Kerry Katona
Bones	Sticks & Stones
Bones	Tom Jones
Bong	Ding Dong
Bonkers (crazy)	Marbles and Conkers
Boobies	Red Red Rubies
Book	Captain Cook
Book	Captain Hook
Book	Fish Hook
Book	Jackdaw and Rook
Book	Joe Hook
Bookie (betting shop)	Biscuit & Cookie
Bookie (betting shop)	Cream Cookie
Boots	Bamboo Shoots
Boots	Daisy Roots
Boots	German Flutes
Booze	Penelope Cruz
Booze	River Ouse
Booze	Tom Cruise
Boozer (pub)	All Time Loser
Boozer (pub)	Battle Cruiser
Boozer (pub)	Cabin Cruiser
Boozer (pub)	German Cruiser
Boozer (pub)	Perpetual Loser
Boss	Dead Loss
Boss	Joe Goss
Boss	Pitch and Toss
Bottle	Aristotle
Bottle	Jerry Cottle

Bouncing Cheque (Check)	Rubber Gregory
Bowler	Bottle of Cola
Box	Charles Fox
Box	Darky Cox
Boy	Rob Roy
Bra	Master McGrath
Bra	Tung Chee Hwa
Braces	Airs and Graces
Braces	Ascot Races
Braces	Epsom Races
Brain	Watch & Chain
Brains	Down The Drains
Brake	Veronica Lake
Brakes	Francis Drakes
Brandy	Andy Pandy
Brandy	Fine and Dandy
Brandy	Jack the Dandy
Brandy	Mahatma Ghandi
Brandy	Sugar Candy
Bread	Uncle Fred
Bread (money)	Poppy Red
Bread (money)	Right Said Fred
Bread and Dripping	Doctor Crippen
Breast	East West
Breasts	Georgie Bests
Breath	King Death
Breath	Life & Death
Breath	True 'Til Death
Brogues	Kylie Minogues
Broke	Coals & Coke
Broke (financial)	Hearts of Oak
Brokers	Engineers & Stokers
Brother	Manhole Cover
Brother	One and the Other
Brown	Camden Town
Brown	Circus and Clown
Bruise	Tom Cruise
Brush	Ian Rush
Brussels	Cockle & Mussels

Brussel Sprout	Doubt
Brussel Sprout	Shout
Bug	Steam Tug
Bullshitter	Little Critter
Bum	Bottle of Rum
Bum	Deaf & Dumb
Bum	Fife & Drum
Bum	Kingdom Come
Bum	Queen Mum
Bum	Tom Thumb
Bum	Wrigley's Gum
Bummer	John Selwyn Gummer
Bunion	Sage & Onion
Bunion	Spanish Onion
Bunk (bed)	Pineapple Chunk
Burger King	Itchy Ring
Burp	Wyatt Earp
Burst (urinate)	Geoff Hurst
Bus (coach)	So Say All Of Us
Bus (coach)	Uncle Gus
Businesses	Bees Knees
Bust	Prince's Trust
Bus Timetable	Aesop's Fable
Bustle	Lord John Russell
Butter	Johnny Rutter
Butter	Mutter & Stutter
Butter	Pull Down The Shutter
Butter	Stammer and Stutter
Butter	Talk and Mutter

C

Cab (taxi)	Andy McNab
Cab (taxi)	Bob McNab
Cab (taxi)	Flounder & Dab
Cab (taxi)	Left Jab
Cab (taxi)	Sherbet Dab
Cab (taxi)	Smash & Grab
Cabbage	Joe Savage
Cadge (borrow)	Coat & Badge
Café	Colonel Gadaffi
Café (caff)	Riff Raff
Cake	Joe Blake
Cake	Sexton Blake
Can (beer)	Jackie Chan
Cans (headphones)	Desperate Dans
Cancel	Nigel Mansell
Cancer	Private Dancer
Cancer	Sunny Dancer
Candle	Jack Randle
Candle	Harry Randall
Candle	Saucepan Handle
Cans (headphones)	Desperate Dans
Cap	Butter Flap
Caps	Baby Paps
Cappuccino	Al Pachino
Car	Danny Marr
Car	Jam Jar
Car	Kareem Abdul Jabbar
Car	La-Di-Da
Car	Leamington Spa
Car	Near & Far
Car	YoYo Ma
Card	Bladder of Lard
Cardy (cardigan)	Linda Lusardi

Car Key	Fergal Sharkey
Carling (lager)	Roger Starling
Cash	Arthur Ashe
Cash	Bangers and Mash
Cash	Crosby, Stills & Nash
Cash	Dot & Dash
Cash	Harry Nash
Cash	Jumping Jack Flash
Cash	Oscar Asche
Cash	Pie & Mash
Cash	Sausage and Mash
Cash	Slap Dash
Cat	Cooking Fat
Cat	This & That
Catholic	Cow's Lick
Cell	Flowery Dell
Chair	Fred Astaire
Chair	Lion's Lair
Chair	Tony Blair
Chairs	Owen Nares
Chalk	Duke of York
Chancer	Ballet Dancer
Chancer	Bengal Lancer
Change	Rifle Range
Chapel	Chipped Apple
Chapel	Pineapple
Charlie(cocaine)	Andy Farley
Charlie(cocaine)	Bob Marley
Charlie(cocaine)	Boutros Boutros Gali
Charlie(cocaine)	Gianluca Vialli
Charlie(cocaine)	Lemon Barley
Charlie (cocaine)	Oats & Barley
Charlie(cocaine)	Salvador Dali
Charmer	Jeffrey Dahmer
Chassis	Shirley Bassey
Chat	Bowler Hat
Chat	Chew the Fat
Chat	Frank & Pat
Chat	Top Hat

Cheap	Meryl Streep
Cheat	Shredded Wheat
Cheating	Angus Deayton
Cheating	Ronan Keating
Cheek	Hide and Seek
Cheek	Once a Week
Cheese	Bended Knees
Cheese	Evening Breeze
Cheese	John Cleese
Cheese	Stand at Ease
Cheque	Ant and Dec(s)
Cheque	Bushel & Peck
Cheque	Goose's Neck
Cheque	Gregory Peck
Cheque	Jeff Beck
Cheque	Nervous Wreck
Chest	Bird's Nest
Chest	Bristol & West
Chest	George Best
Chest	Pants and Vest
Chicken	Charlie Dicken
Chicken Korma	Jean & Norma
Chicken Jahlfrezi	Duke & Daisy
Child	Wet & Wild
Child Molester	Charlie Chester
Child Molester	Uncle Fester
Chilly	Uncle Billy
Chin	Biscuit Tin
Chin	Dusty Bin
Chin	Errol Flynn
Chin	Gunga Din
Chin	Harry Lin
Chink (Chinese)	Fizzy Drink
Chink (Chinese)	Kitchen Sink
Chink (Chinese)	Limehouse Link
Chink (Chinese)	Missing Link
Chink (Chinese)	Rink-a-dink
Chink (Chinese)	Tiddley Wink
Chip	Jockey Whip

Chips (French fries)	Hairy Nips
Chips (French fries)	Jockey Whips
Choice	Rolls Royce
Choker (freeze up)	Bram Stoker
Chopper (penis)	Gobstopper
Chuckle	Belt Buckle
Chum	Fruit Gum
Chunder (Aus; throw up)	Stevie Wonder
Church	Lean And Lurch
Church	Left in the Lurch
Cider	Deep Sea Glider
Cider	Easy Rider
Cider	Knight Rider
Cider	Sean Ryder
Cider	Sue Ryder
Cider	Winona Ryder
Cigar	La-di-da
Circle	Angela Merkel
Civilian	Samba Brazilian
Clanger (mistake)	Coat Hanger
Claret (blood)	Boiled Beef & Carrot
Class	Bottle and Glass
Clean	Billy Jean
Clink (jail)	Kitchen Sink
Clock	Dickory Dock
Clock	Tick Tock
Clown	Charlie Brown
Clown	Gordon Brown
Clucking (craving)	Donald Ducking
Clue	Danny LaRue
Clue	Pot of Glue
Clue	Scooby-Doo
Clue	Tube of Glue
Clue	Vindaloo
Clutch	Starsky & Hutch
Coach	Cockroach
Coat	All Afloat
Coat	Nanny Goat
Coat	Quaker Oat

Coat	Weasel and Stoat
Cocaine	Mary Jane
Cock (penis)	Ayers Rock
Cock (penis)	Blackpool Rock
Cockney	David Hockney
Cockney slang	Chitty Chitty Bang Bang
Cockney Slang	Matheson Lang
Code	A La Mode
Coffee	Bill Roffie
Coffee	Chewy Toffee
Coffee	Everton Toffee
Coffee	Molten Toffee
Coffee	Sticky Toffee
Cold	Boris the Bold
Cold	Cheltenham Bold
Cold	Potatoes in the Mould
Cold	Soldiers Bold
Cold	Stevey Bold
Cold	Taters in the Mould
Collar	Holler Boys Holler
Collar	Oxford Scholar
Come	Rattle & Hum
Computer	Car & Scooter
Computer	Pistol & Shooter
Conk (nose)	Glass of Plonk
Contraceptive (pill)	Jack & Jill
Cook	Babbling Brook
Cool	Harry Kewell
Coon (black person)	Alfie Moon
Coon (black person)	Egg & Spoon
Coon (black person)	Silvery Moon
Coon (black person)	Silvery Spoon
Cop	John Hop
Cop It Hot	Cop a flower pot
Copper (police)	Grasshopper
Copper (police)	Space Hopper
Coppers (police)	Bottles and Stoppers
Coppers (police)	Joe Hoppers
Cork	Duke of York

Corner	Johnnie Horner
Corner	Little Jack Horner
Costermonger, (seller)	Split Asunder
Couch (sofa)	Kangaroo Pouch
Cough	Boris Karloff
Cough	Darren Gough
Cough	Vincent van Gogh
Cousin	Baker's Dozen
Cow	Chairman Mao
Coward	Frankie Howard
Crabs (pubic lice)	Andy McNabs
Crabs (pubic lice)	Dibs & Dabs
Crabs (pubic lice)	Jim Bob Babs
Crabs (pubic lice)	Marble Slabs
Crabs (pubic lice)	Sandy McNabs
Crap	Jamie Redknapp
Crap	Horse & Trap
Crap	Macca
Crap	Pony and Trap
Crap	Von Trappe
Crap	Watford Gap
Crash	Sausage and Mash
Crazy	Chicken Jalfrezi
Crazy	Gert & Daisy
Crazy	Patrick Swayze
Crime	Lemon & Lime
Cripple	Raspberry Ripple
Crook	Babbling Brook
Crust	You Must
Crutch	Double Dutch
Crutch (crotch)	Rabbit Hutch
Crutch (crotch)	Screaming Lord Such
Cry	Drip Dry
Cry	Pipe in Your Eye
Crystal Palace	Screaming Alice
Cuddle	Mix and Muddle
C*nt	Anthony Blunt
C*nt	Back and Front
C*nt	Back to Front

C*nt	Bargain Hunt
C*nt	Berkshire Hunt
C*nt	Charlie Hunt
C*nt	Ethan Hunt
C*nt	Eyes Front
C*nt	Gareth Hunt
C*nt	Grumble and Grunt
C*nt	James Blunt
C*nt	James Hunt
C*nt	Jeremy Hunt
C*nt	Jo Blunt
C*nt	Oxford Punt
C*nt	Shirt Front
C*nt	Shop Front
C*nt	Struggle and Grunt
Cupboard	Mother Hubbard
Cupboard	Old Mother Hubbard
Cup of Tea	Jay Z
Curry	Andy Murray
Curry	Bill Murray
Curry	Fred MacMurray
Curry	Ruby Murray
Curry	Shit in a Hurry
Curtains	Richard Burtons
Customs & Excise	Church Boys
Cycle (menstrual)	George Michael

D

Daft	Fore & Aft
Dance	Isle of France
Dance	Jack Palance
Dance	Kick and Prance
Dandy	Andy Pandy
Danger	Stewart Granger
Dark	Gorky Park
Dark	Jurassic Park
Darkey (black)	Fergal Sharkey
Darlin'	Barney Marlin
Darlin'	Briney Marlin
Darts (pub game)	Martial Arts
Daughter	Bottle of Porter
Daughter	Bricks and Mortar
Daughter	Bucket of Water
Daughter	Didn't oughta
Daughter	Lamb to the Slaughter
Day	Load of Hay
Dead	Born & Bred
Dead	Brown Bread
Dead	Father Ted
Dead	Hovis Bread
Dead	Right said Fred
Dead	Simon Said
Deaf	Corned Beef
Deaf	Mutt and Jeff
Deal	Jellied Eel
Decks (turntables)	Posh 'n Becks
Denial	River Nile
Dense (stupid)	Garden Fence
Devil	Henry Neville
Diarrhea	Tia Maria
Dice	Choc Ice

Dice	Rats & Mice
Dick (penis)	Candle Wick
Dick (penis)	Hampton Wick
Dick (penis)	Lolly Lick
Dick (penis)	Three Card Trick
Dictionary	Tom, Dick and Harry
Diet	Brixton Riot
Dinner	Frank Skinner
Dinner	Glorious Sinner
Dinner	Jim Skinner
Dinner	John Skinner
Dinner	Lilly and Skinner
Dinner	Michael Winner
Dinner	Yul Brynner
Dirty	Two Thirty
Doctor	Gamble & Procter
Doddle (easy)	Glenn Hoddle
Dog	Cherry Hogg
Dog	London Fog
Dole (welfare)	Adrian Mole
Dole (welfare)	De La Soul
Dole (welfare)	Ear'ole (Ear Hole)
Dole (welfare)	George Cole
Dole (welfare)	Jam Roll
Dole (welfare)	Nat King Cole
Dole (welfare)	Old King Cole
Dole (welfare)	Rock and Roll
Dole (welfare)	Sausage Roll
Dollar	Oxford Scholar
Door	Henry Moore
Door	Roger Moore
Door	Rory O'Moore
Dope (marijuana)	Bob Hope
Dope (marijuana)	Slippery Slope
Do So	Robinson Crusoe
Dose	Half a Gross
Doss	Hugo Boss
Double	Barney Rubble
Dough (money)	Russell Crowe

Dozen	Country Cousin
Draft	George Raft
Drama	Bananarama
Draught	George Raft
Draw (tie)	Dennis Law
Draw (cannabis)	Jack McGraw
Draw (cannabis)	Jack Straw
Drawers	Early Doors
Drink	Cuff Link
Drink	Ice Rink
Drink	Kitchen Sink
Drink	Lily the Pink
Drink	Tiddly Wink
Drink	Tumble Down the Sink
Drink	Weakest Link
Drive	Bee Hive
Drugs	Fur Rugs
Drugs	Kisses & Hugs
Drugs	Persian Rugs
Drugs	Spark Plugs
Drunk	Elephant's Trunk
Drunk	Mickey Monk
Drunk	Pineapple Chunk
Dumb	Tom Thumb
Dump (shit)	Camel's Hump
Dump (shit)	Donald Trump
Dump (shit)	Foot Pump
Dump (shit)	Forrest Gump
Dump (shit)	Gravy Lump
Dump (shit)	Ten Ounce Rump
Dwarf	Canary Wharf
Dyke (Lesbian)	Magnus Pike
Dyke (Lesbian)	Mountain Bike
Dyke (Lesbian)	Raleigh Bike
Dyke (Lesbian)	Rusty Spike
Dyke (Lesbian)	Three Wheel Trike

E

Eager	Christian Ziege
Ear	Bottle of Beer
Early	Liz Hurley
Earner	Anthea Turner
Earner	Bunsen Burner
Ear	King Lear
Ears	Britney Spears
Ears	Donald Peers
Ears	Lords & Peers
Ears	Ten Speed Gears
Easy	Bright & Breezy
Easy	Ham & Cheesy
Easy	Lemon Squeezy
Ecstasy	Bumble Bee
Egg	Borrow & Beg
Egg	Clothes Peg
Eighth	Henry the Eighth
Email	Alexei Sayle
Email	Holy Grail
Email	Jimmy Nail
Engineer	German Beer
Engineer	Ginger Beer
Erection	Standing Election
Evening Post	Beans on Toast
Evens (betting term)	Kirk Stevens
Evens (betting term)	Major Stevens
Evens (betting term)	Shakin Stevens
Exam	Green Eggs & Ham
Excited	Sheffield United
Eyes	Mince Pies
Eyes	Puddings and Pies

F

Fable	Bus Timetable
Fable	Railway Timetable
Face	Bib & Brace
Face	Boat Race
Face	Brendan Grace
Face	Cod & Plaice
Face	Chevy Chase
Face	Drum & Bass
Face	Hale & Pace
Face	Jem Mace
Face	Ricky Gervais
Facts	Brass Tacks
Fag (cigarette)	Cough and Drag
Fag (cigarette)	Harry Wragg
Fag	Jet Lag
Fag (cigarette)	Melvyn Bragg
Fag (cigarette)	Oily Rag
Fag (cigarette)	Spit & a Drag
Fag (cigarette)	Toe Rag / Tow Rag
Faggot (gay man)	Inspector Taggart
Fair Enough	Furry Muff
Fair Enough	Hairy Muff
Fairy	Canary
Fairy	Julian Clairy
Fake	Ricky Lake
Fake	Sexton Blake
Fan	Frying Pan
Fanny	Auntie Annie
Fanny (sex)	Jackie Danny
Fanny (backside)	Jack and Danny
Fanny (sex)	Shereen Nanjiani
Farden (farthing)	Covent Garden
Fare	Grey Mare

Farmer	Arnold Palmer
Farrahs (trousers)	Bow and Arrows
Fart	Cupid's Dart
Fart	D'Oyly Carte
Fart	Horse and Cart
Fart	Jam Tart
Fart	Joe Hart
Fart	Orson Cart
Fart	Raspberry Tart
Farting	George Martin
Fat	Postman Pat
Favour	Cheesy Quaver
Fax	Nails & Tacks
Feel	Orange Peel
Feel	Jellied Eel
Feet	Dogs Meat
Feet	Plates of Meat
Fever	Robinson & Cleaver
Fib	Maurice Gibb
Fibs (lies)	Scott Gibbs
Fiddle	Hey Diddle Diddle
Fields	Live Eels
Fifty	Nifty
Fight	Read and Write
Fighter	Typewriter
Fine	Calvin Klein
Fine Girl	Wind Do Twirl
Finger	Mal Maninga
Fingers	Bell Ringers
Fingers	Longers & Lingers
Fingers	Melody Lingers
Fire	I Desire
Fire	Jeremiah
Fire	Obediah
First Uni degree	Damien Hirst
First Uni degree	Geoff Hurst
Fish	Lilian Gish
Fist	Oliver Twist
Fit	Brad Pitt

Five	Jack's Alive
Fiver (£5 note)	Deep Sea Diver
Fiver (£5 note)	Lady Godiva
Fiver (£5 note)	Minnie Driver
Fiver (£5 note)	Muff Diver
Fiver (£5 note)	Pam Shriver
Fiver (£5 note)	Pearl Diver
Fiver (£5 note)	Sky Diver
Fiver (£5 note)	Taxi Driver
Fix	Hans Blix
Fix	Tom Mix
Fix	Two & Six
Flag (fourpence)	Castle Rag
Flares (trousers)	Lionel Blairs
Flash (natty)	Harry Dash
Flash	Lemon & Dash
Flat	French Plait
Fleas	Jenny Lee
Flicks (cinema)	Stevie Nicks
Flies	Morecombe & Wise
Flight	Read and Write
Floor	Rory O'Moore
Flowers	April Showers
Flowers	Early Hour(s)
Flu	Alan Pardew
Flu-ey	Hong Kong Fooey
Flush (having money)	Snow & Slush
Fly	Steak & Kidney Pie
Flying Squad	Sweeney Todd
Foil	Jimmy Boyle
Food	In the Nude
Fool	Garden Tool
Fool	Lump of School
Fool	Two Foot Rule
Footie (football)	Pirate Booty
Footpath	Oats and Chaff
Fork	Duke of York
Fork	Roast Pork
Four of a Kind	Cheese Rind

Freak	Ancient Greek
Freezer	Bacardi Breezer
Frenchies	Park Benches
Fridge	Lightning Ridge
Fridge	Stamford Bridge
Frown	Barry Brown
Frown	Jammed Brown
Fruit of the Loom	Mop & Broom
F*ck	Aylesbury Duck
F*ck	Bombay Duck
F*ck	Cattle Truck
F*ck	Crispy Duck
F*ck	Daffy Duck
F*ck	Donald Duck
F*ck	Farmers Truck
F*ck	Friar Tuck
F*ck	Fuzzy Duck
F*ck	Hockey Puck
F*ck	Push in the Truck
F*ck	Rubber Duck
F*ck	Tom & Huck
F*ck	Uncle Buck
F*cked	Holborn Viaduct
F*cked	Lady Mucked
F*cker	Chicken Plucker
F*cker	Darius Rucker
F*cker	Tommy Tucker
F*cking Hell	Clucking Bell
F*ck Her	Tommy Tucker
F*ck Off	Vincent van Gogh
F*ck It	Bayne & Duckett
F*ck It	Charlie Bucket
F*ck It	Rusty Bucket
F*ck It	Spade & Bucket
F*ck It	Tear in a Bucket
Full of Shit	Pirate Ship
Fun	Currant Bun
Function	Spaghetti Junction
Funny	Easter Bunny

G

Gal	Bob, My Pal
Gamble	Glen Campbell
Gamble	Naomi Campbell
Gamble	Sol Campbell
Garage	Steve Claridge
Garden	Bin Laden
Gargle (drunk)	Arthur Scargill
Gash (vagina)	Kate Nash
Gay (homosexual)	Bale of Hay
Gay (homosexual)	Darren Day
Gay (homosexual)	Doctor Dre
Gay (homosexual)	Doris Day
Gay (homosexual)	Finlay Quaye
Gay (homosexual)	First of May
Gay (homosexual)	Fromage Frais
Gay (homosexual)	Home & Away
Gay (homosexual)	Julian Ray
Gay (homosexual)	Milky Way
Gay (homosexual)	Oyster Bay
Gay (homosexual)	Peter Kay
Gay (homosexual)	Ted Ray
Gear	King Lear
Geezer	Bacardi Breezer
Geezer	Fridge Freezer
Geezer	Ice Cream Freezer
Geezer	Julius Caesar
Geezer	Lemon Squeezer
German	Ben Sherman
Ghost	Pillar and Post
Giggles	Flight Lieutenant Biggles
Gin	Ann Boleyn
Gin	Brian O'linn
Gin	Mother's Ruin

Gin	Needle and Pin
Gin	Nose and Chin
Gin	Thick & Thin
Gin	Vera Lynn
Gin & Tonic	Philharmonic
Girl	Cadbury Swirl
Girl	Ocean Pearl
Girl	Mother of Pearl
Girl	Twist and Twirl
Girl Guide	Blushing Bride
Giro (dole payment)	Man from Cairo
Giro (dole payment)	Nightboat to Cairo
Git (bad person)	Strawberry Split
Glass	Hackney Marsh
Gloves	Turtle Dove's
Go	Scapa Flow
Goal	Sausage Roll
Gob (mouth)	Gang and Mob
Goggle box (TV)	Nervo & Knox
Good	Robin Hood
Gory	God's Glory
Gossip	Rex Mossop
Go to Sleep	Plough the Deep
Gout	In and Out
Gout	Twist & Shout
Gramme	Leg of Lamb
Grand (£1000)	Bag of Sand
Grand (£1000)	Rio Ferdinand
Grass	Ducks Arse
Grass	Ernie Marsh
Gravy	Army and Navy
Gravy	Merchant Navy
Gravy	Royal Navy
Greek	Bubble and Squeak
Greif	Lee van Cleef
Greif	Omar Sharif
Grouch	Peter Crouch
Ground	Penny a Pound
Ground	Tuppence a Pound

Grout	Salmon & Trout
Growler (vagina)	Arthur Fowler
Growler (vagina)	Pauline Fowler
Grumble	Rhubarb Crumble
Guilty	Clonakilty
Gullet	Ruud Hullit
Gut	King Tut
Guts	Fruit & Nuts
Guts (stomach)	Newington Butts
Gutter	Bread and Butter
Gym	Fatboy Slim

H

Haddock	Fanny Craddock
Hail	Jimmy Nail
Hair	Barnet Fair
Hair	Biffo the Bear
Hair	Bonney Fair
Hair	Fanny Blair
Hair	Fred Astaire
Hair	Tony Blair
Hair	Yogi Bear
Hairy	Bloody Mary
Half (a pint)	Cow and Calf
Ham	Uncle Sam
Hammer	Franz Klammer
Hammer	Windjammer
Hand	Ivory Band
Hand	Jimmy Shand
Hand	St. Martins-Le-Grand
Handkerchief	Charley Lancaster
Hands	Alice Bands
Hands	Brass Bands
Hands	Brighton Sands
Hands	Elastic Bands
Hands	German Bands
Hands	Jazz Bands
Handsome	Marilyn Manson
Handy	Jack & Dandy
Hangover	Ben Dover
Hanky	Widow Twanky
Hard (erection)	Marquis de Sade
Harsh	Jodie Marsh
Harsh	Kym Marsh
Harsh	Rodney Marsh
Hash	Jack Flash

Hash	Johnny Cash
Hat	Tit for Tat (Titfer)
Hazy	Riccardo Patrese
Head (Blow Job)	Blood Red
Head	Crust of Bread
Head	Loaf of Bread
Head	Lump of Lead
Head	Uncle Ned
Head (fellatio)	Blood Red
Head In (annoy)	Otis Reading
Heart	Horse & Cart
Heart	Jam Tart
Heart	Raspberry Tart
Heart	Strawberry Tart
Heater	Blue Peter
Hell	Ding Dong Bell
Hell	Gypsy Nell
Hemorrhoid	Clement Freud
Hemorrhoids	Emma Freuds
Hemp	Martin Kemp
Heroin	Vera Lynn
Hill	Jack and Jill
Hips	Fish & Chips
Hiss	Cuddle & Kiss
Hole (home)	Drum Roll
Hole (sex)	Nat King Cole
Home	Gates of Rome
Home	Pope in Rome
Home	Top of Rome
Homo (gay man)	Perry Como
Honours	Jimmy Connors
Hooter (nose)	Pea Shooter
Horse	Bottle of Sauce
Horse	Charing Cross
Host	Pillar and Post
Hot	Alan Knott
Hot	Auntie Dot
Hot	Peas in the Pot
House	Cat and Mouse

House	Mickey Mouse
House	Rat & Mouse
Howler (mistake)	Robbie Fowler
Hump (huff)	Donald Trump
Hump (huff)	Petrol Pump
Hymen	Bill Wyman
Hype (drug paraphernalia)	Sky the Wipe
Hyper	Billie Piper
Hyper	Pied Piper

I

Ice	Blind Mice
Ice	Vincent Price
Ice	White Mice
Incredible	Anchor Spreadable
Insane	David Blaine
Insane	John McCain
Insane	Saddam Hussein
Internet	Sportsman's Bet
Irish Stew	Bonnets So Blue

J

Jacket	AJ Hackett
Jacket	Desmond Hackett
Jacket	Grant Hackett
Jacket	Steam Packet
Jacket	Tennis Racquet
Jail	Bucket and Pail
Jail	Ginger Ale
Jail	Jimmy Nail
Jap	Bathroom Tap
Jap	Cheese Bap
Jap	Kitchen Tap
Jaw (chat)	Jackdaw
Jeans	Baked Beans
Jeans	Bethnal Greens
Jeans	Dixie Deans
Jeans	Harpers and Queens
Jeans	Milton Keynes
Jeans	Runner Beans
Jeans	Steve McQueens
Jehovah's (witness)	Vauxhall Novas
Jesus Christ	Cheese & Rice
Jew	Chelsea Blue
Jew	Five to Two
Jew	Four by Two
Jew	Stick of Glue
Jewelry	Tom Foolery
Jin (card game)	Sport And Win
Jive	Duck and Dive
Job	Corn on the Cob
Job	Dog's Knob
Job	Uncle Bob
Jock (Scot)	Sweaty Sock
Joke	Egg Yoke

Joke	Rum and Coke
Joker	Bram Stoker
Joker	Double Yoker
Journey	Burt & Ernie
Judge	Barnaby Rudge
Judge	Cadbury's Fudge
Judge	Chocolate Fudge
Judge	Inky Smudge
Jugs (breasts)	Carpets and Rugs
Jumper	Kuala Lumpur
Jungle	Zippy & Bungle

K

Kebab (shish kebab)	Phil Babb
Kebabs	Andy McNabs
Keek (peek, quick look)	Mozambique
Keen	James Dean
Keen	Torvill and Dean
Kettle	Hansel & Gretel
Kettle	Stinging Nettle
Key	Brenda Lee
Key	Vivian Lee
Keys	Bruce Lee's
Keys	Cheddar Cheese
Keys	Dancing Fleas
Keys	Honey Bees
Keys	John Cleese
Keys	Knobbly Knees
Keys	Macaroni Cheese
Keys	Mushy Peas
Kick-Off	Paul Dickov
Kid	Bin Lid
Kid	Saucepan Lid
Kidney	Bo Diddley
Kids	Dustbin Lids
Kids	God Forbids
Kids	Teapot Lids
Kids	Tin Lids
Kip (sleep)	Feather & Flip
Kip (sleep)	Jockey Whip
Kip (sleep)	Lucky Dip
Kip (sleep)	Sherbet Dip
Kipper	Jack the Ripper
Kiss	Heavenly Bliss
Kiss	Hit and Miss
Kiss	Snake's Hiss

Kitchen	Stop yer Bitchin'
Kitty (cash)	InterCity
Kitty	Walter Mitty
Khazi (toilet)	Ille Nastase
Knackered (tired)	Cream Crackered
Knackered (tired)	Christmas Crackered
Knackered (tired)	Kerry Packer (ed)
Knackers (testicles)	Cream Crackers
Knackers (testicles)	Jacobs Crackers
Knackers (testicles)	Michael Schumachers
Knees	Biscuits and Cheese
Knees	Chips & Peas
Knickers	Alan Whickers
Knife	Drum & Fife
Knob (penis)	Uncle Bob
Knock	Tick Tock
Knockers (boobs)	Mods & Rockers
Kraut (German)	In and Out
Kraut (German)	Rainbow Trout
Kraut (German)	Short & Stout
Kraut (German)	Twist & Shout

L

Labour (Exchange)	Beggar My Neighbour
Ladder	Bullock Bladder
Lager	Forsythe Saga
Lager	Mick Jagger
Lambourghini	Martini
Lardy	Oliver Hardy
Lark	Bushey Park
Lark (fun)	Tufnell Park
Late	Blind Date
Late	Terry Waite
Later	Alligator
Later	Baked Potat'er
Later	Christian Slater
Laters	Fish 'n' Taters
Lather	How's Your Father
Laugh	Bird Bath
Laugh	Bubble Bath
Laugh	Cow & Calf
Laugh	Giraffe
Laugh	Hat & Scarf
Laugh	Jimmy Giraffe
Laugh	Rory McGrath
Laugh	Steffi Graf
Laugh	Tin Bath
Laugh	Turkish Bath
Laugh	Wally's Scarf
Laugh	Wooly Hat & Scarf
Lavatory	Family Tree
Lazy	Patrick Swayze
Leeds	String of Beads
Legs	Bacon and Eggs
Legs	Clothes Pegs
Legs	Cribbage Pegs

Legs	Dolly Pegs
Legs	Ham & Eggs
Legs	Mumbley Pegs
Legs	Mystic Megs
Legs	Nutmegs
Legs	Pins and Pegs
Legs	Scotch Eggs
Legs	Scotch Pegs
Leicester Square	Euan Blair
Lesbian	West End Thespian
Level	Gary Neville
Liar	Barry Cryer
Liar	Bob Cryer
Liar	Deep Fat Fryer
Liar	Dunlop Tyre
Liar	Holy Friar
Lie	Cherry Pie
Lies	Pork Pies
Life	Nelly Duff
Life (term)	Porridge Knife
Light	Fly My Kite
Light (ale)	Day and Night
Light (beer)	Isle of Wight
Lighter	German Fighter
Lighter	Kung-fu Fighter
Lighter	Street Fighter
Line (of cocaine)	Patsy Cline
Lips	Filter Tips
Lisp	Quentin Crisp
Liver (meat)	Cheerful Giver
Liver	Swanee River
Liverpool	Poor Man's Gruel
Living Room	Bride & Groom
Loan Shark	Cutty Sark
Lodger	Artful Dodger
Loner	Jack Joner
Long	Donkey Kong
Look	Butcher's Hook
Look	Captain Cook

Look	Captain Hook
Looking Glass (mirror)	Snake In The Grass
Loony	Wayne Rooney
Loose	Mother Goose
Loot (money)	Fibre of your fabric
Lose	Tom Cruise
Lost	Jonathan Ross'ed
Lost	Kate Mossed
Lot (a share)	Hopping Pot
Louder	Beecham's Powder
Love	Push & Shove
Love	Rubber Glove
Love	Turtle Dove
Love Handle	Derek Randall
Lover	Danny Glover
Lover	Funk Soul Brother
Luck	Donald Duck
Luck	Friar Tuck
Lug (ear)	Toby Jug
Lunch	Brady Bunch
Lunch	Kidney Punch

M

Mad	Mum and Dad
Maggie Thatcher	Manky Snatcher
Magistrate	Garden Gate
Mail	British Rail
Maltesers	Small Geezers
Man of the World	Flag Unfurled
Marble Mason	Sugar Basin
Marge (margarine)	Little & Large
Mark	Finsbury Park
Marker	Ronnie Barker
Marriage	Horse and Carriage
Married	Cash and Carried
Married	Cut & Carried
Mason	David Jason
Master	Lath and Plaster
Matches	Cuts and Scratches
Mate	China Plate
Mate	Dinner Plate
Mate	Empire State
Mate	Garden Gate
Mate	Paper Plate
Mates	Gareth Gates
Mean	Sean Bean
Meat Pie	Dog's Eye
Medecin	Thomas Edison
Meetin' (meeting)	Buster Keaton
Meeting	Central Heating
Meeting	Ronan Keating
Memory	Dick Emery
Mental(crazy)	Radio Rental
Mental (crazy)	Chicken Oriental
Menu	Me & You
Mercy	Piccadilly Percy

Merry	Tom and Jerry
Mess	Elliot Ness
Mess	Slits in a Dress
Mild (beer)	Oscar Wilde
Milk	Acker Bilk
Milk	Lady in Silk
Milk	Satin and Silk
Milk	Tom Silk
Mind	Bacon Rind
Mind	Chinese Blind
Minge (vagina)	Edinburgh Fringe
Minger (smelly)	Dear Ringer
Minger	Jerry Springer
Mini (car or skirt)	Fat and Skinny
Minute	Cock Linnet
Miss	Cuddle and Kiss
Missus (Mrs)	Cheese & Kisses
Missus (Mrs)	Cows and Kisses
Missus (Mrs)	Love and Kisses
Missus (Mrs)	Plates and Dishes
Mistake	Cadbury's Flake
Mistake	Jaffa Cake
Moan	Darby and Joan
Moans	Catherine Zeta Jones
Mobi (cell/mobile)	Obi Wan Kenobi
Mobi (cell/mobile)	Uncle Toby
Money	Bees and Honey
Money	Bread and Honey
Money	Bugs Bunny
Money	Fluffy Bunny
Money	Sugar and Honey
Moody	Punch & Judy
Moddy	Richard & Judy
Mormon	Jerry O'Gorman
Morning	Day's Dawning
Morning	Gipsy's Warning
Morning	Maids a Dawning (maids adorning)
Motor (car)	Haddock and Bloater
Motor (car)	Tea, Two and a Bloater

Motor (car)	Yarmouth Bloater
Mouth	North and South
Mouth	Salmon Trout
Mower	Blower (telephone)
Mug	Steam Tug
Mug (chump)	Toby Jug
Mum	Darky's Bum
Mum	Finger & Thumb
Mush (face)	George Bush
Mutton	Billy Button
Mutton	Jenson Button

N

Nails	Monkey's Tails
Nark	Grass in the Park
Nasty	Cornish Pastie
Navy	Peas & Gravy
Navy	Soup & Gravy
Neck	Bushel and Peck
Neck	Gregory Peck
Neck	Jeff Beck
Neck	Three Quarters Of A Peck
Needle	Jeremy Beadle
Nerves	West Ham Reserve
Nervous	Peter Purves
News	Jelly Roll Blues
News	Wooden Pews
Newspaper	Linen Draper
Newspaper	Long Acre
Nice	Chicken & Rice
Nice	Creamed Rice
Nice	Katy Price
Nice	Obie Trice
Nick (prison)	Shovel and Pick
Nicker (British pound)	Alan Whicker
Nigger	Mechanical Digger
Nigger	Tommy Hilfiger
Night	Take a Fright
Nightmare	Lionel Blair
Nightmare	Trevor Sinclair
Nightmare	Weston Super-Mare
Nip (Japanese person)	Micro Chip
Nips (nipples)	Tord Gripps
Nipple	Raspberry Ripple
Nippy (cold)	Chinese Chippy
Nippy (cold)	George and Zippy

No	Brown Joe
No Good	Chump (Or Chunk) Of Wood
Noise	Box of Toys
Nonce (pedophile)	Bacon Bonce
Nookie (sex)	Biscuit & Cookie
Nose	Axel Rose
Nose	Duke of Montrose
Nose	Fireman's Hose
Nose	Fray Bentos
Nose	Hairy Toes
Nose	I Suppose
Nose	Irish Rose
Nose	Mary Rose
Nose	Red Rose
Nosh	Becks & Posh
Nowt (nothing)	Brussel Sprout
Number	Samantha Mumba
Numbers	Cucumbers
Number '2' (poop)	Bottle of Glue
Nun	Current Bun
Nun	Hot Cross Bun
Nutter (crazy)	Bread & Butter
Nutter (crazy)	Roll and Butter
Nutter (crazy)	Peanut Butter
Nutty	Bacon Butty
Nutty	Chip Butty
Nutty	Jam Butty

O

Obscene	James Dean
Odd	Ken Dodd
Odds	Ken Dodds
Off (take off, leave)	Frank Bough
Oil	Bodie and Doyle
Old Bailey (high court)	Arthur Daley
Old Boll (police)	Cold Chill
Old Man (Father)	Frying Pan
Old Man (Father)	Peter Pan
Old Man (Father)	Pot and Pan
Once Over	Kornikova
On My Own	Toblerone
On the Knocker (salesman)	Mozzle and brocha
On the Street	Short of a Sheet
Oral Sex	Ant and Dec(s)
Orbit	Ronnie Corbett
Organ	Molly O'Morgan
Out of Order	Allan Border
Overcoat	I'm Afloat

P

Paddy	Tea Caddy
Pager	John Major
Pain	Frasier Crane
Pain	Michael Caine
Paki	Joe Daki
Pakistani	Bacon Sarnie
Pakistani	Reg Varney
Pakistani	Sausage Sarnie
Pants (underwear)	Adam and the Ants
Pants (underwear)	Beetles and Ants
Pants (underwear)	Insects & Ants
Pants (underwear)	Pirates of Penzance
Pants (underwear)	Surrey & Hants
Pants (underwear)	Uncles & Aunts
Paper (newspaper)	Linen Draper
Parcel	Elephant and Castle
Pardon	Osama Bin Laden
Park	Light & Dark
Park	Noah's Ark
Park	Plimsole Mark
Parka (jacket)	Neil Sedaka
Parking Warden	Gay Gordon
Parky	David Starkey
Party	Gay and Hearty
Party	Hale & Hearty
Party	Moriarty
Party	Russell Harty
Party	Todd Carty
Pawn	Bullock's Horn
Pawn	Frankie Vaughn
PC Plod (police)	Fishing Rod
Peas	John Cleese
Peas	Knobbly Knees

Peck (measurement)	Tooting Bec
Pecker (penis)	Black & Decker
Pecker (penis)	Boris Becker
Pedophile	Cousin Kyle
Pee	Bruce Lee
Pee	C'est La Vie
Pee	Fiddle De Dee
Pee	Gypsy Rose Lee
Pee	Jet Li
Pee	Ken Smee
Pee	Patrick McNee
Pee	Rusty Lee
Peelers (policemen)	Pittsburg Steelers
Pen	Bill & Ben
Pen	Laying Hen
Penalty Fare	Cherie Blair
Penny	Abergavenny
Penny	Kilkenny
Penny Faggot	Any Racket
Penis	Mars & Venus
Pension	Shawshank Redemption
Pension	Stand to Attention
Perve	Dodge & Swerve
Perve	Optic Nerve
Pest	Fred West
Phone	Al Capone
Phone	Dog and Bone
Phone	Eau de Cologne
Phone	Herring Bone
Phone	Jelly Bone
Phone	Joey Ramone
Phone	Molly Malone
Phone	Nina Simone
Phone	Sharon Stone
Phone	Trombone
Piano (pee-ana)	Joanna
Pickles	Harvey Nichols
Pictures (cinema)	Dolly Mixtures
Pictures (cinema)	Fleas & Itches

Piddle (urinate)	Jimmy Riddle
Piddle (urinate)	Lauren Riddle
Piddle (urinate)	Malcolm in the Middle
Pie	Isle of Skye
Piece (sandwich)	Merlyn Rees
Pikey (gypsy)	Do As You Likey
Piles	Air Miles
Piles (hemorrhoids)	Bathroom Tiles
Piles (hemorrhoids)	Belinda Carlisle's
Piles (hemorrhoids)	Bernard Miles
Piles (hemorrhoids)	Chalfont St Giles
Piles (hemorrhoids)	Farmer Giles
Piles (hemorrhoids)	Four Minute Miles
Piles (hemorrhoids)	Jeremy Kyles
Piles (hemorrhoids)	Mammy's Smiles
Piles (hemorrhoids)	Metric Miles
Piles (hemorrhoids)	Michael Miles
Piles (hemorrhoids)	Nobby Stiles
Piles (hemorrhoids)	Nuremberg Trials
Piles (hemorrhoids)	Plymouth Argyles
Piles (hemorrhoids)	Rockford Files
Piles (hemorrhoids)	Shetland Isles
Piles (hemorrhoids)	Sieg Heils
Piles (hemorrhoids)	Slay 'em in the aisles
Piles (hemorrhoids)	Tate & Lyles
Piles (hemorrhoids)	Topps Tiles
Pill (birth control)	Harry Hill
Pill (birth control)	Jack and Jill
Pillow	Aston Villa
Pillow	Tit Willow
Pillow	Weeping Willow
Pill	Jimmy Hill
PILL	Rhubarb Hill
Pill	Strawberry Hill
Pills	Benny Hills
Pills	Jack 'n Jills
Pills	Mick Mills
Pills	Scott Mills
Pin	Huckleberry Finn

Pinch (steal)	Half Inch
Pint (beer)	Top Jint
Pipe	Cherry Ripe
Pirate	Millwall in Riot
Pish (pee)	Single Fish
Piss	Arthur Bliss
Piss	Gypsy's Kiss
Piss	Hit and Miss
Piss	Matt le Tiss
Piss	Mickey Bliss
Piss	Sir Arthur Bliss
Piss	Snake's Hiss
Pissed (drunk)	Adrian Quist
Pissed (drunk)	Brahms and Liszt
Pissed (drunk)	Greatly Missed
Pissed (angry)	Hit List
Pissed (drunk)	Mozart & Liszt
Pissed (drunk)	Oliver Twist
Pissed (drunk)	Schindlers List
Pissed (drunk)	Scotch Mist (nothing).
Pistol	Lady from Bristol
Pitch	Hedge & Ditch
Pizza	Omer Riza
Place	Drum & Bass
Plan	Jackie Chan
Plan	Manfred Mann
Plant	Eddy Grant
Plate	Alexander the Great
Play	Grass & Hay
Please	Hairy Knees
Please	On Your Knees
Pleb	Spider's Web
Plonker	Willy Wonka
Pocket	Davey Crocket
Pocket	Lucy Locket
Pocket	Sky Rocket
Poker	Orinoko (orinoker)
Pole	Jam Roll
Ponce	Alphonse

Ponce	Charlie Ronce
Pong	Hum & Song
Pony	Macaroni
Poo	Betty Boo
Poo	Four by Two
Poof (homosexual)	Horse's Hoof
Poof (homosexual)	Iron Hoof
Poof (homosexual)	Tin Roof
Poofter	Wooly Woofter
Pools	April Fools
Poo Poo	Efan Ekuku
Poor	On the Floor
Poorly	Sue Lawley
Pope	Bar of Soap
Pork	Dwight Yorke
Pork	Mickey Rourke
Porker (fat person)	Native New Yorker
Porn	Goldie Hawn
Porn	Frankie Vaughan
Porn	Johnny Vaughn
Portuguese	Pork & Cheese
Post (mail)	Sunday Roast
Poster	Roller Coaster
Potato (potater)	Spanish Waiter
Pot of Ale	Ship in Full Sail
Pot (of beer)	Sir Walter Scott
Pot of Porter	Hod of Mortar
Pound (money)	Lost & Found
Pound (money)	Merry Go Round
Pound (money)	Plymouth Sound
Powder (cocaine)	Nikki Lauder
Pox (the)	Band in the Box
Pox (the)	Cardboard Box
Pox (the)	Holly Hox
Pox (the)	Nervo & Knox
Pox (the)	Surrey Docks
Prat (arse)	Paper Hat
Prayer	Weavers' Chair
Preggers (pregnant)	Keith Cheggers

Price	Anekka Rice
Price	Condoleezza Rice
Prick (penis)	Hampton Wick
Prick (penis)	Lolly Lick
Prick (penis)	Moby Dick
Pride	Jekyll and Hyde
Priest	Bag of Yeast
Priest	Dirty Beast
Priest	Far East
Printer	Alan Minter
Printer	Bernie Winter
Prison	Boom and Mizzen
Prostitute	Brass Flute
Pruno (prison booze)	San Bruno
Pub	Bath Tub
Pub	Nuclear Sub
Pub	Rub-a-Dub
Pub	Wormwood Scrubs
Pube (pubic hair)	Rubik's Cube
Puff (gay)	Brian Clough
Puff (gay)	Collar and Cuff
Puff (marijuana)	Mickey Duff
Punter	Billy Bunter
Punters (gambler)	Hillman Hunters
Purse	Gypsy's Curse
Pyjamas	Barack Obama's
Pyjamas	Simon Schamas

Q

Quarter	Farmers Daughter
Quarter (of drugs)	Bottle of Water
Quarter (of drugs)	Glass of Water
Quarter (of drugs)	Janet Street-Porter
Quarter (of drugs)	Mother & Daughter
Quarter (of drugs)	Vicar's Daughter
Queen	Runner Bean
Queen	Smoke Screen
Queen (homosexual)	Torvill & Dean
Queer (homosexual)	Bottle of Beer
Queer (homosexual)	Brighton Pier
Queer (homosexual)	Chandelier
Queer (homosexual)	Chelsea Pier
Queer (homosexual)	Ginger Beer
Queer (homosexual)	King Lear
Queer (homosexual)	Tyne & Wear
Queer (homosexual)	Vauxhall Cavalier
Queer (odd)	Ginger Beer
Queue	Bernard Matthew
Quid	Bin Lid
Quid	Ocean-Going Squid
Quid	Real Madrid
Quid	Saucepan Lid
Quid	Squid
Quid	Squiddly Did
Quid	Teapot Lid

R

Rabbits	Nuns & Habits
Race Track	Tick Tack
Rail	Toby Ale
Railway Guard	Christmas Card
Rain	Ache and Pain
Rain	Alacompain
Rain	Andy Caine
Rain	Cynthia Payne
Rain	Duke of Spain
Rain	Pleasure and Pain
Rally	Manchester Scally
Ramble	Sol Campbell
Rave (dance)	Comedy Dave
Raver	Cheesy Quaver
Raw	Bale of Straw
Razor	Malky Fraser
Readies (cash)	Duane Eddies
Readies (cash)	Nelson Eddy's
Real	Ian Beale
Reasons	Four Seasons
Red (Communist)	Better Off Dead
Redundance (paid off)	Ticket to the Dance
Reek	Ancient Greek
Rent	Burton on Trent
Rent	Clark Kent
Rent	Duke of Kent
Rich	Scratch & Itch
Ride	Charlie Pride
Right	Isle of Wight
Ring	Highland Fling
Ring	Jonathan King
Ring On Finger	Ling and Linger
River	Shake and Shiver

Road	Frog and Toad
Road	Kermit
Robbing	Apple Bobbing
Rocks	Salford Docks
Roof	Gawds Truth
Roof	Horse's Hoof
Rookie	Biscuit & Cookie
Room	Birch Broom
Rotten	Bobbins and Cotton
Rotten	Dot Cotton
Rotten	Nick Cotton
Rotten	Reels of Cotton
Rough	Barry Cluff
Rough	Damien Duff
Row (argument)	Barn(ey) Owl
Row (argument)	Bull and Cow
Rum	Finger & Thumb
Rum	Tom Thumb
Rummage	Worzel Gummidge
Run Away	Botany Bay

S

Sack (fired)	Last Card in the Pack
Sack (fired)	Tin Tack
Safe	Adam Faith
Saloon Bar	Balloon Car
Sandals	Roman Candles
Sandals	Vandals
Sargy (sergeant)	Onion Bagi
Sarnie (sandwich)	Georgio Armani
Sarnie (sandwich)	Reg Varney
Sauce	Dead Horse
Sauce	Inspector Morse
Sauce	Rocking Horse
Saucer	Geoffrey Chaucer
Saveloy (sausage)	Girl And Boy
Saw	Bear's Paw
Say So	Cocoa
Scar	Mars Bar
Scarf	Centre Half
Scary	Mariah Carey
School	Jah Rule
Scoff (food)	Frank Bough
Score	Ali McGraw
Score	Bobby Moore
Score	Hampden Roar
Score	Ronald de Boer
Score (£20)	Apple Core
Score (£20)	Dudley Moore
Scotch	Gold Watch
Scotch	Pimple and Botch
Scotch (Whisky)	Gold Watch
Scotch (Whisky)	Pimple & Blotch
Scotch (Whisky)	Pocket Watch
Scouse	Mickey Mouse

Scouser (Liverpool)	Mickey Mouser
Scouts	Brussel Sprouts
Scram (run away)	Cheese & Ham
Scran (food)	Jackie Chan
Scran (food)	Tommy O'Rann
Screw	Didgeridoo
Scrummage	Worzel Gummidge
Sea	Housemaid's Knee
Seen	Pearly Queen
See Ya Later	Spanish Waiter
Sense	Eighteen Pence
Sent for Trial	Over the Stile
Severn Bridge	Hotpoint Fridge
Sex	Bendy Flex
Sex	Liberty X
Sex	Oedipus Rex
Sex	Posh 'n Becks
Sexy	Long & Flexy
Shabby	Westminster Abbey
Shades (sunglasses)	Virginia Wades –
Shag	Billy Bragg
Shag	Melvyn Bragg
Shag	Zig & Zag
Shakes	Hatti Jaques (Jakes)
Shaky	Currant Cakey
Shambles	Jakki Brambles
Shandy	Andy Pandy
Shandy	Mahatma Ghandi
Shank (golf term)	J. Arthur Rank.
Shark	Noah's Ark
Shave	All Night Rave
Shave	Chas and Dave
Shave	Dig a Grave
Shave	Mexican Wave
Shave	Ocean Wave
Shave	Rant & Rave
Sheila	Four Wheeler
Shillin'	Rogue and Villain
Shilling	Able and Willing

Shilling	Abraham's Willing
Shilling	John Dillon
Shilling	Thomas Tilling
Shiner (black eye)	Ocean Liner
Shingles	Mandy Dingles
Shirt	Dicky Dirt
Shirt	Throw Me In The Dirt
Shirt	Uncle Bert
Shit	Bottomless Pit
Shit	Brace and Bit
Shit	Brad Pitt
Shit	English Lit
Shit	Ertha Kitt
Shit	Tom Tit
Shit	Top Ten Hit
Shit	Two Bob Bit
Shit	William Pitt
Shite	Ben Cartwright
Shite	Fly a Kite
Shite	Ian Wright
Shite	Jedi Knight
Shite	Jimmy White
Shite	Tom Kite
Shite	Turkish Delight
Shite	Barry White
Shiter (toilet)	Ronson Lighter
Shits (diarrhoea)	Two-Bob Bits
Shitter	Council Gritter
Shitter	Gary Glitter
Shitter	Light & Bitter
Shitter	Mavis Fritter
Shitter	Radio Transmitter
Shitter	Rick Whitter
Shocker	Barry Crocker
Shocker	Constantino Rocca
Shoe	Winnie the Pooh
Shoes	Canoes
Shoes	Church Pews
Shoes	Dinky Doos

Shoes	How Do You Do's
Shoes	Jimmy Choo's
Shoes	Looby Loo's
Shoes	One and Two's
Shoes	Scooby Doos
Shoes	St. Louis Blues
Shoes	Rhythm and Blues
Shoes	Yabba-Dabba-Doos
Shoot	Put in the Boot
Shop	Bottle of Pop
Shop	Cheggers Plays Pop
Shop	Lollipop
Shoulder	Spark and Smoulder
Shoulders	Noddy Holders
Shout	Brussel Sprout
Shout (round)	Wally Grout
Shovel	Lord Lovell
Shower	Austin Power
Shower	Blackpool Tower
Shower	David Gower
Shower	Eiffel Tower
Shower	Fawlty Tower
Shower	Telecom Tower
Shut	Jabba the Hutt
Sick	Bobby & Dick
Sick	Moby Dick
Sick	Pat & Mick
Sick	Spotted Dick
Sick	Tom and Dick
Sick	Uncle Dick
Sicky (sick day)	Metal Mickey
Sight	Website
Silly	Auntie Lilly
Silly	Daffadown Dilly
Silly	Harry & Billy
Silly	Piccadilly
Silly	Uncle Willie
Silly C*nt	Billy Hunt
Simple	Dolly Dimple

Simple	Haigs Dimple
Single	Mandy Dingle
Sister	Skin and Blister
Sister	Sock & Blister
Sitter (an open chance)	Council Gritter
Six	Tim Mix
Sixteenth	Louis the 16th
Skag (heroin)	Salisbury Crag
Skin	Thick & Thin
Skin	Vera Lynn
Skin (cigarette paper)	Vera Lynn
Skint (broke)	After Eight Mint
Skint (broke)	Bernie Flint
Skint (broke)	Borassic Lint
Skint (broke)	Harry Flint
Skint (broke)	Jackie Flint
Skint (broke)	Lamb & Mint
Skint (broke)	Larry Flint
Skint (broke)	Murray Mint
Skint (broke)	Peppermint
Skint (broke)	Polo Mint
Skive	Duck & Dive
Skiver	Angus MacGyver
Skiver	Pearl Diver
Skoda (Russian car)	Whisky & Soda
Skull	Jethro Tull
Skunk (cannabis)	Thelonious Monk
Slag (prostitute)	Oily Rag
Slag (prostitute)	Porno Mag
Slag (prostitute)	Toe Rag / Tow Rag
Slap	C*nt Flap
Slap	Watford Gap
Slash (piss)	Alex Nash
Slash (piss)	Arthur Ashe
Slash (urinate)	Barry Nash
Slash (urinate)	Charlie Nash
Slash (urinate)	Eye Lash
Slash (urinate)	Frazer Nash
Slash (urinate)	Jack Dash

Slash (urinate)	Johnny Cash
Slash (urinate)	Lemon & Dash
Slash (urinate)	Leslie Ash
Slash (urinate)	Pie & Mash
Slash (urinate)	Mark Ramprakash
Slash (pee)	Ogden Nash
Slash (piss)	Pat Cash
Slash (piss)	Pie and Mash
Slash (pee)	Sausage & Mash
Slash (urinate)	Stock Market Crash
Slaughtered (drunk)	Son & Daughtered
Sleep	Bo-Peep
Sleep	Meryl Streep
Sleep	Sooty and Sweep
Slipper	Chicken Dipper
Slipper	Jack the Ripper
Slippers	Big Dippers
Slippers	Day Trippers
Slippers	Eggs & Kippers
Smart	Lemon Tart
Smack	Hammer & Tack
Smashed (drunk)	Pebble-Dashed
Smell	Aunt Nell
Smile	Carpet Pile
Smile	Roof Tile
Smile	Sandy Lyle
Smitten	Atomic Kitten
Smoke	Laugh and a Joke
Smoke a Pipe	Artichoke Ripe
Snake	Joe Blake
Sneeze	Bread and Cheese
Snide	Bonnie & Clyde
Snide	Jekyll and Hyde
Sniper	Billie Piper
Snout (cigarette)	In and Out
Snout (cigarette)	Salmon and Trout
Snow	Cheryl Crow
Snuff	Hang Bluff
Soap	Band of Hope

Soap	Cape of Good Hope
Soap	Faith and Hope
Soap	No Hope
Sock	Teddington Lock
Socks	Almond Rocks
Socks	Bombay Docks
Socks	Diamond Rocks
Socks	Goldie Locks
Socks	Hickory Docks
Socks	Joe Rocks
Socks	Sara Cox
Socks	Tilbury Docks
Soda	Major Loda
Soft	Lara Croft
Son	Currant Bun
Song	Ding Dong
Sores	Dudley Moore's
Soup	Bowl the Hoop
Soup	Loop de Loop
Sovereign	Jimmy O'Goblin
Spam	Jean Claude van Damme
Spanner (wrench)	Copacabana
Spanner (wrench)	Elsie Tanner
Sparko (asleep)	Donnie Darko
Sparrow	Bow and Arrow
Spatula	Horace Bachelor
Speak	Bubble and Squeak
Specs (spectacles)	Gregory Peck
Specs [Spectacles]	Mikkel Becks
Specs (spectacles)	Posh & Becks
Speed	Harris Tweed
Speed	Lou Reed
Spider	Apple Cider
Splash (urinate)	Bangers and Mash
Spliff (joint)	Scratch 'n' Sniff
Splinter	Alan Minter
Spoon	Daniel Boone
Spoon	David Boon
Spoon	Lorna Doone

Spoon	Man on the Moon
Spot (pluke)	Jelly Tot
Spot (acne)	Randolph Scott
Spot	Selina Scott
Spouse	Boiler House
Spouse	Dangermouse
Sprouts	Twist and Shouts
Spud (potato)	Elmer Fudd
Spuds	Roy Hudd's
Spunk (semen)	Harry Monk
Spunk (semen)	Pineapple Chunk
Spunk (semen)	Thelonious Monk
Squeal	Jellied Eel
Stab	Doner Kebab
Stairs	Apples and Pears
Stairs	Daisy Dancers
Stairs	Dancing Bears
Star	La-Di-Da
Starbucks (Starbies)	Ken & Barbie's
Starbucks	Lisa Tarbuck's
Start	Puff and Dart
Starved	Pear Halved
Starvin'	Hank Marvin
Starvin'	Lee Marvin
Starving	Hank & Lee
State (anguish)	Two and Eight
State (condition)	Harry Tate
State (condition)	Six & Eight
Station	Terry Nation
Steak	Ben Flake
Steak	Charlie Drake
Steak	Joe Blake
Steal	Sexton Blake
Steak and Kidney	Kate and Sydney
Steal	Rod and Reel
Steaming (drunk)	Jan Leeming
Stella Artois (beer)	Cinderella
Stella Artois (beer)	David Mellor
Stella Artois (beer)	Keith Deller

Stella Artois (beer)	Nelson Mandela
Stella Artois (beer)	Ooh Aah
Stella Artois (beer)	Paul Weller
Stella Artois (beer)	Uri Geller
Stench	Judy Dench
Stench	Dawn French
Stew	Battle of Waterloo
Stick (walking)	Hackney Wick
Stick	Paddy Quick
Sticks (countryside)	Pick & Mix
Stink	Pen and Ink
Stinker	Reggie Blinker
Stinking	Abraham Lincoln
Stoned	Al Caponed
Stoned	Dog & Boned
Stools	April Fools
Story	Frankie Dettori
Story	Jackanory
Story	Morning Glory
Stout (beer)	Salmon and Trout
Stranger	Connaught Ranger
Stranger	Queen's Park Ranger
Stranger	Texas Ranger
Strangers	Glasgow Rangers
Stray	Gamma Ray
Streak	Dawson's Creek
Street	Ain't It a Treat
Street	Field of Wheat
Street	Plate of Meat
Strides (trousers)	Donkey Rides
Strides [trousers]	Jekyll and Hydes
Stripper	Chicken Dipper
Stripper	Jack the Ripper
Stripper's Tits	Money Pits
Strong	Annie May Wong
Strong	Ping Pong
Stunner	Air Gunner
Style	Sandy Lyle
Sub (pay advance)	Rub a Dub

Sub (Submarine)	Rub a Dub
Subaru	Scooby-Doo
Suit	Bag of Fruit
Suit	Bowl of Fruit
Suit	Fiddle and Flute
Suit	Piccolo & Flute
Suit	Tin Flute
Suit	Whistle and Flute
Suitcase	Crowded Space
Sun	Current Bun
Suntan Lotion	Billy Ocean
Supper	Tommy Tucker
Sure	Bobby Moore
Sure	Five to Four
Suspenders	No Surrenders
Swear	Lord Mayor
Swear	Orange & Pear
Sweetheart	Treacle Tart

T

Table	Aunt Mabel
Table	Betty Grable
Table	Cain and Abel
Table	Clark Gable
Tablet (pill)	Gary Ablett
Tail	Alderman's Nail
Tailor	Sinbad the Sailor
Tail Toucher (Homosexual)	Terry Butcher
Take Away	Jay Kay
Tale	Daily Mail
Tale	Newgate Jail
Talk	Rabbit and Pork
Talker	Murray Walker
Tall	Bat and Ball
Tan	Charlie Chan
Tan	Peter Pan
Tan	Steely Dan
Tandoori	Kansas & Missouri
Tank	Rattle and Clank
Tanner (sixpence)	Goddess Diana
Tanner (sixpence)	Lord of the Manor
Tanner (sixpence)	Sprarsy Anna
Tanner (sixpence)	Tartan Banner
Tap (borrow)	Cellar Flap
Tap (borrow)	Star's Nap
Tart	Beating Heart
Tart	Horse & Cart
Tart	Kick Start
Tart	Lionel Bart
Tart	Merryheart
Tatty	David Batty
Tax	Ajax
Tax	Bees Wax

Tax	Candle Wax
Taxi	Joe Baxi
Taxi Meter	Dickory Dock
Tea	Bruce Lee
Tea	Half Past Three
Tea	Jack Dee
Tea	Kiki Dee
Tea	River Lea
Tea	Rosy Lee
Tea	Split Pea
Tea	You and Me
Tears	Britney Spears
Tears	Bunny Ears
Teeth	Bexleyheath
Teeth	Corn Beef
Teeth	Edward (Ted) Heath
Teeth	Hampstead Heath
Teeth	Haywards Heath
Teeth	Holly Wreath
Teeth	Hounslow Heath
Teeth	Penelope Keith
Telephone	Al Capone
Telly (TV)	Auntie Nellie
Telly (TV)	Custard and Jelly
Telly (TV)	K Y Jelly
Telly (TV)	Liza Minelli
Telly (TV)	Marie Correlli
Telly (TV)	Matthew Kelly
Telly (TV)	Roger Mellie
Telly (TV)	Wobbly Jelly
Ten	Big Ben
Ten	Bill & Ben
Ten	Cock and Hen
Ten	Dirty Den
Ten	Maggie's Den
Ten	Nigel Benn
Ten	Speckled Hen
Ten	Tony Benn
Ten	Uncle Ben

Tenner (£10)	Ayrton Senna
Tenner (£10)	Bill & Benner
Tenner (£10)	Jim Fenner
Tenner (£10)	Louise Wener
Tenner (£10)	Paul McKenna
Tennis	Les Dennis
Testicles	Barnacle Bills
Testicles	Outings & Festivals
Text (message)	Malcolm X
Text	T-Rex
Thanks	Tom Hanks
Thief	Tea Leaf
Thieves	Jimmy Greaves
Thieving	Tea Leafing
Thick	Paddy Quick
Think	Cocoa Drink
Thirst	Geoff Hurst
Thong	Rigobert Song
Three Months in Jail	Sorrowful Tale
Throat	Billy Goat
Throat	Ferret & Stoat
Throat	John O'Groat
Throat	Nanny Goat
Throat	Weasel & Stoat
Thrums (threepence)	Currants And Plums
Thrush	Basil Brush
Thugs	Spiders & Bugs
Thunder	Crash & Blunder
Ticket	Bat and Wicket
Ticket	Jiminy Cricket
Ticket	Lemony Snicket
Ticket	Wilson Picket
Tie	Peckham Rye
Tights	Fly By Nights
Tile (hat)	Battle Of The Nile
Till (Cash register)	Jack & Jill
Tim	Jungle Jim
Time	Cockney Rhyme
Time (prison)	Bird Lime

Time	Harry Lime
Time	Grease and Grime
Time	Lemon & Lime
Time	Lager & Lime
Tips	Fish & Chips
Tired	Barb Wired
Tit (breast)	Brace & Bit
Tit (breast)	Brad Pitt
Tits (breasts)	Bacon Bits
Tits (breasts)	Ballroom Blitz
Tits (breasts)	Brace and Bits
Tits (breasts)	Ertha Kitts
Tits (breasts)	Fainting Fits
Tits (breasts)	First Aid Kits
Tits (breasts)	Oven Mitts
Tits (breasts)	Thruppenny Bits
Titties (breasts)	Bristol Cities
Titty (breast)	Bristol City
Titty (breast)	Salt Lake City
Titty (breast)	Walter Mitty
Toast	Holy Ghost
Toast	Mickey Most
Toast	Pig and Roast
Toaster	Roller Coaster
Toes	Bromley by Bows
Toes	Edgar Allen Poes
Toes	Marilyn Monroes
Toes	Sebastian Coes
Toilet	Pontius Pilate
Toker	Al Roker
Tomatoes	Stars & Garters
Tongue	Brigham Young
Tongue	Crosby Stills Nash & Young
Tongue	Iron Lung
Tonic	Supersonic
Tools	Crown Jewels
Tools	Judge Jules
Tonic	Philharmonic
Toss (care)	Iron Horse

Toss (care)	Jonathan Ross
Toss (care)	Kate Moss
Toss (care)	Stirling Moss
Tosser (wanker)	Charing Crosser
Tosser (wanker)	Dental Flosser
Tote (carry)	Canal Boat
Totty	Beam Me Up Scotty
Totty	Lanzarote
Tough	Brian Clough
Tout (sell)	Brussel Sprout
Towel	Baden Powell
Town	Bobby Brown
Town	Joe Brown
Town Crier	Town Crier
Traffic Jam	Amsterdam
Train	Daniel Fergus McGrain
Train	Hail & Rain
Train	John Wayne
Train	Michael Caine
Trainers (shoes)	Claire Rayners
Trainers (shoes)	Gloria Gaynors
Tram	Baa Lamb
Tramp (hobo)	Hurricane Lamp
Tramp (hobo)	Oil Lamp
Tramp (hobo)	Paraffin Lamp
Tramp (hobo)	Postage Stamp
Tramp (hobo)	Thirteen Amp
Tramp (hobo)	Wankers Cramp
Tramp (hobo)	Wet & Damp
Transported for Life	Read Of Tripe
Trash	Bangers and Mash
Trash	Basement Jaxx
Treadmill	Can't Keep Still
Trick (con)	Penny-Come-Quick
Trip (on drugs)	Walnut Whip
Trots (diarrhea)	Zachary Scotts
Trouble	Barney Rubble
Trousers	Callard & Bowsers
Trousers	Council Houses

Trousers	Doogie Howsers
Trousers	Lards (short for Callard & Bowsers)
Trousers	Lesley Crowthers
Trousers	Round the Houses
Trowel	Baydon Powell
Trowel	Jennie Powell
Trowel	Simon Cowell
True	Eyes of Blue
Trumper (arsehole)	Bambi and Thumper
Trunks	Chipmunks
Truth	Babe Ruth
Tube (idiot)	Oxo Cube
Tube (idiot)	Rubik's Cube
Tune	Stewed Prune
Turd (shit)	Douglas Hurd
Turd (shit)	Lemon Curd
Turd (shit)	Richard the Third
Turd (shit)	Thora Hird
Turf	Harry Worth
Turk	Captain Kirk
Turk	Second Hand Merc
Turkey	Pinky & Perky
Twat	Ball and Bat
Twat	Bowler Hat
Twat	Granny Flat
Twat	Rabbit in a Hat
Twat	Roland Rat
Twig (understand)	Earwig
Twit	Strawberry Split
Two-One	Atilla the Hun
Twopence	Bottle of Spruce
Tyres	Dorothy Squires

U

Umbrella	Auntie Ella
Umbrella	Isabella
Umbrella	Red 'n' Yella
Undies	Eddie Grundies

V

Vagina	Elizabeth Regina
Vagina	Morris Minor
Van	Slice Pan
Veg	Uncle Reg
Vegan	Kevin Keegan
Veggie	Ronnie & Reggie
Very Best	Hairy Chest
Very Best	John West
Vest	East and West
Vicar	Pie & Liquor
Villain	Bob Dylan
Virus	Billy Ray Cyrus
Voda (cell brand)	Whisky & Soda
Voddy (Vodka)	Bill Oddie
Voice	Hobson's Choice
Volley	Buddy Holly
Vomit	Wallace and Gromit

W

Wad	Ken Dodd
Wager	John Major
Wages	Cat & Cages
Wages	Greengages
Wages	Rock of Ages
Waistcoat	Charlie Prescott
Waiter	Hot Potato
Wales	Canterbury Tales
Walk	Ball of Chalk
Walk	Bowl of Chalk
Wander	Jane Fonda
Wank (masturbate)	Ann Frank
Wank (masturbate)	Armitage Shank
Wank (masturbate)	Barclays Bank
Wank (masturbate)	Hilary Swank
Wank (masturbate)	Iron Tank
Wank (masturbate)	J. Arthur Rank
Wank (masturbate)	Jodrell Bank
Wank (masturbate)	Lamb Shank
Wank (masturbate)	Midland Bank
Wank (masturbate)	Pedal and Crank
Wank (masturbate)	Septic Tank
Wank (masturbate)	Sherman Tank
Wank (masturbate)	Thomas Tank
Wank (masturbate)	Tommy Tank
Wank (masturbate)	Westminster Bank
Wanker	Cab Ranker
Wanker	Casa Blanca
Wanker	Kuwaiti Tanker
Wanker	Merchant Banker
Wanker	Oil Tanker
Wanker	Ravi Shankar
Wanker	Ricky & Bianca
Wanker	Sefton Branker
Wanker	Ship's Anchor
Wanker	Sri Lanker
Wanker	Swiss Banker
Wanker	Walter Anchor
Wanks	Gordon Banks

Wanks	Ham Shanks
Wash	Bish Bash Bosh
Wash	Bob Squash
Wash	Lemon Squash
Watch (fob watch)	Kettle and Hob
Water	Darling Daughter
Water	Fisherman's Daughter
Water	Ten Furlongs (Mile and a quarter)
Watch	Gordon & Gotch
Wazz (pee)	Keith Vaz
Web Site	Wind and Kite
Wedding	Otis Reading
Wee	Rusty Lee
Wee (urine)	Dairylea
Weed (drugs)	Dog & Lead
Weed (drugs)	Happy Feed
Weed (drugs)	Harris Tweed
Weed	Oliver Reed
Week	Bubble and Squeak
Weight	Alfred the Great
Weight	Pieces of Eight
Wench	Monkey Wrench
Wench	Tramp on a Bench
Wet	Boba Fett
Where Abouts	Furry Boots
Whiff	Jimmy Cliff
Whisky	Gay and Frisky
Whore	Brass Door
Whore	Doug McClure
Whore	Forty Four
Whore	Four by Four
Whore	Roger Moore
Whore	Sloop Of War
Whore	Thomas Moore
Wife	Bag for Life
Wife	Bread Knife
Wife	Carving Knife
Wife	Duchess of Fife
Wife	Trouble and Strife

Wig	Farmers Pig
Wig	Irish Jig
Wig	Oil Rig
Wig	Syrup of Figs
Window	Burnt Cinder
Window (winder)	Jenny Linder
Window (Winda)	Kevin & Linda
Window (wind'er)	Tommy Trinder
Windscreen Wiper	Billie Piper
Windy	Mork and Mindy
Wine	Calvin Klein
Wine	Porcupine
Winner	Chicken Dinner
Wishes	Pots & Dishes
Wog	Chocolate Frog
Wog	Kermit the Frog
Woman	Gooseberry Puddin'
Woods	Do me Goods
Word	Dicky Bird
Word	Lemon Curd
Work	Captain Kirk
Work	Dunkirk
Work	Kathy Burke
Worry	Chicken Curry
Worry	Fred MacMurray
Wrench	Judy Dench
Wrist	Schindler's List
Wristwatch	Bottle of Scotch
Wrong	Falun Gong
Wrong	Pete Tong

Y

Yank	Anti-Septic
Yank	Septic Tank

Yank	Wooden Plank
Yanks	Ham Shanks
Yanks	Petrol Tanks
Yanks	Tom Hanks
Yawn	Johnny Vaughn
Years	Donkey's Ears
Yellow	Marty Pellow
Yes	Brown Bess
Yid (Jew)	Front Wheel Skid
Yid (Jew)	Tea Pot Lid
Yoga	Battle of Saratoga

Z

Zits	Candlesticks
Zoo	Coochie Coo

Made in United States
North Haven, CT
13 December 2023

45628708R00214